Immunizations &Infectious Diseases

An Informed Parent's Guide

Margaret C. Fisher, MD, FAAP,
Editor in Chief

American Academy of Pediatrics

DEDICATED TO THE HEALTH OF ALL CHILDREN™

American Academy of Pediatrics Department of Marketing and Publications Staff

Maureen DeRosa, MPA
Director, Department of Marketing and Publications

Mark Grimes
Director, Division of Product Development

Jeff Mahony
Manager, Product Development

Eileen Glasstetter, MS
Manager, Consumer Publishing

Sandi King, MS
Director, Division of Publishing and Production Services

Kate Larson
Manager, Editorial Services

Jason Crase
Editorial Specialist

Theresa Wiener
Manager, Editorial Production

Linda Diamond
Manager, Graphic Design

Jill Ferguson
Director, Division of Marketing and Sales

Library of Congress Control Number: 2004101466
ISBN: 1-58110-139-2
CB0033

9-130/0905

1 2 3 4 5 6 7 8 9 10

Reviewers/Contributors

Editor in Chief
Margaret C. Fisher, MD, FAAP
Professor of Pediatrics
Drexel University College of Medicine
Philadelphia, PA
Chair, Department of Pediatrics
Monmouth Medical Center
Long Branch, NJ

American Academy of Pediatrics Board of Directors Reviewer
Robert M. Corwin, MD, FAAP

American Academy of Pediatrics
Errol R. Alden, MD, FAAP
Executive Director/CEO

Roger F. Suchyta, MD, FAAP
Associate Executive Director

Maureen DeRosa, MPA
Director, Department of Marketing and Publications

Mark Grimes
Director, Division of Product Development

Jeff Mahony
Manager, Product Development

Reviewers
Louis M. Bell, Jr, MD, FAAP
Henry H. Bernstein, DO, FAAP
Deborah R. Faccenda, MD, FAAP
S. Michael Marcy, MD, FAAP
Gail L. Rodgers, MD, FAAP
Edward P. Rothstein, MD, FAAP
Joseph A. Zenel, Jr, MD, FAAP

Additional Reviewers

Deborah A. Borchers, MD, FAAP
Danette S. Glassy, MD, FAAP
Nancy G. Powers, MD, FAAP
Judith T. Romano, MD, FAAP

Writer

Richard Trubo

Illustrator

Anthony Alex LeTourneau

Book Design

Linda J. Diamond

Copy Editor

Jason Crase

Additional Assistance

Holly Kaminski
Eileen Glasstetter, MS
Stacey Willis

This book is dedicated to the thousands of pediatricians and nurses throughout the United States who strive daily to improve the health and well-being of our children, the future of our country. On a personal basis, I dedicate the book to Susan, Beth, Ed, Meg, Catie, Chris, and John—all very special people!

—MCF

Acknowledgments

The editor wishes to thank the following people for their thoughtful reviews and insightful comments and corrections: Lou Bell, MD, FAAP; Hank Bernstein, DO, FAAP; Deb Faccenda, MD, FAAP; Mike Marcy, MD, FAAP; Gail Rodgers, MD, FAAP; Ed Rothstein, MD, FAAP; and Joe Zenel, MD, FAAP. Special thanks to Jeff Mahony for his patience and guidance and Martha Cook for her help and encouragement.

Please Note

The information contained in this book is intended to complement, not substitute for the advice of your child's pediatrician. Before starting any medical treatment or program, you should consult with your pediatrician, who can discuss your child's individual needs and counsel you about symptoms and treatment. If you have any questions about how the information in this book applies to your child, speak to your pediatrician.

The information and advice in this book applies equally to children of both sexes (except where noted). To indicate this, we have chosen to alternate between masculine and feminine pronouns throughout the book.

This book has been developed by the American Academy of Pediatrics. The authors, editors, and contributors are expert authorities in the field of pediatrics. No commercial involvement of any kind has been solicited or accepted in the development of the content of this publication.

Table of Contents

Foreword

The American Academy of Pediatrics (AAP) welcomes you to the latest in its series of books for parents, *Immunizations & Infectious Diseases: An Informed Parent's Guide.*

This book will help inform readers about the prevention and treatment of infectious diseases in children, including everyday prevention measures, recommended immunizations, and the appropriate use of antibiotics and other medicines. It is my hope that this book will become an invaluable resource and reference guide for you as parents and caregivers. The book should be used in concert with the advice and counsel of your pediatrician, who will provide individual guidance and assistance related to the health of your child.

Under the direction of Margaret C. Fisher, MD, FAAP, the material in this book was developed with the assistance of numerous reviewers and contributors from the AAP. This book is the parent's guide to match the pediatrician's guide—*Red Book®*, the essential medical resource on pediatric infectious diseases, authored by the AAP Committee on Infectious Diseases.

Because medical information related to these topics is constantly changing, every effort has been made to ensure that this book contains the most up-to-date findings. Readers are encouraged to visit the AAP Web site, www.aap.org, to keep current on these important topics and more.

The AAP is an organization of 60,000 primary care pediatricians, pediatric medical subspecialists, and pediatric surgical specialists dedicated to the health, safety, and well-being of infants, children, adolescents, and young adults. *Immunizations & Infectious Diseases: An Informed Parent's Guide* is part of the ongoing educational efforts of the AAP to provide parents and caregivers with high-quality information on a broad spectrum of children's health issues.

Errol R. Alden, MD, FAAP
Executive Director/CEO
American Academy of Pediatrics

Introduction

Immunizations & Infectious Diseases: An Informed Parent's Guide is designed to provide you with information about infections and infecting agents such as bacteria, viruses, fungi, and parasites. Not all infections could be included, so the most common problems were selected. You will also find information on some unusual infections that we felt were of special importance or interest to you.

This book is based on *Red Book®: Report of the Committee on Infectious Diseases*. *Red Book* provides information to pediatricians and others who provide care for children. This book is written for parents.

Whenever possible, the guidance given in this book is *evidence based,* meaning it comes from the results of scientific studies. This is important because "the way it's always been done" or "the way Mom used to do it" isn't always the best way to keep your child healthy. For example, when a child had diarrhea in the past, a pediatrician was likely to recommend stopping milk and giving only clear fluids and the so-called "brat" diet (bananas, rice, apples, toast). We now know that there is no need to stop milk or change the diet. You may have heard things like "Milk and formula make coughing worse by producing phlegm." Again, there is no evidence to show that is true. Lots of over-the-counter medicines are available for many infections, including cough medicines, sinus medicines, and a variety of combination medicines. There is no evidence that these help with the common cold, and there is plenty of evidence that all of these medicines can do harm. We have tried to base the recommendations in this book on the evidence.

Immunizations & Infectious Diseases: An Informed Parent's Guide is divided into 4 subject areas—immunizations, prevention, antibiotics, and summaries of infectious diseases. Part 1, "Keeping Your Child Healthy Through Immunizations," provides information on the history and successes of immunizations and explanations of how vaccines work, how safe they are, and which vaccines your child needs.

Part 2, "Preventing and Controlling Infections in Your Child," tells you about things you can do to help stop the spread of infections. It also provides information about infections in child care, contaminated food, animal bites, travel, international adoptees, teenagers who are sexually active, blood transfusions, and bioterrorism attacks.

✓ Part 3, "Understanding the Use of Antibiotics When Your Child Is Sick," provides you with information about antibiotics, including how they work and when they should be used. You will learn that there are antibiotics for bacteria (antibacterials), viruses (antivirals), fungi (antifungals), and parasites (antiparasitics).

✓ Part 4, "Getting the Facts About Infectious Diseases," starts with an overview and continues with individual chapters about the germs (bacteria, viruses, fungi, and parasites) that cause illnesses. Chapters provide information about the agent, the illness, how the diagnosis is made, what treatment is used, when to call your pediatrician, and what you can do to prevent the infection.

There also is a section on additional resources to help you find more detailed information and a glossary to help you understand some of the medical terminology used in the book. An index is provided to allow you to find topics of interest quickly.

We hope you will find this information useful. Clearly, this book is neither comprehensive nor complete. It should not be used to diagnose your child. We suggest you let your pediatrician make diagnoses and provide you with specific advice about the care of your child. We hope you will use this book to become more informed about infectious diseases, their treatment, and when possible, their prevention.

Part 1

Keeping Your Child Healthy Through Immunizations

CHAPTER 1

Immunizations:
History and Achievements

Before the modern era of childhood immunizations, parents would have been surprised at the thought that future generations would be able to protect their children from many of the most serious childhood infectious diseases. After all, there was a time when diphtheria was one of the most feared childhood diseases, claiming more than 10,000 lives a year in the United States during the 1920s. In the 1940s and 1950s, polio paralyzed and even killed children by the thousands. At one point in time, the measles affected nearly a half-million US children every year. Almost everyone in the United States got it at some point during childhood—and it sometimes caused complications such as pneumonia and encephalitis.)

(Fortunately, times have changed. Today, most children in the United States lead much healthier lives and parents live with much less anxiety and worry over infections during childhood. Yet vaccines are a relatively recent development.)Barely more than 200 years ago in the United Kingdom, Edward Jenner noticed that some dairymaids seemed protected from smallpox if they had already been infected by the much less dangerous virus that caused cowpox. In 1796, Jenner conducted an experiment, scratching the arm of an 8-year-old boy named James Phipps using material from a cowpox sore in one of these dairymaids. Then he repeated the same experiment, but this time added a small amount of smallpox into the same child. He hoped that the procedure would immunize the child against the deadly smallpox infection. In fact, it did.)

> The terms *vaccine* and *vaccination* were actually derived from Edward Jenner's initial discoveries using the cowpox virus. The Latin term vaccinus means "of or from cows."

Jenner's experiment began the immunization age. The next major advance occurred almost 100 years later when Louis Pasteur, MD, showed that disease could be prevented by infecting humans with weakened germs. In 1885, Dr Pasteur used a vaccine to successfully prevent rabies in a boy named Joseph Meister who had been bitten by a rabid dog.

By the mid-20th century, regular progress in immunizations was made. Jonas Salk, MD, and Albert Sabin, MD, made what are perhaps the best-known advances—they developed the inactivated polio vaccine and live polio vaccine, respectively. Their discoveries have saved countless children worldwide from polio, a disease that often left youngsters dependent on wheelchairs or crutches for life.

Today, immunizations are one of the success stories of modern medicine. Smallpox was declared eradicated from the world in 1977. Polio was officially eliminated from the United States and the rest of the Western Hemisphere in 1991. Whereas 13,000 to 20,000 cases of polio were reported every year in the United States before the availability of the vaccine, *no* cases were reported in 2000! While there were 12,230 deaths from diphtheria in the United States in 1921 (long before the availability of a vaccine), there was only 1 case of diphtheria reported in 1998. The list of serious diseases that have been eradicated, or whose numbers have been dramatically reduced by immunizations, continues to grow—from the mumps to the measles, from rubella to tetanus (see Table on page 7).

Vaccines for Your Child

Immunizations routinely recommended for all children can prevent many major diseases, including

- Chickenpox (varicella)
- Diphtheria
- The flu (influenza)
- German measles (rubella)
- *Haemophilus influenzae* type b infections (meningitis, sepsis, pneumonia, arthritis, epiglottitis, and other serious infections)
- Hepatitis B
- Measles
- Meningococcal infections (meningococcemia, meningitis)
- Mumps
- Pneumococcal infections (meningitis, sepsis, pneumonia, arthritis, and other serious infections)
- Polio
- Tetanus
- Whooping cough (pertussis)

Several other immunizations are used in certain circumstances (eg, hepatitis A, rabies). The opportunities to protect the health of children and teenagers have never been greater.

Today's generation of parents may feel safe from diseases that threatened millions of children many years ago. Although the number of sick patients has greatly decreased, it's important to remember that all of these diseases still exist and can harm children who have not been immunized. Routine, up-to-date vaccinations are as important today as they have ever been.

Then and Now: Incidences of Illness From 10 Vaccine-Preventable Diseases (Includes Vaccines Recommended Before 1990 for Universal Use in Children in the United States)[a]

Disease	Baseline 20th Century Annual Incidences of Illness	2001 Incidences of Illness	% Decrease
Smallpox	48,164[b]	0	100
Diphtheria	175,885[c]	2	>99
Whooping cough (pertussis)	147,271[d]	7,580	95
Tetanus	1,314[e]	37	97
Polio (paralytic)	16,316[f]	0	100
Measles	503,282[g]	116	>99
Mumps	152,209[h]	266	>99
German measles (rubella)	47,745[i]	23	>99
Congenital rubella syndrome	823[j]	3	>99
Haemophilus influenzae type b	20,000[k]	181[l]	>99

[a]Adapted from Centers for Disease Control and Prevention. Impact of vaccines universally recommended for children—United States, 1990–1998. *MMWR Morb Mortal Wkly Rep.* 1999; 48:243–248; and Centers for Disease Control and Prevention. Notice to readers: final 2001 reports of notifiable diseases. *MMWR Morb Mortal Wkly Rep.* 2002;51:710.

[b]Average annual number of cases during 1900–1904.

[c]Average annual number of reported cases during 1920–1922, 3 years before vaccine development.

[d]Average annual number of reported cases during 1922–1925, 4 years before vaccine development.

[e]Estimated number of cases based on reported number of deaths during 1922–1926, assuming a fatality rate of 90%.

[f]Average annual number of reported cases during 1951–1954, 4 years before vaccine was licensed.

[g]Average annual number of reported cases during 1958–1962, 5 years before vaccine was licensed.

[h]Number of reported cases in 1968, the first year reporting began and the first year after vaccine was licensed.

[i]Average annual number of reported cases during 1966–1968, 3 years before vaccine was licensed.

[j]Estimated number of cases based on seroprevalence data in the population and on the risk that women infected during a childbearing year would have a fetus with congenital rubella syndrome.

[k]Estimated number of cases from population-based surveillance studies before vaccine was licensed in 1985.

[l]Represents invasive disease in children younger than 5 years and includes *H influenzae* strains that were not serotyped.

Adapted from Pickering LK, ed. *Red Book: 2003 Report of the Committee on Infectious Diseases.* 26th ed. Elk Grove Village, IL: American Academy of Pediatrics; 2003:2

The Success of the Measles Vaccine

Measles is a perfect example of a disease that, at least in the United States, has nearly been conquered by a vaccine. A 10th-century Persian doctor named Rhazes described the measles as "more to be dreaded than smallpox." Barely more than 40 years ago, the measles was still a normal part of childhood. Its distinctive rash was well known to parents and pediatricians. Even though most children got and survived the illness with no lasting effects, there were problems at times.

- About 10% of children with the measles developed an ear infection.
- Five percent contracted pneumonia.
- Less than 1% developed a swelling of the brain that caused mental retardation or deafness.

From 1953 to 1963, an average of 450 deaths per year related to measles was reported in the United States. Then, in 1963, a vaccine was licensed to protect against the disease, and children by the millions were immunized. Very rapidly, there was a dramatic decrease in the number of new cases. Today, pediatricians go years without seeing a single child with measles. Some pediatricians have never seen a case. In fact, there are less than 100 cases of measles each year in the entire country.

Do Immunizations Really Work?

Despite the absence of diseases like polio, diphtheria, and tetanus in entire communities, some parents remain unconvinced about the importance of immunizations. Yes, it's true that a few children do not respond to one vaccine or another—no vaccine has a record of 100% effectiveness. But depending on the study being cited, childhood vaccines are 85% to 98% effective. That's a remarkable track record, particularly when you take into account the serious nature of many of these infections. When you have an opportunity to give your child up to a 98% chance of avoiding a disease like chickenpox that can lead to dehydration or pneumonia or a serious illness like whooping cough that can cause seizures, brain disease, and death, that's a convincing reason to vaccinate.

Today's Parents Talking about "Yesterday's" Diseases

- "I had the worst case of chickenpox my pediatrician had ever seen. Chickenpox also killed my grandfather—he died of varicella encephalitis caused by shingles."
- "Whooping cough still concerns me. It's still around, and it's awful. I just hope that people don't forget how bad it is."
- "Both my dad and my husband's dad nearly died of diphtheria in the mid-1930s. We are strong believers in immunization."

Nevertheless, despite the easy availability and the proven effectiveness of vaccines, some children are still not properly immunized. A few parents are unaware that the initial shots need to be given in the early days and weeks of infancy. Other parents have made a conscious decision to avoid having their child vaccinated, believing one myth or another about the safety of immunizations (you can read more about this in Chapter 3). But when children are not immunized, the results can be devastating. Each year, thousands of children in the United States become seriously ill with diseases that could have been prevented with proper immunizations.

Immunizations are among the most effective medical interventions of all time. Short of basic sanitation and nutrition, no medical intervention has done more to save lives and prevent disease than immunizations. Immunizations are the cornerstone of preventive health, and the American Academy of Pediatrics believes strongly that every child needs and deserves the protection that immunizations provide.

CHAPTER 2

How Do Vaccines Work?

Most of the vaccines your child receives are given by shots. One can be given in a nasal spray (a version of the influenza vaccine). In the past, the polio vaccine was placed on a sugar cube and given by mouth (this form of the polio vaccine is no longer available in the United States). But no matter how they are given, the general ideas of the vaccines are all the same.

To help you understand how immunizations work, here's a little background on the body's immune system and the way it functions.

When your child becomes infected, his body relies on his immune system to fight the invading organism. White blood cells activate and begin making proteins called *antibodies* that locate the infectious agent and create a counteroffensive. By this time, the germs may have already had time to cause a few symptoms. In some cases, the antibody response will be too late to be helpful and the invading organism can cause a severe or life-threatening infection. Even so, by going on the attack, the immune system and its antibodies can eventually help stop many infections and help your child get well.

There's another important point to keep in mind about this process. Even after they've done their work, these antibodies don't disappear. They remain in the bloodstream, always on the lookout for the return of the same invaders. If these germs reappear, whether it's a few weeks or many years later, the antibodies are ready to protect. They can often prevent the infection altogether or stop the infection even before the first symptoms appear. That's why if you had the mumps or measles as a child, you never got it again, no matter how often you were exposed to the same infectious agent. The antibodies are pretty specific. If they've been created in response to, for example, the measles virus, they're not going to work against chickenpox. There are some antibodies that are not so specific and can protect you from similar types of bacteria.

So how does this scenario apply to childhood vaccines? The principle is very similar, even if the details are somewhat different. Immunizations rely on antibodies to fight off infections. But after a vaccination, antibodies go to work *before* a first infection develops. Here's how vaccines make that possible.

Live vaccines are made up of a weakened version of the bacteria or virus responsible for the disease. In some, vaccines are made from dead forms of the organism. These dead organisms were killed in a way to preserve their ability to provide immunity or protection. In other cases, an inactivated toxin that is made by the bacteria or a piece of the bacteria or virus is used. When the vaccine is given, the body's immune system detects this weakened or dead germ or germ part and reacts just as it would when a new full-blown infection occurs. It begins making antibodies against the vaccine material. These antibodies remain in the body and are ready to react if an actual infectious organism attacks. In a sense, the vaccine tricks the body into thinking it is under assault, and the immune system makes weapons that will provide a defense when a real infection becomes a threat.

Sometimes one dose of a vaccine is enough to protect a person, but often more than one dose is needed. Some antibodies protect for a lifetime, but others need boosting. For example, measles antibody lasts a lifetime, but antibody to tetanus can fall below a level that protects you, so booster doses are needed. Some viruses such as the flu can change enough to make the existing antibodies ineffective. That's why influenza vaccine is needed every year.

To repeat, the vaccine-generated antibodies stay in your child's bloodstream and are prepared to fight off infections for months, years, and even a lifetime. If and when your child is exposed to the actual infectious disease, these antibodies will recognize and attack the germs, destroying them and preventing or greatly weakening the illness.

By the way, newborns are immune to some infections because they've received antibodies from their mothers. But that immunity begins to fade in the first months of life. For that reason, it's very important to follow the immunization schedule that appears in Chapter 4 and that your pediatrician will recommend. Also, keep in mind that children do not gain *any* immunity from their mothers against some of the infectious diseases covered by childhood vaccines, including whooping cough and hepatitis. This is another important reason to follow the American Academy of Pediatrics immunization guidelines.

Immunizations: Active Vs Passive

Pediatricians can protect your child by administering not only the vaccines that most of this section of the book is devoted to (called *active immunizations*), but sometimes they can use what physicians call *passive immunizations*.

If you hear your pediatrician use these terms, this is what they mean.

- When your child receives an active immunization, the vaccine prevents an infectious disease by activating the body's production of antibodies that can fight off invading bacteria or viruses.
- Passive immunization, in which antibodies against a particular infectious agent are given directly to the child or adult, is sometimes appropriate. These antibodies are taken from a donor and then processed so the final preparation contains high antibody concentrations. At that point, they are given in the vein or by shot to the patient.

Passive immunization is often used in children and adults who have weakened immune systems or may not be good candidates for routine vaccinations for other reasons. It can be used with people who haven't been vaccinated against a disease to which they've been exposed. For example, the passive rabies immunization (rabies immune globulin) is commonly used after a certain type of wild animal bites a child. Passive immunizations for hepatitis A *(gamma globulin)* may be helpful for people traveling to a part of the world where hepatitis A is common. They are typically given before children or adults leave on their trip. These are used less now that there is a vaccine for hepatitis A. If there is enough time, the active vaccination is preferable.

Keep in mind that passive immunizations provide only short-term protection that often lasts just a few weeks before the antibodies are worn down and removed from the bloodstream. By contrast, active immunizations can produce antibodies that last a lifetime.

CHAPTER 3

How Safe Are Vaccines?

If you believed everything you heard on TV talk shows or read on anti-vaccine Internet sites, you might never allow your child to become vaccinated. In one warning after another, vaccine opponents often exaggerate or even make up immunization risks, with no scientific evidence to support their claims. They may imply that vaccines aren't effective. At the same time, they downplay or don't discuss the serious diseases that vaccines can eliminate or reduce in frequency. No wonder some parents are left feeling anxious and, in some cases, keep their youngster unvaccinated at the risk of their child's health.

You've probably heard some of the arguments made by immunization skeptics. One vaccine or another is said to cause autism, or brain damage, or multiple sclerosis, or seizures. Sometimes the alarmists warn that the vaccines are so unreliable that they leave children just as vulnerable to diseases as they were before they were vaccinated.

These claims would be upsetting if they were based on fact. But they're not, and they create plenty of fear among concerned parents. Panels of experts have confirmed again and again that today's vaccines are safer than ever. In fact, the greatest risks come when children are *not* immunized.

As a responsible parent, it's important for you to be fully informed. You can talk to your pediatrician if you have any concerns. In this chapter, let's get the facts straight.

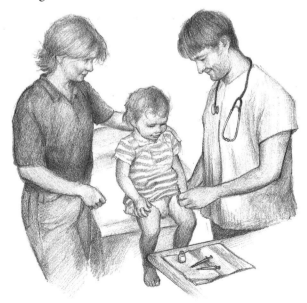

Gaining Perspective

Before a vaccine is ever approved and licensed, it goes through years of testing for safety and effectiveness. Neither the American Academy of Pediatrics (AAP) nor government agencies like the Centers for Disease Control and Prevention would recommend a vaccine that had not passed the tests for safety and effectiveness.

Of course, no vaccine or medicine is perfect. Some boys and girls who are immunized will experience reactions. Fortunately, when they occur, most are mild and short lived. Your child may experience redness, pain, or swelling at the site of the injection. She may develop a slight fever. After a few days, however, these minor symptoms will disappear, with no lasting effects. In the next chapter, you'll find vaccine-by-vaccine descriptions that include the side effects that have been associated with immunizations.

Managing Your Child's Pain

For most children, the mere thought of having a needle inserted into their arms is very upsetting. Anxiety before receiving a shot is common, no matter how old your child is. That worry is often heightened when more than one vaccine is given at a time. In some cases, 4 or more injections are given during a single doctor's visit.

Yet in most cases, the bark is worse than the bite. The pain associated with the majority of immunizations is minor. By 5 years of age, most children object only minimally, if at all, to receiving a shot. If there are any tears, they rarely last for more than a few minutes.

To make the experience as acceptable as possible, prepare your child in advance for the vaccines that she'll be receiving, no matter how old she is. Be honest; show her that you care. If your child is old enough to understand, explain how the shots will help her avoid becoming sick. *Never* describe the shots as punishment or use them as a threat.

In a newborn, you might try placing sugar on her tongue or a pacifier. This can often ease her worry. In an older infant, however, this approach generally doesn't work. For most young children, you can soothe and stroke them to help them get through an immunization and rock them afterward to decrease their crying. Holding your child on your lap may help calm her.

For older children, it may help to distract them during and after each shot. Try "blowing away the pain" or use soap bubbles, pinwheels, or music to divert their attention. Telling them stories or reading books to them may help as well. Some older children feel better hugging their parent, chest to chest, when the shot is given. If your doctor believes it is appropriate, let your older kids choose the site of the injections, giving them a sense that they have a degree of control over the process. Afterward, if a mild fever develops, ask your doctor about giving your child acetaminophen to make her more comfortable.

Through it all, keep reminding yourself that guarding your child against serious health risks is worth the short-term discomfort and tears that may be part of getting immunized.

When the Side Effects Are Serious

What about serious side effects? How often do they occur, and should you worry about them? This is an issue that has been studied repeatedly and intensively. Here are some facts that should help put your mind at ease.

Yes, there are reports of serious side effects that have been blamed on vaccines. But proving that the vaccine caused these side effects is often hard to do. In many cases, children simply develop illnesses around the time they've received a vaccine, and the immunizations get blamed unfairly. Don't forget that infants and children are given vaccinations at a time in life when certain health conditions begin and become apparent to both parent and doctor. In most cases, the evidence just isn't there to support a cause-and-effect link with vaccines.

That's the case with the myth linking the diphtheria-tetanus-pertussis (DTP) vaccine with sudden infant death syndrome (SIDS). The first dose of the vaccine is administered when a baby is 2 months old, which coincides with the time of life when the risk of SIDS is highest. Thus, you would expect some SIDS deaths to occur in this age group, whether children receive the immunization. In fact, a number of studies dating back to the 1980s looked at the incidence of SIDS deaths occurring at the time of the DTP vaccine. The researchers concluded that the number of deaths was at a level about equal to the number that would be expected to take place by chance. In short, there just isn't any scientific evidence linking the vaccine with SIDS.

Even so, many of the myths surrounding vaccines seem to have a life of their own. In the box below, you'll find a description of some of these unfounded claims, as well as a look at what the scientific evidence shows.

The Claims of Serious Side Effects—and the Facts

"I have heard a number of frightening stories about vaccinations, including the one about the MMR vaccine being potentially linked to autism. As a parent who does vaccinate, I often wonder if these stories are true."

Measles-Mumps-Rubella Vaccine and Autism

Autism is made up of many chronic developmental disorders and is often first diagnosed in toddlers. The number of cases of autism is reportedly on the rise, and some critics insist that the measles-mumps-rubella (MMR) vaccine is to blame. Others say the increase can be attributed to better reporting of autism cases by doctors. In 2001 and again in 2004, the Institute of Medicine (IOM) Immunization Safety Review Committee, an independent body of experts who have no conflict of interest with pharmaceutical companies or organizations that make vaccine recommendations, studied a possible MMR-autism link and found *no* evidence supporting such a connection. A panel of experts brought together by the AAP reached the same conclusion. Most of the authors of the original study linking MMR to autism have retracted their support of the study.

Risks of Thimerosal?

Since the 1930s, some vaccines have included a mercury-containing preservative called *thimerosal.* It has been used as an additive to vaccines because of its ability to prevent contamination by bacteria or fungi. Critics have argued that thimerosal-containing vaccines are the cause of a number of neurologic and developmental disorders, ranging from autism to attention-deficit/hyperactivity disorder and speech and language delays.

The IOM safety committee studied this issue and concluded that the evidence favors rejection of a causal relationship between thimerosal-containing vaccines and autism. Since the end of 2001, most of the vaccines recommended by the AAP are available in thimerosal-free formulations. Some vaccines, such as the MMR, polio, and chickenpox vaccines, have never contained thimerosal.

Multiple Immunizations and Immune Disorders
Because some immunizations are given together, parents are often concerned that multiple vaccines might trigger health problems associated with the immune system. Can they increase your child's risk of infections? Can they lead to the development of type 1 diabetes or various allergic diseases including asthma?

After looking at this issue, the IOM committee concluded that there is no evidence of a cause-and-effect relationship between multiple immunizations and a greater risk of infections and/or type 1 diabetes. As for a link with asthma and other allergic disorders, there simply isn't enough evidence to either accept or reject a connection with multiple vaccinations given together.

Hepatitis B Vaccines and Multiple Sclerosis
Although critics have claimed that hepatitis B immunizations can cause or trigger a relapse of multiple sclerosis, the IOM safety committee could find no scientific support for this theory. The same report also concluded that there is no evidence that the hepatitis B vaccine causes other types of nervous system problems, including Guillain-Barré syndrome.

Weighing the Risks *and* Benefits

If you've ever hesitated to have your child vaccinated, you need to keep in mind the risks of not getting these vaccines. The immunization of US children is so widespread and successful that the serious diseases that once caused severe illnesses and lasting disabilities have, in some cases, disappeared. That has left some parents asking, "If the disease is wiped out, why should I immunize my child against it?"

Here's what you need to keep in mind. If the rates of immunizations decline even a little, it can cause a comeback of the infectious diseases that have nearly been wiped out in the United States. Remember, even though many vaccine-preventable illnesses now occur in extremely low numbers, the germs that cause them are still around us, particularly in other parts of the world that are as close as a jet plane ride away.

Because of the success of immunizations, most parents have never seen a child with whooping cough or tetanus, so they aren't aware of how serious these diseases can be. They probably don't know of anyone who has died from these diseases (although in past years, many people did—see Table in Chapter 1 on page 7). As a result, they may not feel it is as necessary to get their kids vaccinated as their own parents might. But not vaccinating one's children can be very dangerous. In 1999, when rates of immunization were lower, there was a measles outbreak in the United States, and one out of every 500 people who developed the disease died. If we stop vaccinating children, the epidemics of previous eras will quickly return, causing serious illnesses and taking lives.

Meanwhile, researchers are looking at ways to make sure that vaccines are as safe as possible. For example, many parents may worry about the pertussis (whooping cough) part of the DTP vaccine. It's important for parents to know that the older version of the DTP vaccine is no longer used. It has been replaced by a newer DTaP vaccine (the *a* stands for *acellular pertussis*). In this vaccine, only a segment of the pertussis bacteria required for immunity is used. The old vaccine used whole cells of the bacteria responsible for pertussis. This is a significant improvement in vaccine safety. In 2005, a new vaccine, Tdap, was licensed for use in teenagers and adults. It has a smaller amount of the diphtheria and pertussis portions of the vaccine. The reason for the smaller amount is that less is needed to boost immunity in teenagers and adults because they received several doses of vaccine as young children.

Meanwhile, from time to time, adjustments are made in the immunization recommendations by public health agencies and the AAP to increase effectiveness and safety. For instance, in the past, the *oral* polio vaccine was associated with a very rare complication in which a few children actually developed polio after being immunized. (How rarely did this happen? In about one of every million children receiving the live oral doses.) In recent years, the recommendations have changed. Only the use of the *inactivated* polio vaccine (IPV), which carries absolutely *no* risk of causing polio itself, is advised. The evidence could not be clearer—your child is at much greater risk from the infectious diseases themselves than from the vaccines.

Some parents choose not to immunize because they don't want to take any risks. But choosing not to immunize your child is not without risk.

Your child can contract the illness and suffer problems. Your child can transmit the disease to others, including those who may be particularly vulnerable, like young infants or relatives with immune problems (many cancer patients, for example, can't be immunized). And your child will need to stay out of child care or school during disease outbreaks, even if she doesn't have the disease.

Reporting Side Effects

If your child has side effects after an immunization, talk it over with your pediatrician, especially before another dose of the same vaccine is given to your child.

Your doctor should not only write this information on your child's medical chart, but also report reactions to the Vaccine Adverse Event Reporting System (VAERS). The federal government established this organization to keep track of vaccine safety. You can also submit the report of a vaccine reaction to VAERS on your own. (For more information, call 800/822-7967.) It isn't necessary for you or the pediatrician to be sure the vaccine caused the event, nor does the event have to be serious in nature. The reason for this reporting system is to gather information and identify unrecognized negative events.

The National Vaccine Injury Compensation Program was established by the government to provide funds for the care of anyone who has been hurt by a vaccination. You can get information about this program on the Internet (www.hrsa.gov/osp/vicp) or by calling 800/338-2382.

Reporting Side Effects, *continued*

WEBSITE: www.vaers.org   E-MAIL: info@vaers.org   FAX: 1-877-721-0366

VAERS

VACCINE ADVERSE EVENT REPORTING SYSTEM	For CDC/FDA Use Only
24 Hour Toll-Free Information 1-800-822-7967 P.O. Box 1100, Rockville, MD 20849-1100 **PATIENT IDENTITY KEPT CONFIDENTIAL**	VAERS Number _____ Date Received _____

Patient Name:	Vaccine administered by (Name):	Form completed by (Name):
Last First M.I.	Responsible Physician _____	Relation ☐ Vaccine Provider ☐ Patient/Parent to Patient ☐ Manufacturer ☐ Other
Address	Facility Name/Address	Address (*if different from patient or provider*)
City State Zip	City State Zip	City State Zip
Telephone no. (___) _____	Telephone no. (___) _____	Telephone no. (___) _____

1. State	2. County where administered	3. Date of birth / / mm dd yy	4. Patient age	5. Sex ☐ M ☐ F	6. Date form completed / / mm dd yy

7. Describe adverse events(s) (symptoms, signs, time course) and treatment, if any	8. Check all appropriate: ☐ Patient died (date __/__/__) mm dd yy ☐ Life threatening illness ☐ Required emergency room/doctor visit ☐ Required hospitalization (_____days) ☐ Resulted in prolongation of hospitalization ☐ Resulted in permanent disability ☐ None of the above

9. Patient recovered ☐ YES ☐ NO ☐ UNKNOWN	10. Date of vaccination / / mm dd yy Time _____ AM PM	11. Adverse event onset / / mm dd yy Time _____ AM PM
12. Relevant diagnostic tests/laboratory data		

13. Enter all vaccines given on date listed in no. 10

	Vaccine (type)	Manufacturer	Lot number	Route/Site	No. Previous Doses
a.					
b.					
c.					
d.					

14. Any other vaccinations within 4 weeks prior to the date listed in no. 10

	Vaccine (type)	Manufacturer	Lot number	Route/Site	No. Previous doses	Date given
a.						
b.						

15. Vaccinated at: ☐ Private doctor's office/hospital ☐ Military clinic/hospital ☐ Public health clinic/hospital ☐ Other/unknown	16. Vaccine purchased with: ☐ Private funds ☐ Military funds ☐ Public funds ☐ Other/unknown	17. Other medications

18. Illness at time of vaccination (specify)	19. Pre-existing physician-diagnosed allergies, birth defects, medical conditions (specify)

20. Have you reported this adverse event previously?	☐ No ☐ To doctor	☐ To health department ☐ To manufacturer	*Only for children 5 and under*
			22. Birth weight _____ lb. _____ oz.	23. No. of brothers and sisters

21. Adverse event following prior vaccination (check all applicable, specify)	*Only for reports submitted by manufacturer/immunization project*

	Adverse Event	Onset Age	Type Vaccine	Dose no. in series
☐ In patient				
☐ In brother or sister				

24. Mfr./imm. proj. report no.	25. Date received by mfr./imm.proj.
26. 15 day report? ☐ Yes ☐ No	27. Report type ☐ Initial ☐ Follow-Up

Health care providers and manufacturers are required by law (42 USC 300aa-25) to report reactions to vaccines listed in the Table of Reportable Events Following Immunization. Reports for reactions to other vaccines are voluntary except when required as a condition of immunization grant awards.

Form VAERS-1(FDA)

CHAPTER 4

What Immunizations Does Your Child Need?

As you've already read, immunizations can be lifesaving for children and adults. Keep that in mind as you read about the vaccines that will protect your child from diseases.

Initially, some parents worry about the number of recommended vaccinations or shots. Sometimes they wonder if they're all really necessary. As your pediatrician will tell you, the answer is a definite "yes." Pediatricians and public health officials speak in a united voice on this issue. As a result of ongoing advances in medical science, new vaccines continue to be developed and the number of recommended immunizations keeps on growing. The American Academy of Pediatrics (AAP) immunization schedule represents an agreement among not only the AAP, but also the Advisory Committee on Immunization Practices of the Centers for Disease Control and Prevention and the American Academy of Family Physicians.

The high number of necessary vaccines may seem overwhelming at times. Don't forget the fact that each shot represents protection for your child from a major disease that, in previous generations, commonly caused serious illness, permanent disability (eg, severe mental retardation, deafness, blindness, seizures), and sometimes even death.

In this chapter, we'll describe the most important immunizations that your child needs, when he should get them, and other information that you should know to help you better understand the vaccines. You'll also learn how to ask any questions you may have for your pediatrician. As you'll see or as your doctor may have already explained, your baby's initial vaccination should be given at birth or, in some cases, at your baby's first doctor's visit. Additional shots are given during follow-up visits to the doctor's office before your child starts school. Each vaccine should be given at specific ages, based largely on when its use is likely to produce the greatest response and show the most effectiveness. For some vaccines, your child will need multiple injections over a period of time or booster shots along the way.

For more information about the diseases that the vaccines protect against, see Part 4, "Getting the Facts About Infectious Diseases."

Chickenpox (Varicella) Vaccine

This vaccine protects against chickenpox, a viral illness that affects the skin and other organs. It is recommended for all children between 12 and 18 months of age. In a small number of youngsters, redness and pain at the site of the shot may occur. A mild rash—a few tiny bumps or pimples—may appear, most often where the shot was given. This rash sometimes occurs up to 1 month after the immunization and lasts for a few days. A fever may develop, as well.

Nostalgia for Chickenpox?!?

Some people feel almost a kind of nostalgia toward their encounters with potentially dangerous infectious diseases, especially with chickenpox.

- "I had the chickenpox when I was in third grade. Got to stay home from school for a week and take oatmeal baths! I am sure it was a mild case because it did not bother me much."
- "I had chickenpox—they came; they itched; they went away. And I got to stay out of school for several days."
- "Chickenpox was a breeze. A few days of downtime and then back to normal."

Thankfully, these people did not suffer any long-term effects of chickenpox. But remember, what's mild for one person may be deadly for another. Other parents don't look back so fondly on this disease, which used to be an uncomfortable "rite of passage" for young children.

- "I had chickenpox as a child and it was awful. My son has been vaccinated against chickenpox so he will not have to experience this disease."
- "I had chickenpox as an adult—I never caught it as a child. It would have been very severe if not for the antiviral medication I was able to take. I'd prefer a vaccination and skip the whole thing!"

Diphtheria, Tetanus, and Acellular Pertussis Vaccine

When your baby is 2 months old, he should be given his first vaccine against diphtheria (D), tetanus (lockjaw) (T), and acellular pertussis (whooping cough) (aP). This single shot will provide protection against all 3 diseases. It will be the first of 5 DTaP injections given before your child enters school. The entire series is given at the following times:

- Two, 4, and 6 months of age
- Six to 12 months after the third dose (typically at 18 months of age)
- Between 4 and 6 years of age (before he enters school)

Different vaccine formulations are used as your child gets older. When your child is 11 to 12 years old, he should receive a shot of tetanus, diphtheria, and acellular pertussis (Tdap) vaccine if at least 5 years have passed since the last dose of the DTaP vaccine. This preteen dose of Tdap was recommended in 2005 to protect older children from pertussis. Subsequent Td boosters are advisable every 10 years.

Now, what about side effects? In the first 24 hours after the DTaP shot, you may notice some normal and expected reactions to the shot in your child, including irritability and sleepiness. He might also experience some of the general side effects described in Chapter 3, such as redness and soreness in the area where the shot was given and a low-grade fever. These reactions should last no more than a couple of days. Until they run their course, ask your doctor about giving your child acetaminophen to make him more comfortable.

Serious side effects are rare, occurring in less than 1% of children receiving the DTaP vaccine. They may include continuous and sometimes high-pitched crying for more than 3 hours, paleness or limpness, excessive sleepiness, a high temperature (105°F or higher), or seizures, which are usually associated with the high fever. Swelling of the brain has occurred in very rare cases (1 in every 110,000 shots), but it is not clear whether the vaccine is responsible or whether there is some other cause such as an infection totally unrelated to the vaccine but occurring soon after the vaccination.

Haemophilus influenzae type b Vaccine

This vaccine protects your child against *Haemophilus influenzae* type b (Hib) bacteria, which causes meningitis, pneumonia, and infections of the joints, throat, bloodstream, and soft tissue. This immunization should be given to your child beginning at 2 months of age. Reactions at the site of the injection, including soreness, redness, or swelling, occur in about 25% of children who receive this immunization.

There are 3 types of Hib vaccines available in the United States. Depending on the type chosen, you child should receive one of the following:

- Three doses given at 2, 4, and 6 months of age
- Two doses given at 2 and 4 months of age

An additional booster shot is recommended between ages 12 and 15 months.

An Incredible Success Story

The Hib vaccine is a relatively recent vaccine. It was added to the recommended immunization schedule in 1990 and has had a dramatic positive effect on child health. Among other illnesses, Hib infections cause meningitis, which can lead to mental retardation, deafness, and sometimes death. Since the introduction of the vaccine, these types of illnesses caused by Hib have quickly decreased by more than 98%!

Source: Baker JP, Pearson HA, eds. *Dedicated to the Health of All Children.* Elk Grove Village, IL: American Academy of Pediatrics; 2005

Hepatitis B Vaccine

This vaccine protects against irritation and swelling (inflammation) of the liver (hepatitis) caused by the hepatitis B virus. The infection can occur at any time during childhood and can even be spread from an infected mother to a newborn at birth. It can also be spread from one member of a household to another by sharing toothbrushes or razors.

Your child should be immunized with the hepatitis B vaccine during early infancy. The vaccine should be given in 3 doses according to the following guidelines:

- In an infant whose mother is infected with or hasn't been tested for the hepatitis B virus
  — First shot: Shortly after birth and before discharge from the hospital
  — Second shot: Between 1 and 2 months of age
  — Third shot: At 6 months of age
- In an infant whose mother is not infected with the hepatitis B virus
  — First shot: Between birth and 2 months of age
  — Second shot: Between 1 and 4 months of age, at least 1 month after the first dose
  — Third shot: Between 6 and 18 months of age
- In an older child or teenager
  — First shot: Any time
  — Second shot: 1 to 2 months after the first dose
  — Third shot: At least 8 weeks after the second dose and 4 to 6 months after the first dose

■ Alternate 2-dose schedule for teenagers aged 11 to 15 years, using the
adult version of the vaccine
— First shot: Any time
— Second shot: 4 to 6 months after the first dose

The hepatitis B vaccine is very safe. Minor reactions to it may occur in
a small number of children and can include fussiness as well as redness,
soreness, or swelling where the shot is given. A mild fever may occur as
well. More serious side effects are extremely rare.

Why Should We Vaccinate Our Newborn Against Hepatitis B?

Some parents wonder why their child needs to be vaccinated for
hepatitis B, a virus that is commonly associated with intravenous
drug use and sexual contact. Hepatitis B can be spread to children
in several ways, including from infected people living with young
children. Thirty percent of all people with hepatitis B have no
known risk factors.

Hepatitis B can also be spread from infected mothers to their babies
during birth. But even those newborns can benefit from proper immunization, which can prevent the disease from developing. Infancy
is the best time to begin immunizing against hepatitis B because an
infection acquired early in life is most likely to cause chronic liver
disease. This can lead to liver failure or liver cancer later in life. Infancy
is also the best time for pediatricians to give this immunization because frequent routine office visits take place during the first year
of life.

Simply put, the hepatitis B vaccine is safe. It provides the best possible protection against hepatitis B infection, which may lead to liver
problems including infection, failure, or cancer. Prior to routine immunization, every year in the United States more than 300,000 people
developed hepatitis B infections and 5,000 of them died from
related causes.

Influenza Vaccine

This vaccine protects your child against influenza, commonly referred to as *the flu,* and must be given every year.

- The influenza vaccine is recommended for all children aged 6 to 23 months, as well as for other people in their household. Youngsters in this age group have a greater risk of health problems if they contract the flu and may need to go to the hospital.
- It is also presently recommended for children who have medical conditions such as asthma, diabetes, heart disease, human immunodeficiency virus (HIV), and sickle cell disease.

If a child is younger than 9 years and is receiving the influenza vaccination for the first time, he will need 2 doses given at least 4 weeks apart.

Despite popular myths, the traditional influenza vaccine *cannot* cause the flu. It is made from an *inactivated* or killed influenza virus. When children get cold symptoms that mimic mild flu within a few days after influenza immunization, they are caused by the common cold virus, which they already had at the time of immunization. Local reactions at the site of the shot are not common. Fever is rare in children younger than 13 years, although it sometimes occurs in children younger than 24 months about 6 to 24 hours after the shot is given.

An alternative to the inactivated influenza vaccine became available in 2003 with the approval of a nasal spray influenza vaccine. This vaccine is a live virus that has been changed so that it can't survive at body temperature. It can grow locally in the nose so that the person makes antibody to the virus. This spray vaccine is currently licensed for use in healthy children aged 5 years and older, as well as adults up to age 49 years. Side effects of the live attenuated nasal spray (cold-adapted influenza vaccine) include a runny nose and low-grade fever, symptoms similar to a very mild flu infection.

Measles-Mumps-Rubella Vaccine

This is a combination vaccine that provides protection against the measles (M), mumps (M), and rubella (R) (German measles) in a single shot. Your child should receive 2 doses of this vaccine at

- Twelve to 15 months of age
- Four to 6 years of age (before he enters school)

Beginning 5 to 10 days after this vaccine is given, your child may develop a mild rash, a low-grade fever, and mild joint pains. Less commonly, there may be mild swelling of the lymph nodes in the neck or diaper region. Other rare side effects are sometimes reported and include tingling of the arms or legs. Allergic reactions are rare and usually mild. In the past, there had been some concerns about egg allergies, but this is no longer considered a problem.

Meningococcal Vaccine

This vaccine protects your preteen against most (but not all) types of the meningococcal bacteria. This bacteria causes overwhelming infections (sepsis) and meningitis. The newest version of the vaccine was licensed in 2005 and is a conjugate vaccine that includes 4 of the 5 types of meningococcus that cause disease.

Currently, a single dose of the vaccine is given at 11 to 12 years of age or entry to high school or college. In the future, these recommendations will change to include younger children.

Pneumococcal Vaccine

This vaccine protects your child against meningitis, pneumonia, and joint infections caused by *Streptococcus pneumoniae*. This is the most common type of bacterial pneumonia. The newest versions of pneumococcal vaccines, which were licensed for use in the United States in 2000, are called conjugated vaccines. A series of 4 shots should be given to all children at the following ages

- Two months
- Four months
- Six months
- Between 12 and 15 months

Some children are thought to have a higher risk of getting a pneumococcal infection because they have sickle cell disease, HIV infection, or other health conditions. These children should be given an extra dose of the original pneumococcal vaccine, which protects against more strains of *S pneumoniae*, between 24 and 59 months of age.

A few children receiving this vaccine have redness and swelling at the site where the shot is given. Some may get a mild fever that can occur within the first 1 to 2 days after the shot.

Polio Vaccine

Children should receive 4 doses of the inactivated poliovirus (IPV) vaccine before starting school. It should be given at

- Two months of age
- Four months of age
- Between 6 and 18 months of age
- Between 4 and 6 years of age (before the child starts school)

You may remember the oral polio vaccine, which was once a common alternative to giving the vaccine as a shot. In fact, the oral polio vaccine eliminated polio from the entire Western hemisphere and most of the world. Since 2000, the AAP stopped recommending use of the oral vaccine in the United States because of a very small risk of a serious side effect called vaccine-associated paralytic polio (VAPP). This side effect occurred in about 1 of every million children receiving the live oral vaccine. The vaccine used today (IPV) is made with inactivated poliovirus and cannot cause VAPP. The oral vaccine is no longer available in the United States.

There are very few side effects associated with the IPV vaccine, and none of them are serious. Your child might have some mild soreness at the site where the shot was given.

Additional Vaccines

In addition to protecting your child with the vaccines already described, some children may need additional immunizations.

Hepatitis A Vaccine

This vaccine is recommended in certain parts of the country where hepatitis A is common, as well as for children who are considered to be at high risk of getting the infection. The vaccine is approved for youngsters 2 years and older. It requires 2 doses that should be given at least 6 months apart. The first dose can be given during any visit to the pediatrician's office. No serious side effects have been reported with the hepatitis A vaccine. Some children have mild pain at the site of the shot.

Rabies Vaccine and Rabies Immune Globulin

Active and passive immunizations are used to prevent rabies in a person who has been bitten by an animal suspected to have rabies.

Vaccines for Travel

Vaccines needed for travelers vary depending on a person's age and itinerary. More information is provided in chapters 7 and 14.

Recommended Childhood and Adolescent Immunization Schedule UNITED STATES · 2005

Vaccine ▼ / Age ▶	Birth	1 month	2 months	4 months	6 months	12 months	15 months	18 months	24 months	4-6 years	11-12 years	13-18 years
Hepatitis B[1]	HepB #1	HepB #2			HepB #3						HepB Series	
Diphtheria, Tetanus, Pertussis[2]			DTaP	DTaP	DTaP		DTaP	DTaP		DTaP	Td	Td
Haemophilus influenzae type b[3]			Hib	Hib	Hib	Hib						
Inactivated Poliovirus			IPV	IPV	IPV	IPV				IPV		
Measles, Mumps, Rubella[4]						MMR #1				MMR #2	MMR #2	MMR #2
Varicella[5]						Varicella				Varicella		
Pneumococcal[6]			PCV	PCV	PCV	PCV	PCV		PCV	PPV		
Influenza[7]						Influenza (Yearly)				Influenza (Yearly)		
Hepatitis A[8]										Hepatitis A Series		

█▌▌▌▌█ Vaccines below dashed line are for selected populations

This schedule indicates the recommended ages for routine administration of currently licensed childhood vaccines, as of December 1, 2004, for children through age 18 years. Any dose not given at the recommended age should be given at any subsequent visit when indicated and feasible. ▨ Indicates age groups that warrant special effort to administer those vaccines not previously given. Additional vaccines may be licensed and recommended during the year. Licensed combination vaccines may be used whenever any components of the combination are indicated and the vaccine's other components are not contraindicated. Providers should consult the manufacturers' package inserts for detailed recommendations. Clinically significant adverse events that follow immunization should be reported to the Vaccine Adverse Event Reporting System (VAERS). Guidance about how to obtain and complete a VAERS form can be found on the Internet: **www.vaers.org** or by calling **800-822-7967**.

Range of recommended ages	Only if mother HBsAg(−)
Preadolescent assessment	▨ Catch-up immunization

The *Recommended Childhood and Adolescent Immunization Schedule* is updated on a regular basis, typically in January. Please refer to the latest schedule, available online at www.cispimmunize.org or www.aapredbook.org.

1. Hepatitis B (HepB) vaccine. All infants should receive the first dose of hepatitis B vaccine soon after birth and before hospital discharge; the first dose may also be given by age 2 months if the infant's mother is hepatitis B surface antigen (HBsAg) negative. Only monovalent HepB can be used for the birth dose. Monovalent or combination vaccine containing HepB may be used to complete the series. Four doses of vaccine may be administered when a birth dose is given. The second dose should be given at least 4 weeks after the first dose, except for combination vaccines, which cannot be administered before age 6 weeks. The third dose should be given at least 16 weeks after the first dose and at least 8 weeks after the second dose. The last dose in the vaccination series (third or fourth dose) should not be administered before age 24 weeks.

Infants born to HBsAg-positive mothers should receive HepB and 0.5 mL of Hepatitis B Immune Globulin (HBIG) within 12 hours of birth at separate sites. The second dose is recommended at age 1–2 months. The last dose in the immunization series should not be administered before age 24 weeks. These infants should be tested for HBsAg and antibody to HBsAg (anti-HBs) at age 9–15 months.

Infants born to mothers whose HBsAg status is unknown should receive the first dose of the HepB series within 12 hours of birth. Maternal blood should be drawn as soon as possible to determine the mother's HBsAg status; if the HBsAg test is positive, the infant should receive HBIG as soon as possible (no later than age 1 week). The second dose is recommended at age 1–2 months. The last dose in the immunization series should not be administered before age 24 weeks.

2. Diphtheria and tetanus toxoids and acellular pertussis (DTaP) vaccine. The fourth dose of DTaP may be administered as early as age 12 months, provided 6 months have elapsed since the third dose and the child is unlikely to return at age 15–18 months. The final dose in the series should be given at age ≥4 years. **Tetanus and diphtheria toxoids (Td)** is recommended at age 11–12 years if at least 5 years have elapsed since the last dose of tetanus and diphtheria toxoid-containing vaccine. Subsequent routine Td boosters are recommended every 10 years.

3. *Haemophilus influenzae* type b (Hib) conjugate vaccine. Three Hib conjugate vaccines are licensed for infant use. If PRP-OMP (PedvaxHIB or ComVax [Merck]) is administered at ages 2 and 4 months, a dose at age 6 months is not required. DTaP/Hib combination products should not be used for primary immunization in infants at ages 2, 4, or 6 months but can be used as boosters following any Hib vaccine. The final dose in the series should be given at age ≥12 months.

4. Measles, mumps, and rubella vaccine (MMR). The second dose of MMR is recommended routinely at age 4–6 years but may be administered during any visit, provided at least 4 weeks have elapsed since the first dose and both doses are administered beginning at or after age 12 months. Those who have not previously received the second dose should complete the schedule by the visit at age 11–12 years.

5. Varicella vaccine. Varicella vaccine is recommended at any visit at or after age 12 months for susceptible children (i.e., those who lack a reliable history of chickenpox). Susceptible persons aged ≥13 years should receive 2 doses, given at least 4 weeks apart.

6. Pneumococcal vaccine. The heptavalent **pneumococcal conjugate vaccine (PCV)** is recommended for all children aged 2–23 months. It is also recommended for certain children aged 24–59 months. The final dose in the series should be given at age ≥12 months. **Pneumococcal polysaccharide vaccine (PPV)** is recommended in addition to PCV for certain high-risk groups. See *MMWR* 2000;49(RR-9):1–35.

7. Influenza vaccine. Influenza vaccine is recommended annually for children aged ≥6 months with certain risk factors (including but not limited to asthma, cardiac disease, sickle cell disease, HIV, and diabetes), healthcare workers, and other persons (including household members) in close contact with persons in groups at high risk (see *MMWR* 2004;53[RR-6]:1–40) and can be administered to all others wishing to obtain immunity. In addition, healthy children aged 6–23 months and close contacts of healthy children aged 0–23 months are recommended to receive influenza vaccine, because children in this age group are at substantially increased risk for influenza-related hospitalizations. For healthy persons aged 5–49 years, the intranasally administered live, attenuated influenza vaccine (LAIV) is an acceptable alternative to the intramuscular trivalent inactivated influenza vaccine (TIV). See *MMWR* 2004;53(RR-6):1–40. Children receiving TIV should be administered a dosage appropriate for their age (0.25 mL if 6–35 months or 0.5 mL if ≥3 years). Children aged ≤8 years who are receiving influenza vaccine for the first time should receive 2 doses (separated by at least 4 weeks for TIV and at least 6 weeks for LAIV).

8. Hepatitis A vaccine. Hepatitis A vaccine is recommended for children and adolescents in selected states and regions and for certain high-risk groups; consult your local public health authority. Children and adolescents in these states, regions, and high-risk groups who have not been immunized against hepatitis A can begin the hepatitis A immunization series during any visit. The 2 doses in the series should be administered at least 6 months apart. See *MMWR* 1999;48(RR-12):1–37.

Your Child's Immunization Record

It's important to keep up-to-date records of all your child's immunizations, beginning at birth and continuing through adolescence. Make entries into this chart each time your child receives a vaccination by filling in the date.

Record of Immunizations

	Date Given	Where Given	Reaction
Hepatitis B			
Diphtheria, Tetanus, Pertussis			
H influenzae type b			
Inactivated Poliovirus			
Pneumococcal			
Measles, Mumps, Rubella			
Varicella			
Influenza			
Meningococcal			
Hepatitis A— in selected areas			
Other			

Timing Is (Almost) Everything

The AAP strongly recommends that you get your child immunized at the ages that have been carefully selected for each vaccination. The first immunizations should be given at birth or in infancy, followed by shots at the designated intervals.

But what if your child falls behind? What if he hasn't gotten all the recommended vaccines? If that's the case, he'll be at risk for becoming sick with a potentially life-threatening illness. Also, he could spread that infection to other children and adults.

Despite the dangers of not getting vaccinated on time, studies have shown that about 20% of very young children aged 19 to 35 months are under-immunized. This means that they are not up-to-date with their shots. If your child falls into this category, it's time to catch up. If he hasn't received a particular vaccine (or vaccines) at the recommended age(s) or hasn't received *any* vaccines, it's never too late to get started or pick up where you left off. Ask your pediatrician to start giving vaccines during your next office visit or when your doctor decides it's appropriate. Find the point in the recommended schedule where your child should be, figure out which vaccines he's missing, and follow your pediatrician's advice on how to get back on track. There's no need to start all over again, but you need to make sure that your child is fully protected.

It's always a good idea to keep your own records of the immunizations your child has received. Yes, they're part of your child's medical file in your pediatrician's office. But if you move to a different city or change pediatricians for any reason, it's helpful to have your own records to make sure that your child continues to receive the right immunizations at the proper times. Also keep in mind that every state requires that you give proof that your child has been properly vaccinated before she enrolls in school.

CHAPTER 5

Immunizations in Special Circumstances

Most parents are convinced that immunizations are important to the present and future health of their children. They make sure that their children's vaccinations are current. Even so, there are special circumstances that come up in a child's life that often have parents wondering whether the recommended immunization schedule still applies. In this chapter, let's look at these special situations and how they may affect the vaccines your child receives.

Preterm Babies

Some parents of preterm and low birth weight babies are concerned about immunizing their newborns according to the standard schedule created by the American Academy of Pediatrics (AAP) and other medical organizations. Their main worry is whether the recommendations were made with full-term, normal weight babies in mind and whether the same guidelines apply to their own newborns. Parents may think that their newborns are just too fragile to be vaccinated because of low birth weight and possible health problems that came with their baby's preterm birth.

Your pediatrician will tell you that all of these babies should be given the routinely recommended childhood vaccinations. They should get every immunization on the standard schedule when they reach the ages at which these shots are normally given to all children.

If you're uncertain, keep in mind that if preterm babies get the infections that vaccines can prevent, they have a greater chance of having disease-related problems. All of the available vaccines are safe when given to preterm and low birth weight babies. Any side effects associated with the vaccines are similar in both full-term and preterm babies.

The hepatitis B immunization deserves special mention. In most circumstances, the AAP recommends this particular vaccine at birth or before the baby is discharged from the hospital to return home. In other words, this vaccine should be given in the first hours or days of life. But if your baby weighs less than 2.2 pounds (2,000 grams) at birth, your pediatrician may decide to change the timetable for the hepatitis B vaccine, perhaps waiting to give it until the baby is a little older. Nevertheless, medically stable preterm babies weighing more than 2.2 pounds at birth should be treated like full-term babies and receive the first dose of the hepatitis B immunization according to the recommended schedule.

Weakened Immune Systems

Some children have weakened immune systems because of chronic diseases or medications they're taking. These include

- Children born with abnormalities of the immune system
- Children infected with human immunodeficiency virus, which causes acquired immunodeficiency syndrome (AIDS), including those who have full-blown AIDS
- Children who have cancer
- Children who have had organ transplants
- Children with diseases that require them to take certain medicines, including corticosteroids

If your child falls into one of these categories, your pediatrician may decide that the benefits of giving certain vaccines outweigh the risks that your youngster's immune system problems pose. Your doctor also may choose to wait until your child's immune system is stronger before giving these vaccines.

Here are a few points to keep in mind and discuss with your doctor.

- For a child with a weakened immune system, your pediatrician may suggest delaying or not using immunizations containing live viruses in particular because of the risk of serious effects from the vaccine. These include vaccines such as measles-mumps-rubella (MMR), chickenpox (varicella), and the nasal spray influenza vaccine. (Although the oral polio vaccine contains a live virus, it is no longer used in the United States.) If a child has had chemotherapy, live-virus vaccines are often given 3 months or more after the treatment is completed.

■ In general, vaccines with inactivated viruses and bacteria can be used in children who have weakened immune systems with no increased risk. However, the effectiveness of these immunizations can vary in these children and may be reduced in some cases. Vaccines with inactivated viruses or parts of bacteria that do not have an increased risk of side effects in children with weakened immune systems include diphtheria, tetanus, and acellular pertussis; hepatitis A; hepatitis B; polio; *Haemophilus influenzae* type B; pneumococcal; meningococcal; and the killed influenza vaccines (those given by shot).

■ Children taking corticosteroids can have weakened immune systems. The decision of whether to use vaccines in these youngsters often depends on the dose of steroids taken, as well as how these medicines are given. For example, when steroids are given in the form of topical medicines (applied directly to the skin), or if they're inhaled in an aerosol formulation (often to treat asthma or allergies), they don't interfere with the immune system. This means live-virus vaccines can be given to these youngsters. Also, children taking steroid pills in low or moderate doses can safely be given live-virus vaccines.

Other Circumstances for *Not* Vaccinating

Although the vaccines described in Part 1 are meant for every child, there may be some other exceptions to giving the immunizations as scheduled. Ask your pediatrician whether there is anything else in your child's medical history that makes her a poor candidate for one or more immunizations. Your pediatrician will examine your child's condition and decide whether she will be given the vaccines or if they should be rescheduled.

Here are some examples of circumstances that may require postponing the use of one or more vaccines or even avoiding them completely.

■ If your child has had a severe reaction to a particular vaccine with symptoms such as shortness of breath, wheezing, or hives, she should not be given further doses of that vaccine.

- If your child has a progressive illness and the diagnosis is unknown, immunizations may be postponed until your child's problem becomes clear.
- Because the influenza vaccine is made with egg proteins, it should not be given to your child if she is severely allergic to eggs. (This is no longer considered a factor for the MMR vaccine). Also, if your child is severely allergic to yeast, she should not be given the hepatitis B vaccine.
- If your child is moderately to severely ill with or without a fever at the time of a scheduled vaccination, the immunization should be postponed until she's feeling better. The symptoms of a serious illness could interfere with determining whether your child has had a reaction to the vaccine. A fever itself and mild illness are not reasons to avoid immunizations. If otherwise well enough, a child who is receiving antibiotics may be immunized with any of the recommended vaccines.

CHAPTER 6

Common Parent Questions and Concerns

There is plenty of information available about immunizations—and lots of misinformation, too. As a result, parents are often confused about the use of vaccines, including their safety and effectiveness, and may come to the pediatrician's office with a list of questions for their doctor.

Here are just a few of the questions that commonly arise among parents, and the authoritative answers to them.

I'm breastfeeding my baby. Does he still need to be immunized?
Yes, your baby needs all of the recommended vaccines even when the mother is breastfeeding. Breastfeeding supplies your child with the best possible nutrition and even some antibodies from the mother. However, it will not protect him from infectious illnesses the way that immunizations do. Serious diseases such as polio, whooping cough, tetanus, and diphtheria are best prevented with vaccines. Your baby's immune system will make its own antibodies and stimulate the blood cells to be ready to fight these illnesses.

I know a child who has gotten all of her vaccines, but she caught one of the diseases that she was vaccinated against. Doesn't that show that these vaccines don't work?
No. It's true that occasionally children will not have a response to vaccines. But in 85% to 98% of cases, the vaccines are effective. Sometimes the vaccines don't totally prevent the infection but weaken it so the child gets a mild case. This is especially true with influenza and chickenpox vaccines. Most people who get the full-blown disease have not received the full series of immunizations against that infection.

Why is my pediatrician recommending that my newborn receive vaccines? Can't we wait until he's a little older?
Vaccines are recommended beginning in infancy because infectious diseases can begin at this early age. When they affect an infant or young child, they are often more serious and create more problems than when they strike older children. Vaccines are only recommended for newborns after testing to see if they are safe and effective.

I'm really worried. . . I heard that there are batches of vaccines referred to as "hot lots" that might be dangerous. Do hot lots exist?
No. There is no evidence that there are safety differences from one vaccine batch to another. Vaccine reactions are routinely reported to the federal

government Vaccine Adverse Event Reporting System (VAERS). While there's a common belief that large numbers of VAERS reports come from certain batches of vaccine (so-called hot lots), the VAERS data have never found a vaccine lot to be unsafe. Keep in mind that every vaccine lot is tested for safety by its maker. Both the Food and Drug Administration and the Centers for Disease Control and Prevention (CDC) conduct ongoing surveillance to make sure vaccines are safe.

My child has a cold and fever. Can she receive any vaccinations while she's sick?

Yes. If an otherwise healthy child only has a mild illness such as a runny nose, a low-grade fever, an ear infection, a cough, or mild diarrhea, she can safely be vaccinated.

My child is scheduled to receive more than one immunization at his next office visit. Do any vaccines interfere with each other when given at the same time?

The vaccines recommended by the American Academy of Pediatrics (AAP) for use in all children do not interfere with each other and, as needed, can be safely given together during a single visit. Research has shown that when multiple vaccines are given together, the side effects are no greater than when immunizations are given individually. In fact, the only 2 vaccines that can't be given together are yellow fever and cholera vaccines. This is really no longer a concern because the cholera vaccine is no longer recommended for use and the yellow fever vaccine is used mostly for travelers to certain areas of the world.

The time you should wait between your infant's routine vaccines depends on the type of vaccine used. In general, you wait at least a month. Be sure to tell your doctor if your child receives a vaccine at school, in an emergency department, or elsewhere.

What vaccine side effects should concern me?

If your child has negative effects after being vaccinated, let your pediatrician know about them at your next office visit. A few side effects are signs of a serious reaction, and if you see them, call your pediatrician immediately. They include

- Hives
- Difficulty breathing

The following symptoms could be reactions to the vaccine or signs of an infection, so call your pediatrician right away:

- Extreme irritability
- A very high fever (above 104°F)
- A generalized rash

If your child has a large amount of swelling at the site where the shot was given, let your pediatrician know before the next immunization.

My child has missed some of her vaccinations. In fact, the time when she was supposed to get them passed long ago. Do we have to start all over again at the beginning?

No. If a particular immunization such as the diphtheria, tetanus, and acellular pertussis or hepatitis B vaccine is given in a series of doses and your child has missed one or more of them, just pick up where you've left off. The vaccines she has already received still count. At the next doctor's visit, she can restart her childhood vaccinations until she's caught up.

What are the next steps being undertaken to make vaccines even safer for the future?

Vaccine safety is continually looked at by reviewing reports made to VAERS and by independent researchers. As new methods of immunization become available, such as oral vaccines or genetically altered foods that can act as vaccines, safety issues are considered above all else. If it is safe for animals, careful trials are done with people. If safety and effectiveness is confirmed, large-scale trials take place. Even after a vaccine is licensed for use, there are ongoing studies by drug companies, the CDC, and independent scientists. If outbreaks of illness occur, they are studied to determine the effectiveness of vaccines.

How do the AAP-recommended vaccines compare to what is done in other countries?

In the United States, we are fortunate to have a number of vaccines that are not normally used in other countries. Many countries of the world do not have the resources to provide immunizations to their children. Our vaccine schedule is a bit different than that of other countries. In some cases, this is because the timing of infections is earlier. For example, infections caused by *Haemophilus influenzae* type B occur very early in Native Americans and Alaska Natives.

The types of vaccines recommended for an area are based on the infections common in that area. In Asia, children receive a vaccine against Japanese encephalitis virus. This is not needed in the United States, where this virus is very rare. Travelers often need additional vaccines for diseases like Japanese encephalitis or typhoid fever. Before you take your child on an international vacation, check with your pediatrician to see if your child needs any additional vaccines.

How long does the vaccine for chickenpox last, and should it be given again in adulthood?

Immunity following the chickenpox vaccine lasts for at least 20 years. However, there are cases of chickenpox in children who have been given the vaccine. These cases are called *breakthrough* cases and are almost always mild and short lasting. There isn't enough information at this time to know if booster doses would prevent these breakthrough cases. It is possible that the recommendations will change.

There is currently a trial going on to study whether a dose of the chickenpox vaccine given to 50-year-olds who had chickenpox as children will prevent shingles. The chickenpox virus can live in the nerve cells of a person, become active again, and cause shingles, a very painful rash. The trial is not yet completed. Stay tuned for the results and any follow-up vaccine recommendations.

What would it mean for my child if another child—say one whose parents don't believe in immunization—brings measles to preschool?

The answer to this question depends on whether your child has been immunized. If so, your child will be protected. The exception to this is a child who doesn't respond to the vaccination. This occurs in about 5% of children and it is the reason that all children receive a second shot. Therefore, there would be a small risk that a child who received a single shot might get measles after being exposed. What is even more important is what could happen to a child with an immune problem who couldn't be immunized. That child would not only get measles but would probably have a serious case.

Should parents of small children make sure they are up-to-date on their own vaccinations? Are side effects in adults different than for their kids?

Everyone should receive immunizations. Check with your doctor to see which vaccines are important for you. It is important that parents are protected so that they do not bring infections home to their children and they are well enough to take care of their children! Parents and siblings of children younger than 2 years should receive influenza vaccine. Adults should receive a booster dose of tetanus and diphtheria every 10 years, or sooner if you have an injury that can lead to tetanus. All adults older than 50 years should receive influenza vaccine yearly. People older than 65 years should receive the older version of the pneumococcal vaccine (the polysaccharide vaccine).

Adults who did not have chickenpox should consider getting the vaccine (although, interestingly, most adults who don't remember having chicken-pox are actually found to be already protected when their blood is tested for the presence of antibodies). Adults who may be exposed to blood or who are adopting children from areas of the world where hepatitis B is common should get the hepatitis B vaccine. Travelers should consider hepatitis A vaccine and others depending on where you are traveling. You can find country-specific information on the CDC Web site at www.cdc.gov/travel.

My child has already had more vaccinations at 9 months than I have had in my entire life. Why are there so many more now, and why weren't these necessary when I was a child?
Because of scientific studies and new techniques, more vaccines have been developed. Children can now be protected against more infections than they were in the past. In the future, there will be even more vaccines! Just like seat belts and infant car seats, you survived without them, but many others didn't. You don't want to take a chance with your child!

Why is there a standard dose for all infants for vaccinations? Most medications use weight as a guide for amount being administered. Could a 5-pound baby really be the same as a 10-pound baby?
The dose for vaccination was determined by studies, first in animals and then in people. Small amounts of vaccine are used to protect children. These have been shown to be safe and effective in preterm and low birth weight babies and in teenagers, who are obviously much larger. Although the patients aren't the same, the immune system response is similar. For most vaccines, it is one size fits all! Of course, there are exceptions. For example, the dose of hepatitis B vaccine for adults is higher than that used in infants. Sometimes the number of doses is different depending

on the age of the patient. Children younger than 9 years receive 2 doses of influenza vaccine. People 13 years and older get 2 doses of chickenpox vaccine.

Why is polio still on the list of recommended vaccines when it has been eradicated in its natural form in nearly every country, including the United States, for years?

Although polio has been eliminated from most of the world, it has not been eliminated from the entire world. There are pockets of polio in India and parts of Africa. The poliovirus can live in the gut of vaccinated people so a person could travel and pick up the virus without being ill or aware that they are carrying the virus. The vaccine protects a person against the disease but the virus can still live in the gut and could come back to the United States with the traveler. Children will continue to be vaccinated until polio has been eliminated from the entire world.

Which vaccines are required for school attendance?

This varies depending on your location. The best way to get the answer is to call your local school and ask the school nurse. This information is often available on a state or city Web site.

CHAPTER 7

More About Immunizations

Immunizations for Teenagers and Young Adults

Many parents tend to think of vaccines as something needed for infants and young children but less important later in life. In fact, teenagers and young adults often get a number of vaccine-preventable diseases, including hepatitis B, measles, German measles, and chickenpox. They need protection against infectious illnesses as well.

Teenagers should continue to see their pediatricians or other physicians on a regular basis. All teens (or their parents) should keep an updated record of their immunizations. Many will need more vaccinations as teenagers, particularly if they haven't been previously vaccinated against hepatitis B or chickenpox, for example, or if they're fallen behind on some of their other immunizations.

Here are guidelines for specific vaccines for teenagers as established by the American Academy of Pediatrics (AAP) and other medical organizations.

- *Hepatitis B.* Most people who have a hepatitis B infection got the virus as teenagers or young adults. If teenagers have not been previously immunized with the 3-dose hepatitis B vaccine, they should be given this

vaccination. Teenagers older than 18 years who have an increased risk for hepatitis B infection—perhaps because they are sexually active, live in the same household as a person infected with hepatitis B, or were exposed on the job—are candidates for hepatitis B immunization.

- *Measles-mumps-rubella (MMR).* Check your teenager's immunization records to be sure he received 2 doses of the MMR vaccine. If not, he should receive the second dose of this combination vaccine.
- *Tetanus-diphtheria-acellular pertussis (Tdap) or tetanus-diphtheria (Td) booster.* The Tdap vaccine was licensed for use in 2005. It should be given to children aged 11 to 12 years if at least 5 years have passed since the last dose. The Td booster is used in children who should not get pertussis vaccine. Booster doses of Td are recommended every 10 years for adults.
- *Chickenpox.* This vaccine should be given to teens that have never had chickenpox and have never received this immunization. If a teenager is 13 years or older, 2 doses given a month apart will be needed.
- *Influenza.* The influenza vaccine is recommended each year for teenagers who have a medical condition that places them at higher risk of problems if they get the flu. It is also recommended if they have close contact with anyone who is at high risk for complications of the flu, such as a younger brother or sister. Finally, it is recommended for anyone who wants to lower risk for the flu.
- *Meningococcal.* The new conjugate meningococcal vaccine is recommended for children aged 11 to 12 years, those entering high school, and students entering college, especially those who will be living in dormitories.
- *Pneumococcal.* This vaccine should be given to teenagers who have a condition that makes them more likely to get pneumococcal disease and the problems associated with it.
- *Hepatitis A.* The vaccine against hepatitis A infections is appropriate for teenagers who fall into any number of categories, including those who live in a community with a high rate of hepatitis A infections or are planning to travel to or attend school in a country or state with a high rate of hepatitis A infections.

What if You're Pregnant?

At their doctor's recommendation, pregnant women often try to limit the number of medicines they're taking, stop drinking alcohol, and stop smoking to protect the baby developing in their wombs. But what about vaccinations? If a pregnant women needs to be immunized, is it safe for her to do so?

Keep in mind that some infections that take place during pregnancy can cause birth defects in the fetus. Diseases like the measles can increase the risks of a pregnant woman having a miscarriage or delivering a premature baby. But many high-risk infections can be prevented if women get the recommended vaccinations before trying to become pregnant.

Once a woman is pregnant, a key factor in immunizing her is whether the vaccine is made with live or inactivated (killed) viruses. Because of the theoretical risk of transmitting the virus to the fetus, pregnant women should not be immunized with live vaccines (eg, MMR and chickenpox). As a general guideline, you should avoid becoming pregnant for 28 days after being given either the MMR or chickenpox vaccine.

Other immunizations, however, are especially important for pregnant women to consider having. For example, women in the second and third trimesters of pregnancy have a greater risk of problems from the flu. Because the presently available influenza shot (but not the influenza nasal spray) is made from an inactivated virus, the vaccine itself is safe for pregnant women. The Centers for Disease Control and Prevention (CDC) recommends the influenza vaccine for women who are beyond the first trimester of pregnancy during the flu season.

By the way, all vaccines can be given safely to breastfeeding mothers.

Immunizations for International Travel

Before your child travels abroad, make sure he is up-to-date with all recommended childhood vaccinations. Even though certain vaccine-protected diseases may be rare in the United States, they may occur much more often in other countries.

Talk with your pediatrician about other immunizations that may be needed, depending on the parts of the world to which you and your child will be traveling, your planned activities, and the length of your stay. Your pediatrician may recommend vaccines to prevent, for example, hepatitis A, yellow fever, meningococcal disease, typhoid fever, rabies, and Japanese encephalitis.

- A vaccine for yellow fever is required by some nations before allowing entry into the country. Yellow fever is a potentially fatal disease that can occur year-round, primarily in rural parts of South America and sub-Saharan Africa. If possible, however, immunization for yellow fever should not be given to children younger than 9 months to reduce the risk of serious side effects, including vaccine-associated encephalitis or brain swelling.
- If a child is traveling to a part of the world where there are rabid animals and he is likely to be taking part in activities in which he might encounter rabid animals, you should consider rabies immunization. The rabies vaccine is given in a series of 3 shots.
- The influenza vaccine may be recommended, depending on travel destinations, the season of travel, duration of travel, and other factors. However, the strains that cause the flu in the United States may be different than those in other countries. This means that the composition of the vaccine needed for protection in other parts of the world may be different from the one generally offered in the United States.
- The Japanese encephalitis virus, which is spread by mosquitoes, is prevalent in parts of southeast Asia, China, eastern Russia, and the Indian subcontinent. A 3-dose vaccine is available and should be considered for people who will spend extended time in high-risk areas. There is no information on its safety and effectiveness in children younger than 1 year.

For complete and timely information from the CDC about current travel recommendations, call 877/394-8747 or visit the CDC travel Web site, www.cdc.gov/travel.

The Future of Vaccines

More than 200 years after the development of the first vaccine, immunizations have saved millions of lives and prevented much human suffering. Although many of the most feared diseases of our times can now be avoided, pediatricians and other physicians know that there's more research to be done. Many efforts are directed toward developing new vaccines for serious infectious diseases for which there are still no immunizations.

Not only do today's scientists have a better understanding of infectious diseases than ever before, but they also have more tools at their disposal to conduct research that may produce future vaccines. Genetic engineering and other technological advances are already speeding progress on vaccines that could eliminate acquired immunodeficiency syndrome (AIDS), malaria, certain cancers, and other diseases, as well as improve the effectiveness and safety of the immunizations that already exist. As a result, the health and well-being of millions of children may be even better in the years ahead.

Part 2

Preventing and Controlling Infections in Your Child

CHAPTER 8

General Prevention Guidelines: Things *You* Can Do to Prevent Infections

Disease prevention is an important part of maintaining your child's overall good health. Yes, your pediatrician can help your child get well from one sickness or another, but often only after a trip to the doctor's office; a 5-, 7-, or 10-day course of medicine; and some time spent resting and recovering. With that in mind, it makes sense to keep your youngster as healthy as possible, particularly because many preventive strategies are so simple, safe, and effective.

In Part 1, you learned just how powerful immunizations can be for keeping your child safe from serious and, in some cases, deadly diseases. In Part 2, we'll look at more preventive approaches to protecting your youngster at home, in school, and in child care settings. You will learn how to guard against a variety of potentially serious illnesses, from food-borne diseases to infections caused by ticks and animal bites. These guidelines can help you and your child fight off germs and stay healthy.

Hand Washing: A Powerful Antidote to Illness

How many times have you and your child washed your hands today? You might not have given it much thought. It's either part of your routine, done frequently without thinking, or maybe you don't do it much at all. But as your pediatrician may have told you, hand washing may be the single most important act you and your child have for disease prevention.

As early as possible, get your child into the habit of washing her hands often and thoroughly. All day long, your child is exposed to bacteria and viruses—when touching a playmate, sharing toys, or petting the cat. Once her hands pick up these germs, she can quickly infect herself by rubbing her eyes, touching her nose, or placing her fingers in her mouth. The whole process can happen in seconds, and cause an infection that can last for days, weeks, or even longer.

Hand washing can stop the spread of infection. The key is to encourage your child to wash her hands throughout the day. For example, help her or remind her to wash her hands

- Before eating (including snacks)
- After a trip to the bathroom
- Whenever she comes in from playing outdoors
- After touching an animal like a family pet

- After sneezing or coughing if she covers her mouth
- When someone in the household is ill

Studies on hand washing in public restrooms show that most people don't have very good hygiene habits. "Hand washing" may mean just a quick splash of water and perhaps a squirt of soap, but not nearly enough to get their hands clean.

So what does a thorough hand washing involve? The Centers for Disease Control and Prevention recommends the following steps:

- Wet your child's hands.
- Apply clean bar soap or liquid soap to the hands, and then place the bar on a rack where it can drain before the next hand washing.
- Rub the hands vigorously together. Scrub every surface completely.
- Keep rubbing and scrubbing for 10 to 15 seconds to effectively remove the germs.
- Rinse the hands completely, then dry them.

Drugstore shelves are full of trendy antibacterial soaps, but studies have shown that these antibacterial products are no better at washing away dirt and germs than regular soap. Some infectious disease experts have even suggested that by using antibacterial soaps, you may actually kill off normal bacteria and increase the chances that resistant bacteria may grow. The best

solution is to wash your child's hands with warm water and ordinary soap that does not contain antibacterial substances (eg, triclosan). Regular use of soap and water is better than using waterless (and often alcohol-based) soaps, gels, rinses, and hand rubs when your child's hands are visibly dirty (and with children, there usually is dirt on the hands!). However, when there is no sink available (eg, the car), hand rubs can be a useful alternative.

Keep in mind that although 10 to 15 seconds of hand washing sounds like an instant, it is much longer than you think. Time yourself the next time you wash your hands. Watch your child while she's washing her hands to make sure she's developing good hygiene behaviors. Pick a song that lasts for 15 seconds and sing it while you wash. Encourage your child to wash her hands not only at home, but also at school, at friends' homes, and everywhere else. It's an important habit for her to get into, and hopefully one that's hard to break!

Other Hygiene Strategies

When your child or another family member has a cold or cough, there are extremely important steps in addition to frequent hand washing that can lower the risk of spreading the infection to others. Some experts call these strategies *respiratory hygiene,* and they can be very effective if followed carefully. For example, to keep your sick child from blowing secretions into the air, where they can land on other people or on toys and other objects

- Encourage her to cough or sneeze into a tissue or, if a tissue isn't available, onto her sleeve.
- Discourage your child from covering her mouth with her hands while coughing or sneezing because this will leave germs on the hands that can be spread by touching other people or objects. Most often, germs are spread by the hands, not through the air.
- Throw away tissues immediately after each use, putting them in a nearby wastebasket or other container.
- Once your child is old enough, teach her how to blow her nose into a tissue.
- Don't allow your child to share pacifiers, drinking cups, eating utensils, towels, or toothbrushes whether she is sick.

Clean and Disinfect

Housecleaning may not be the most enjoyable activity in your day. If you spend a few minutes killing germs, especially those in the kitchen and bathroom, it can go a long way toward keeping your child healthy.

After you've prepared a meal, wash the kitchen counters with hot, soapy water and disinfect them using a household bleach solution or other disinfectant. Infectious bacteria can thrive in foods like uncooked beef and chicken. In the bathroom, use the same cleaning and disinfecting routine on the toilet, sink, and other surfaces. This is especially important when a family member is sick with an infectious disease, particularly one that causes diarrhea. Also, frequently clean the area where you change diapers, including the changing table. (Be sure you keep the bleach and all cleaning products out of the reach of infants and young children.) Avoid changing diapers in areas where food is being prepared or consumed.

Some Target Areas for Cleaning
- In the kitchen
- In the bathrooms
- Near diaper-changing areas

Some germs can survive and thrive for hours unless you take steps to wipe them away. After using soap and disinfectant, dry the cleaned surfaces with paper towels or a clean cloth. After you clean up, be sure to wash your own hands.

Handle Food Safely

We'll talk about avoiding food-borne infections in detail in Chapter 11. But because it's so important, it also deserves a mention here. Food can become contaminated with bacteria and other germs that can cause stomach pain, vomiting, and worse. To limit problems

- Make sure your hands are washed and the kitchen surfaces are clean before and after preparing meals.
- Clean your cutting board or kitchen surface after preparing raw meats for cooking and clean before using the surface to prepare any food that is not to be cooked such as salads, fruits, or vegetables.
- Cook ground meat all the way through.

- Wash raw vegetables and fruit thoroughly before eating.
- Avoid eating raw or undercooked eggs.
- Cook frozen food right after it's defrosted.
- Clean utensils frequently during food preparation, washing them after they're used on raw foods and before using them again on cooked foods.
- When it comes to leftovers, store them properly and get them into the refrigerator or freezer right away to prevent germ growth. Don't leave perishable items out for more than a couple hours.

Collectively, Americans are sick more than 4 *billion* days a year—and many of those sick days can be prevented by taking the steps described previously and in the following chapters. If you follow the guidelines found in these pages, you will go a long way toward helping your child, as well as the rest of your household, have fewer infections; fewer missed days of child care, school, and work; less frequent visits to the doctor; and lower medicine costs.

CHAPTER 9

Children in Child Care and School

In today's world of two-income families and single parents, many young children spend a lot of their time in child care. When selecting the best type of child care for your own youngster, you can choose from

- *In-home care,* in which the caregiver comes into or lives in your home
- *Family child care,* for which you take your youngster to the caregiver's home
- *Center-based care,* for which you take your child to a facility that is designed and staffed to care for children

When selecting family and center-based care, there are a number of things you'll need to consider and questions to ask.

- Is the home or facility licensed or registered with the appropriate local government agency?
- Is the program accredited by a nationally recognized group such as the National Association for Family Child Care (www.nafcc.org) or the National Association for the Education of Young Children (www.naeyc.org)?
- Is it located close to your home or work?
- Do the hours of care fit your needs?
- Are you welcome to visit anytime during normal operating hours?
- Are the caregivers trained and experienced?
- Are there enough staff members for the number of children?
- Are there age- and developmentally appropriate activities for your child?
- Is it clean and safe?
- Do the staff and children wash their hands frequently?
- Do they have all infants sleeping on their backs?
- How do they support breastfeeding mothers? To help reduce your child's risk of illness, try to continue to pump breast milk for your child to have in child care.

What About Your Child's Health?

In addition to choosing a child care setting using the criteria mentioned previously, there is another crucial factor you need to take into account—what is the policy concerning sick children? Wherever children are together, the risk of spreading infectious diseases exists, especially among infants and toddlers who are likely to put their hands and toys into their mouths and then share their toys.

To reduce the risk of becoming sick, your child, the child care providers, and all the children being cared for must be up-to-date with the recommended immunizations against diseases such as measles, mumps, rubella, chickenpox, diphtheria, tetanus, pertussis, polio, hepatitis B, *Haemophilus influenzae* type b, pneumococcus, hepatitis A, and the flu if eligible for the vaccine.

Even though your child has had his immunizations, he can get other infectious diseases common in youngsters such as colds, sore throats, coughs, vomiting, and diarrhea. For example, the viruses responsible for colds or the flu cause the most common sicknesses in child care facilities and schools. In fact, most children in child care and school settings have as many as 8 to 12 colds a year. Diarrheal episodes occur once or twice a year in the typical child.

Make sure you get answers to questions like

- When your child becomes sick, either at school or in a child care program, will you be notified in a timely manner?
- What plans are in place to lower the chances that your child will get sick from another youngster who is sneezing or sniffling, has diarrhea, or is vomiting?

Reducing Disease Transmission

In many child care programs, as well as public and private schools, parents are contacted right away when their child shows signs of even a mild illness, like a cold. In others, a child is allowed to stay at the facility as long as he doesn't have a fever and can take part in most activities. Either way, be certain that the school or caregiver has a way to reach you at all times—make your phone numbers at home and work available, as well as your cell phone number.

In many child care facilities and schools, the staff simply cannot care for a sick child, although in others, the child is kept comfortable in a separate area so a cold, a cough, or diarrhea doesn't spread throughout the facility. In these programs, a staff member is trained to care for ill children, often in a "get-well room" where they won't pass the disease to others. There may also be a place to lie down while remaining within sight of a staff member if a youngster needs to rest. In some communities, special sick child care centers have been established for children with mild illnesses who should be kept apart from healthy youngsters.

You can help prevent the spread of infectious diseases by keeping your contagious child home from school or child care until he can no longer spread his illness to others. Children should be kept home when they have

- Diarrhea or stools that contain blood or mucus
- An illness that caused vomiting 2 or more times during the previous 24 hours, unless the vomiting is known to be caused by a condition that's not contagious
- Mouth sores with drooling, unless caused by a noncontagious condition
- Pinkeye or red eye with a yellowish or whitish discharge
- Impetigo (a skin infection with erupting sores) until 24 hours after treatment has been started
- Head lice (until after proper treatment has been given)
- Scabies (an itchy skin condition caused by mites) until after treatment has been given
- Conditions that suggest the possible presence of a more serious illness, including a fever, sluggishness, persistent crying, irritability, or difficulty breathing

Even with all these safety measures, it is likely that some infections will be spread in the child care center. For many of these infections, a child is contagious a day or more before he has symptoms. That is another reason why it is important to wash your and his hands frequently. You never know when your child or another child is passing a virus or bacteria.

Fortunately, not all illnesses are contagious (eg, ear infections). In these cases there's no need to separate your sick youngster from the other children. If he's feeling well enough to be at child care or school, he can attend as long as a staff member can give him any medication he's taking. Sometimes your child will become sick while at child care and need to go home. You will need to have a plan so someone can pick him up.

Measures Promoting Good Hygiene

To reduce the risk of disease in child care settings as well as schools, the facility should meet certain criteria that promote good hygiene. For example

- Are there sinks in every room, and are there separate sinks for preparing food and washing hands? Is food handled in areas separate from the toilets and diaper-changing tables?
- Are the toilets and sinks clean and readily available for the children and staff? Are disposable paper towels used so each youngster will use only his own towel and not share with others?
- Are toys that infants and toddlers put in their mouths sanitized before others can play with them?
- Are the child care rooms and equipment cleaned and disinfected at least once a day?
- Is breast milk labeled and stored correctly?
- Are children and their caregivers or teachers instructed to wash their hands throughout the day, including
  — When they arrive at the facility
  — Before and after handling food, feeding a child, or eating
  — After using the toilet, changing a diaper, or helping a child use the bathroom (Following a diaper change, the caregiver's and child's hands should be washed and the diaper-changing area should be sanitized.)
  — After helping a child wipe his nose or mouth or tending to a cut or sore
  — After playing in sandboxes
  — Before and after playing in water that is used by other children

— Before and after staff members give medicine to a youngster
— After handling wastebaskets or garbage
— After handling a pet or other animal

Make sure your own child understands good hygiene and the importance of hand washing after using the toilet and before and after eating.

Giving Medicines at Child Care or School
While at a child care facility or school, your youngster may need to take medicine for an infectious disease, perhaps an ear infection, or a chronic illness like asthma. Provide the caregiver with your written permission to administer the medicine to your child. Make sure the caregiver understands how to give the medicine properly. This includes the amount to be given, how it needs to be given (eg, by mouth, drops into the eyes or ears), and how often the medicine is to be given. Ask the caregiver to keep a written record of each time the caregiver gives your child his medicine. The medicine bottle itself should have a pharmacy label with your child's name on it, as well as the dosage and expiration date. Also, make sure that the caregiver understands how the drug should be stored (does it need refrigeration?), what side effects to look for, and what to do if they occur.

For detailed information about specific diseases that can become problems in schools and child care centers, including the flu, cold sores (herpes simplex), the common cold, and head lice, see the disease descriptions in Part 4.

CHAPTER 10

Breastfeeding

Breastfeeding is the ideal way to provide nourishment for your baby in her first year of life. The American Academy of Pediatrics (AAP) recommends exclusively breastfeeding for the first 4 to 6 months* of life, then continuing breastfeeding until at least the baby's first birthday, along with the addition of solid foods. If you decide to breastfeed, there are not only enormous nutritional benefits for your infant, but at the same time, your breast milk will provide substances that promote the development of your baby's own disease-fighting immune system. It can also help to protect her from a number of infectious diseases. For example, breastfeeding will help safeguard your baby from middle ear infections as well as severe diarrhea and a number of upper respiratory illnesses, including bronchiolitis (an infection of the small breathing tubes of the lungs) and infections caused by *Haemophilus influenzae* type b bacteria (such as a serious throat infection called *epiglottitis*).

Yet despite the proven benefits of breastfeeding, many new mothers still have questions and concerns about it that they often take to their pediatrician. Can certain bacteria or viruses contaminate their breast milk? When they're ill, can those diseases be passed along to their babies through human milk? Can a breastfeeding mother receive the vaccinations that she needs?

In this chapter, we'll discuss these issues and hopefully ease some of your own worries.

Vaccination Guidelines

If you're a breastfeeding mom and you need one or more immunizations, there is no reason to avoid or postpone getting them. Even though some vaccines are formulated with live viruses, there is no evidence that these vaccine viruses can harm your infant. Rubella vaccine virus has been recovered from breast milk. However, it is not a problem because at most, it would immunize the baby.

---

*There is a difference of opinion among AAP experts on this matter. The Section on Breastfeeding supports exclusive breastfeeding for about 6 months. The Committee on Nutrition supports the introduction of complementary foods between 4 and 6 months of age where safe and nutritious complementary foods are available.

To be specific, research shows that breastfeeding women can safely receive vaccines that protect against

- Measles
- Mumps
- Rubella
- Tetanus
- Diphtheria
- Influenza
- *Streptococcus pneumoniae* infection
- Hepatitis A
- Hepatitis B
- Chickenpox (varicella)

The inactivated polio vaccine can also be administered if you haven't been vaccinated against polio in the past and you'll be traveling to a part of the world where polio is prevalent.

Now, what about vaccinations for your baby? Whether your infant is being fed through breastfeeding or with a bottle, your pediatrician should follow the immunization schedule recommended by the AAP (see page 37). Breastfeeding provides your baby with the best possible nutrition and gives some protection from diseases. Vaccines give added protection against serious infections (eg, diphtheria, whooping cough, polio).

Germs and Human Milk

If you become ill with an infection, you might be worried about continuing to breastfeed. You may be concerned that your breast milk will become contaminated with the bacteria or viruses responsible for your illness. But during colds, the flu, bacterial illnesses, and most other infections, you can and should continue breastfeeding. Here are the facts.

Bacteria

A number of infections caused by bacteria often raise questions when they occur in breastfeeding women. For example

- *Mastitis* is an infection in the breast tissue causing swelling, redness, and pain, usually affecting just one breast. Your doctor will treat mastitis with antibiotics and pain medication while also recommending rest, warm or cool compresses, and continued removal of milk from the breast. Although bacteria may be present in your milk, the infection is not passed along to a healthy baby—you can continue breastfeeding. If your baby is premature or has a medical problem, ask your pediatrician if your breast milk is safe for the baby. During mastitis, it is important to drain the breast by feeding or using a breast pump.

■ *Abscesses.* Fortunately, breast abscesses (collections of pus from an infection) occur only rarely, but they often worry breastfeeding mothers. That's because they have the potential to break open, spilling large amounts of bacteria into the breast ducts and mother's milk. If you develop a breast abscess, it may be necessary to stop feeding temporarily from the affected breast, depending on the location of the abscess and other factors. Your doctor will discuss the treatment options for your specific situation with you. If you are told not to breastfeed from that side, continue to remove milk regularly using a breast pump or hand expression.

■ *Tuberculosis.* Mothers with tuberculosis may safely breastfeed their babies if they've been treated for at least 2 weeks and are not considered contagious. If you have an active disease and may be contagious, you should avoid breastfeeding. In fact, you need to avoid any close contact with your baby to keep from spreading the disease by coughing or sneezing.

Viruses

If you're diagnosed with a viral illness, talk to your pediatrician about whether you need to take a break from breastfeeding until the infection is successfully treated. Here is some general information to keep in mind about some common viral infections.

■ *Cytomegalovirus (CMV).* The virus responsible for a mother's CMV infection can get into her breast milk. Because there are also antibodies against the disease in the breast milk, it is uncommon for the baby to get serious CMV disease from the mother this way. The baby may get the infection, but she's unlikely to have any symptoms. If your baby is preterm, however, she may have a greater risk of developing the disease than a full-term infant. Talk to your pediatrician. Your pediatrician will decide if the benefits of breastfeeding outweigh the potential risk of transmitting CMV.

■ *Hepatitis.* Evidence of hepatitis B and C viruses has been found in the breast milk of women infected with these diseases. However, studies have shown that a breastfeeding mother with hepatitis B does not significantly increase her infant's risk of contracting the disease. If your baby receives the hepatitis B vaccine in the first few days after birth, you can safely breastfeed her, even if you have the infection. As for the hepatitis C virus, its transmission through breast milk is theoretically possible, although it has never been documented.

■ *Human immunodeficiency virus (HIV).* The virus that causes acquired immunodeficiency syndrome (AIDS), HIV can be transmitted from mother to baby in breast milk. The risk is higher for mothers who have acquired HIV after the delivery of their babies, compared with those who already had the infection before their infants were born. As a rule, any woman in the United States who tests positive for HIV should not breastfeed her baby.

■ *Herpes simplex virus (HSV).* There have been reports of HSV type 1 being transmitted during breastfeeding when the mother has an open herpes sore on her breast. If you have these breast sores, you should not breastfeed. If you have open sores on other places on your body, they should be covered while breastfeeding.

If You "Bank" Your Milk

In some circumstances, such as when babies are delivered prematurely, babies may be fed milk that has been collected from their mothers or donors. But is the milk from donors really safe?

Many donor milk banks are members of the Human Milk Banking Association of North America and follow guidelines that require screening the milk for antibodies to a number of infectious organisms, including HIV, hepatitis B and C, and syphilis. Donor milk is also heat-treated for 30 minutes to destroy any bacteria or HIV that may be present.

If you want to save some of your own breast milk, store it in a clean container. When it's going to be used to feed your baby within 24 hours, immediately seal and refrigerate it, and then use it within 24 hours if possible. Freeze milk if you will not be using it within 24 hours. Frozen milk is good for at least 3 months (some experts suggest 3 to 6 months if kept in a 0°F freezer).

Antibiotics in Breast Milk

If you're taking antibiotics for a bacterial infection, traces of the medicine may be found in your breast milk. Even so, breastfeeding mothers can take most antibiotics, as well as most other prescription and over-the-counter drugs, without causing any health risks to their babies. However, there are a few exceptions to this general rule.

When your doctor prescribes antibiotics, be sure to let your doctor know that you're breastfeeding. With many of these medicines, your doctor won't need to make any changes in the way they're prescribed. However, if a baby is premature or ill, your doctor will choose certain antibiotics with your breastfeeding in mind. Or your doctor may suggest that you temporarily stop breastfeeding when taking certain specific drugs. Remember that if you temporarily stop breastfeeding, you will want to pump the breasts to drain them (for comfort) and ensure that milk production continues.

Before you start taking any medicine, be sure to tell your doctor that you're breastfeeding your baby. Your doctor can give you the most up-to-date information about drug risks and select the safest medicine taken at the lowest possible dose.

CHAPTER 11

Food-borne Illnesses

Children can become sick from contamination of foods and beverages
that they eat and drink. According to the Centers for Disease Control and
Prevention, there are more than 250 food-borne diseases that cause more
than 76 million cases of illness in the United States each year. Young children have a greater chance of getting these illnesses and having complications associated with them.

Bacteria, viruses, tiny parasites, and sometimes the chemicals they release
can be found in food. They can all cause infectious diseases that are sometimes called *food poisoning.* For instance, bacteria called *Staphylococcus
aureus* are the leading cause of food poisoning. They are the same bacteria
responsible for many skin infections. When an infected person handles food,
the bacteria or poisons produced by the bacteria can be spread to the food.
Symptoms can begin just hours after the contaminated food is eaten. Other
common food-borne bacteria include

- *Salmonella* is responsible for the disease called salmonellosis and most
  often affects foods such as raw meat, unpasteurized milk, and raw or
  undercooked eggs. Thorough cooking, however, can kill *Salmonella*
  organisms. *Salmonella* can also be acquired when handling pets,
  especially reptiles.
- *Clostridium perfringens.* These bacteria are sometimes found in soil
  and sewage and often transferred to food by the people who handle and
  prepare it. The bacteria can multiply in places such as school cafeterias
  when foods such as beef, fish, poultry, stews, and casseroles are left out
  for long periods of time at room temperature.
- *Clostridium botulinum.* These bacteria are not able to grow in the presence of air, but spores are found in the soil. It tends to thrive without
  oxygen, which is the reason it is often found in improperly canned foods.
  Under certain conditions, the spores can become poisonous (toxic). The
  poison causes the potentially deadly disease called botulism.

Food-borne illnesses can also be caused by many other germs, such as
Campylobacter, Escherichia coli (E coli), and the hepatitis A and Norwalk
viruses, and parasites such as *Cryptosporidium.* All of these germs cause illnesses with strikingly similar symptoms such as nausea, vomiting, abdominal cramps, diarrhea, and sometimes fever. Some food-borne illnesses can
cause even more severe symptoms. One example is botulism, which affects
the nervous system, making it hard to breath and swallow, impairing
normal vision, and unless properly treated, even leading to death.

Reducing the Risk

To lower the likelihood that your child will develop a food-borne infectious disease, follow these guidelines for particular types of food:

- *Milk and cheese.* Because of the health risks associated with consuming unpasteurized milk and milk products (eg, cheese, butter), children should drink only pasteurized milk. If the milk is unpasteurized, including certified raw milk, it may contain harmful bacteria that can cause illness associated with germs such as *E coli,* *Salmonella,* and *Campylobacter.*
- *Raw and undercooked meat.* Meat and meat products such as hamburger, poultry, hot dogs, pork, and wild game should not be fed to your child if they are not properly cooked. They may contain bacteria such as *Salmonella, E coli,* or *Listeria* or parasites such as the tapeworm *(Taenia solium)* or roundworm *(Trichinella spiralis).* In the kitchen, reduce the risk of cross-contamination by making sure to thoroughly clean any knives, utensils, plates, and cutting boards that are used for raw meats before they are used again in preparing other foods like fresh fruits and vegetables.

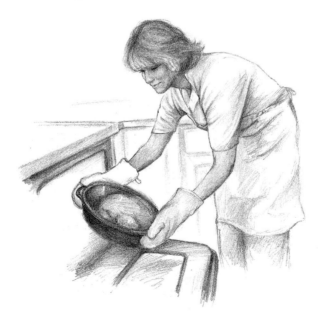

- *Raw shellfish and fish.* Many infectious disease experts advise against feeding raw fish or shellfish to children. Parasites, viruses, and bacteria have been identified in these foods, including oysters, clams, mussels, scallops, and raw fish.
- *Eggs.* Don't allow your child to eat raw or partially cooked eggs, unpasteurized powdered eggs, or products containing raw eggs. Cook eggs until they are firm, not runny. Sometimes eggs are still infectious when they're prepared sunny-side up or undercooked or raw in homemade frostings and mayonnaise, ice cream from uncooked custard, fresh Caesar salad dressing, hollandaise sauce, and cookie or cake batter. All of these foods can be contaminated with *Salmonella* bacteria.
- *Fresh fruit and vegetables and nuts.* To prevent disease, all fruits and vegetables need to be washed before children are allowed to eat them. Raw shelled nuts have been linked with outbreaks of *Salmonella* infections.
- *Seed sprouts.* Because of concerns about the safety of seed sprouts such as alfalfa sprouts, children should not eat them. They can contain bacteria including *Salmonella* and *E coli,* which can cause illness.
- *Unpasteurized juices.* Give your child only pasteurized juice products. There is an exception to this rule, however—it is acceptable to prepare freshly squeezed juices such as orange juice from washed fruit, as long as the juice is consumed immediately after it is prepared.
- *Honey.* If your child is younger than 1 year, he should not be fed honey. In some instances, honey may contain spores of the infectious organism that causes botulism *(Clostridium botulinum).*

Food Preparation

A key to minimizing the risk of food-borne illnesses is cleaning and disinfecting before, during, and after food preparation. For example

- Always wash your hands with soap and hot water before and after handling food. Be sure to wash your hands after using the bathroom and before returning to the kitchen. Do the same after changing your baby's diaper.
- Wear gloves during food handling if you have open cuts or sores on your hands.

- When handling raw meat and poultry, rinse the meat and then wash your hands and all kitchen surfaces that you'll be using with hot, soapy water before continuing with the preparation.
- Inspect all canned foods for any indication of possible contamination, such as a swollen can or lid or a cracked jar. If you suspect a problem, throw out the food.
- Cook meat, poultry, and eggs thoroughly. Cut into meats to make sure they're done (they should be brown inside). Use a meat thermometer to measure the internal temperature of roasts and other large items.
- Don't let prepared foods stand at room temperature for longer than 2 hours.
- When preparing cooked leftovers, reheat them to a temperature of 165°F or greater.

CHAPTER 12

Bite Wounds

Each year, many parents rush their children to the pediatrician's office or the emergency department after their youngsters have been bitten by animals or other humans. Consider the following statistics: there are about 4.5 million dog bites reported annually in the United States, along with 400,000 cat bites and 250,000 human bites. It is likely that the actual number of bites is much higher. While many of these bites cause only minor injuries, others are much more serious. In many cases, these bites produce infections. This occurs in more than 50% of cat bites and 15% to 20% of dog or human bites.

Many people don't realize that most bites come from domesticated animals that the child knows, not from wild or unfamiliar animals. A major concern for parents about animal bites is the child's risk of contracting rabies. Rabies is a very serious viral infection that affects the central nervous system and brain, causing a high fever, swallowing difficulties, convulsions, and eventually, death.

Fortunately, rabies in humans is rare today (most domesticated animals are vaccinated for rabies), but even so, the animal that bit your child may need to be confined and observed for 10 days for the presence of rabies. (Don't attempt to capture the animal yourself. Contact animal control officials.) However, confinement is not always possible, especially when a wild animal is responsible for the bite. The greatest risk for rabies comes from wild animals such as bats, raccoons, foxes, skunks, and coyotes. (For more information about rabies, see Chapter 27.)

Even when rabies isn't present, an infection can develop at the site of the bite. Contact your pediatrician if any of the following signs of an infection are present:

- Pus or drainage from the bite wound
- Swelling and tenderness in the area around the bite
- Red streaks that extend from the bite
- Swollen glands that occur above the bite

Prevention of Bites and Infections

To prevent bites and the infections associated with them, here are some tips to keep in mind.

- Teach your child to avoid contact with wild animals. She also needs to stay away from dead animals, whose nervous system tissues and saliva may contain the rabies virus and who may be infested with fleas or ticks carrying various bacteria, viruses, and other infectious organisms.
- Never leave a young child alone with an animal. Even playful interaction between the child and a pet can overexcite the animal and lead to an unexpected bite.
- Don't allow your child to tease a pet, play roughly with it (eg, pulling its tail), or grab its toys, bones, or food.
- Educate your youngster never to kiss or place her face close to an animal, nor to awaken a pet from sleep or bother it while it's eating. Teach your child how to behave when approached by an unfamiliar dog. She shouldn't run from the dog or make any aggressive movements, but instead face the dog, allow the dog to sniff her, and then back away slowly.
- Instruct older children to recognize the signs of a potentially unsafe dog, including a rigid body, a stiff tail at half-mast, a staring expression, hysterical barking, or a crouched position.
- Cover and secure all garbage containers, which will keep raccoons and other wild animals from being attracted to your home and places where children play.

How Animal Bites Are Treated

Here are some guidelines on treating an animal bite to lower the risk of developing an infection.

- Apply firm pressure to the area of the bite using a clean bandage or towel until the flow of blood ceases. If you can't stop the bleeding, contact your pediatrician.
- Wash the wound gently but thoroughly with soap and water, dry it, and cover it with gauze.

- Contact your pediatrician whenever any animal bite breaks the skin, even if the wound seems minor. Your pediatrician may decide to suture (stitch) the wound and perhaps prescribe antibiotics or treatment to prevent rabies or tetanus. Antibiotics are given most often for moderate to severe bites, puncture wounds, or bites to the face, hand, foot, or genital area. They are also used for children with a weakened immune system.

If the animal is unavailable to be observed and the risk of rabies is considered high, your doctor will give your child a specific type of immune globulin and begin a series of immunizations against the rabies virus, which will prevent the infection from occurring. The immune globulin is injected into the bite wound. It must be given as soon as possible to be most useful.

What should you do in the case of human bites, perhaps from a sibling or playmate? Contact your pediatrician and describe the wound. Your pediatrician will want to know whether the bite has broken the skin and if the injury is large enough to need stitches. If your doctor wants to examine the bite, wash it with soap and water before leaving for the office visit. For minor wounds that barely break the skin, a thorough washing and bandaging may be all that's needed.

CHAPTER 13

Tick-borne Infections

In recent years, parents have become more aware of the health risks associated with tick-borne illnesses. Much of the public attention has focused on Lyme disease, a bacterial infection that was first identified in children with arthritis-like symptoms in Lyme, CT, and nearby communities in the 1970s. But there are other tick-borne infections that also pose risks for children, including those caused by bacteria or viruses such as relapsing fever, tularemia, Rocky Mountain spotted fever, ehrlichiosis, and Colorado tick fever. Specific tick-borne infections vary from one region of the country to another. Unless precautions are taken, they can sometimes cause serious illness.

Lyme disease is transmitted by the deer tick. It is caused by spiral-shaped bacteria called *Borrelia burgdorferi* and can produce arthritis (swelling of the joints), most commonly in the knee (this is often called *Lyme arthritis*). The infection usually begins with a red rash at the site of the tick bite, as well as flu-like symptoms such as a headache, fever, chills, swollen glands, and fatigue.

Reducing Your Child's Risk

To protect your child from tick-borne infections such as Lyme disease

- Keep him away from tick-infested areas such as wooded regions, high grasses, and marshes. He should stay on cleared trails. Ticks can live in your own backyard. Clear away brush and tall grass and remove leaves.
- If your child spends time in a tick-infested area, he should wear clothing that covers bare parts of the body, including arms and legs. Button long-sleeved shirts at the cuff and tuck shirts into pants and pants into socks or boots. Your child shouldn't wear sandals that leave part of the feet exposed when he's in an area where ticks are present. He should wear a hat to keep ticks away from his scalp. If he wears light-colored clothing, it will be easier to spot ticks.
- Spray the insecticide permethrin on his clothes to decrease the chances that ticks will attach to them. Do not spray permethrin directly on the skin.
- Use a tick and insect repellent that contains DEET (diethyltoluamide), applying it lightly to the skin. It needs to be reapplied every 1 to 2 hours. Repellents appropriate for children should contain no more than 20% to 30% DEET. The chemical is absorbed through the skin, so it can be

unsafe for children at very high concentrations. Carefully follow the directions on the repellent's label to avoid any side effects. Do not put repellent on your child's face, hands, or any irritated skin or open sores. Once your child returns indoors, wash the sprayed areas of the skin with soap and water.

■ Take a couple minutes to inspect your child's body, including the head and neck, behind the ears, and along the hairline, each day. Removing ticks promptly will often prevent disease. Remove the tick by grasping it with tweezers as close to the skin as possible. Gently but firmly pull straight up and out until the tick is removed, without using any twisting motion. If you must use your fingers to remove a tick, protect them with tissue or cloth, and then wash your hands once the tick has been removed. Once the tick is removed, wash the bitten area with alcohol or an antiseptic. Sometimes parts of the tick's mouth stay in the skin, and it can often cause more harm than good to try to remove it completely.

■ If you have household pets, they should be kept as tick free as possible to prevent them from bringing ticks into your home. Inspect your pets for ticks when they have spent time in tick-infested areas, checking the fur and skin. Use veterinary products to prevent ticks from attaching themselves to your pets.

Keep in mind that your chance of getting Lyme disease after a tick bite is very low (even in Lyme, CT). If your child gets a Lyme disease treatment with antibiotics, he will be cured. Although a Lyme vaccine was developed, it is no longer made. The best way to protect your child from Lyme disease or any tick-borne disease is to follow the preventive measures described in this chapter.

CHAPTER 14

International Travel

When you and your child are traveling abroad, you want the experience to be fun, educational, and disease free. A good starting point is right in your pediatrician's office many weeks before your trip. Review your child's immunizations with your doctor. Make sure your youngster is up-to-date with the recommended immunizations necessary for her age. These include vaccinations for diphtheria-tetanus-acellular pertussis (DTaP), measles-mumps-rubella (MMR), chickenpox (varicella), hepatitis B, polio, *Haemophilus influenzae* type B, meningococcal and pneumococcal infections, and the flu. Immunizations against diseases such as polio, for example, are especially important when your family travels internationally. Even though the number of countries where travelers face a risk of getting polio is small, outbreaks do occur, and it's important for your child to be fully immunized and protected.

In addition to these routine vaccines, your youngster may need others as well. This will depend on the parts of the world to which you're traveling and the activities in which you and your child will be participating. For instance, if hepatitis A is common at your travel destination, talk to your pediatrician about giving your child the vaccine against that infection. Other immunizations, including those providing protection against yellow fever, typhoid fever, meningococcal disease, rabies, and Japanese encephalitis, may be recommended for certain destinations. Here are some examples.

- Meningococcal vaccine is recommended for travelers to areas of Africa.
- Rabies vaccines may make sense for children who will be traveling to areas such as developing countries where they could meet rabid dogs and other animals. These vaccines are particularly important when going to parts of the world where it could be difficult to quickly obtain rabies immunizations and medical care if needed.
- Yellow fever may be found in parts of South America and Africa. Some countries require the yellow fever vaccine before allowing travelers to enter. Keep in mind, however, that your pediatrician may not have the vaccine available in the office, so plan ahead. Certain vaccines are usually given only at places chosen by state health agencies.
- The typhoid vaccine is recommended for children and other travelers who could be exposed to contaminated food or water.
- An influenza shot may be given to a child traveling abroad, depending on issues such as the youngster's current health and chances of being exposed to the flu. The influenza season is different in the southern hemisphere than it is in the United States.

For other immunizations, such as the MMR vaccine, talk to your pediatrician about the advisability of accelerating the vaccination schedule if your young child hasn't yet been immunized. The first MMR vaccine, usually given at or after 12 months of age, can be given earlier (between 6 and 11 months of age) in children traveling to places where the risk for measles is higher. Before 6 months of age, an infant is protected by antibodies passed from her mother. These are special cases in which your pediatrician's advice is important.

Other Travelers' Diseases

There are no immunizations for some of the diseases that may be found in other countries. There are, however, some steps you can take to protect your child.

- Travelers' diarrhea is the most common illness affecting international tourists. It occurs most often in developing countries in Latin America, Africa, Asia, and the Middle East. Carefully choose foods and drinks for your child to prevent diarrhea. Do not eat anything from street vendors and stay away from food prepared and served in unclean conditions. Also avoid raw or undercooked meat, as well as raw fruit and vegetables. Your child should only drink water that comes from treated sources. Safe drinks include bottled carbonated water and water boiled or treated with chlorine or iodine.
- Preventing mosquito bites can lower the risk of getting certain infections, including malaria and dengue fever. Have your child wear long-sleeved cotton shirts and long pants. Apply insect repellent containing DEET (diethyltoluamide) to bare skin. It should be put on lightly and washed off once the child comes inside. Use bed nets and window screens for added protection. If preventive medicine has been prescribed for malaria, make sure it is taken as directed.

You can obtain up-to-date travel health information and advice from the Centers for Disease Control and Prevention online at www.cdc.gov/travel or by calling a toll-free phone number, 877/394-8747. When traveling, it is a good idea to bring an up-to-date record of your child's vaccinations. This record will be useful when entering a country that asks for proof of immunization against certain infectious diseases.

CHAPTER 15

International Adoptions

Each year, families in the United States adopt more than 18,000 children from foreign countries. More than 90% of these adopted children come from Asia, Central and South America, and Eastern Europe. Sometimes, the health status of these children is unclear because of incomplete or inaccurate medical records, their living conditions (eg, orphanages, foster care), and the limited health care they may have received in the past, particularly in developing countries. Children adopted internationally often have been exposed to alcohol or illegal drugs during the mother's pregnancy. This puts them at risk for diseases spread through blood and developmental and behavioral problems. Many adoption medicine specialists consider all children adopted internationally to be children with special health care needs.

All internationally adopted children, as well as refugee children who may have lived in processing camps for many months, are required to have a medical examination before they are allowed to enter the United States. Although this examination should test for certain diseases, it will not give you a complete picture of your child's health. Therefore, you need to bring your child to his new pediatrician to get a complete physical examination shortly after arriving in this country. According to the Centers for Disease Control and Prevention, up to 60% of internationally adopted children have infectious diseases, although many may not have symptoms of those infections.

The American Academy of Pediatrics (AAP) recommends that each adopted child arriving in the United States be tested for a number of diseases, including

- *Hepatitis B.* All children should have blood tests for hepatitis B. These tests can tell you whether your child has the infection currently or had it at some point in the past. It can also tell if he has had the hepatitis B vaccination. If you're adopting a child from another country, you and all your family members should be immunized against hepatitis B before your child arrives.
- *Hepatitis C.* Although routine screening for hepatitis C is not recommended for all internationally adopted children because this infection occurs in low numbers in most parts of the world, youngsters arriving from certain regions, including China, Russia, Eastern Europe, and Southeast Asia, should be tested for this infection.
- *Intestinal parasites.* As many as 35% of internationally adopted children have parasites of one type or another, from hookworms to amoeba. Your child should have 3 stool samples collected 2 or 3 days apart and tested for parasites and the eggs of parasites.
- *Tuberculosis (TB).* Many children adopted from other countries come to the United States infected with the bacteria that causes TB. Tuberculosis tends to be worse in young children, and it may come back years later. For this reason, tuberculin skin tests are important for these internationally adopted youngsters. The tuberculin skin test is the most accurate test for finding an infection with the TB bacteria. A positive test means there is an infection. If the tuberculin skin test is positive, your child should have a chest x-ray film to look for lung disease that may be present without symptoms. Chest x-ray films are not needed for healthy, symptom-free adoptees with negative TB skin tests.

  Many children living in institutions receive the bacille Calmette-Guérin (BCG) vaccine just after they are born. This vaccine is given to stop the spread of TB throughout a child's body if he is infected with the bacteria. This vaccine is rarely used in the United States. Even if a child has been given the BCG vaccine, he should still be tested for TB. If the skin test is positive, the child needs to be evaluated and considered for treatment.
- *Syphilis.* Babies can get syphilis from their mothers at birth and yet have no symptoms. As a result, they may not have been properly diagnosed or adequately treated. Every adoptee from another country should be tested

for syphilis, even if the medical record says that the child has already been treated for the disease.

■ *Human immunodeficiency virus (HIV)*. Every internationally adopted child should be screened for HIV, the virus responsible for acquired immunodeficiency syndrome (AIDS).

■ *Other infections.* A number of bacterial and fungal skin infections are commonly found in adoptees from developing countries. You can examine your new child for infections such as scabies and head lice.

Immunizations for International Adoptees

When you adopt a baby from another country, he may have papers showing that he has been immunized in his own country or, in some cases, a refugee camp. However, these records cannot always be trusted. Sometimes, there are no records at all. Look over any documents you receive and with your pediatrician's help, make sure your adopted baby has had the vaccines recommended by the AAP (see page 37). Your doctor may check to see if your child has been fully protected by giving him blood tests that measure his antibodies to specific viruses and other infectious germs. A safe choice is to simply repeat all vaccines given, using the recommended schedule. Even if your child has had some immunizations, he may not have been given the full series of recommended vaccines. As a result, he may need more doses of some vaccines.

By the way, if you are going to another country to bring your child home, make sure that your own immunizations are up-to-date. Talk with your doctor about vaccines you may need before traveling. Check with the National Center for Infectious Diseases Travelers' Health Web site at www.cdc.gov/travel. If you have an adopted child or are planning an adoption, the AAP Web site, www.aap.org, also has informational resources for parents.

CHAPTER 16

Sexually Transmitted Diseases in Teenagers

Sexually transmitted diseases (STDs) are infections that are spread by sexual contact. While the incidence of reported STDs has actually declined in the United States in the last decade, the number of these infections in children and teenagers is still very high. About 25% of teenagers will have an STD before they graduate from high school.

Bacteria or viruses cause STDs. Any person who has sex with another person can get them. While STD symptoms can range from mild irritation and soreness to severe pain, many times there are no symptoms at all. The STD called chlamydia, for example, is generally symptom free or causes only mild symptoms. The diagnosis may not be made until complications develop.

Teenagers and young adults have higher rates of STDs than any other age group. One of the main reasons is that they frequently have unprotected sex. They are also biologically more likely to develop an infection. In addition, they may be less likely to use health care services that could give them information on how to protect themselves against STDs.

Prevention of STDs

The best way for teenagers to prevent STDs is to not have sexual intercourse. They should understand that when they choose to have sex, it is a decision that could affect them for the rest of their lives. Teenagers need to know that having sex could lead to pregnancy or an STD. Be certain that your teenager understands the risks. For example, make sure she knows that acquired immunodeficiency syndrome (AIDS), which is caused by human immunodeficiency virus (HIV), is a leading cause of death in people aged 15 to 24 years. The presence of other STDs such as chlamydia, herpes, gonorrhea, and syphilis can increase the chance of getting an HIV infection. According to the Centers for Disease Control and Prevention, people with STDs have at least 2 to 5 times the risk of acquiring HIV through sexual contact.

Sexually transmitted diseases can also cause pelvic inflammatory disease in women (an infection of the uterus and fallopian tubes) and epididymitis in men (inflammation of the coiled tube beside the testes). Complications from STDs can lead to infertility or an ectopic pregnancy (a fertilized egg that grows outside the womb). If a woman is pregnant, an STD can infect her baby.

Teenagers may face peer pressure to have sex. They need to understand that they can resist that pressure, and it's OK to wait to have sex. Remind your teenager that saying "no" may not be easy at times, but saying "no" today is better than doing something she will regret tomorrow. Provide some guidance on what your teenager can say without hurting the feelings of her date, such as

- "I like you a lot, but I'm just not ready to have sex."
- "You're really fun to be with, and I wouldn't want to ruin our relationship with sex."
- "You're a great person, but sex isn't how I prove I like someone."
- "I want to wait until I'm married to have sex."

Also, let your teenager know that using alcohol or drugs can affect her ability to make a good decision. Drugs and alcohol make it more difficult to remain firm about the choice to wait to have sex. Even sexually active teenagers might try high-risk sexual behaviors while drinking alcohol or using drugs.

If a teenager starts having sex, it is important for her to practice safe sex. Safe sex means using a barrier method of birth control (eg, latex condoms) every time, beginning with the first sexual experience. Condoms are not a guarantee against STDs. The only way to truly prevent getting an STD is by not having sex at all. Condoms, however, can significantly reduce the risk of STDs and HIV. Talk to your teenager about how she can reduce her risk of STDs by limiting the number of lifetime sexual partners.

Anyone who is sexually active should get regular tests for STDs. Women should have an annual Pap smear. This is the first line of defense against cervical cancer and precancerous changes caused by papillomaviruses. Many doctors also recommend that every sexually active teenager be tested twice a year for gonorrhea and chlamydia and once a year for syphilis. Regular counseling about HIV is also important. Testing should be performed more frequently if symptoms such as abnormal vaginal discharge, irritation, or pain occur.

Using Condoms Properly

Even though you may have clearly spoken with your teenager about the advantages of waiting to have sex, you need to talk with her about birth control. To prevent the transmission of STDs, teenagers need to be taught how to effectively use condoms. The condom should be made of latex. Laboratory studies have shown that HIV and other viruses can pass through the pores of natural membrane or lambskin condoms. Remind your teenager that other forms of birth control, including birth control pills, shots like Depo-Provera, and implants like Norplant, do not prevent STDs. Only latex condoms offer this protection.

Share the following guidance on correct male condom use with your teenager:

- A new condom should be used every time your teenager has sex.
- Condoms need to be handled with care to prevent tearing or cutting them with fingernails, teeth, or sharp instruments.
- A condom should be placed on the penis after it is erect and before any genital contact.
- Sufficient lubrication should be used during intercourse with a condom. If a lubricant is used on the outside of the condom, it should only be a water-based product such as K-Y Jelly, Astroglide, or Aqua-Lube. Oil-based lubricants such as petroleum jelly or body lotion can weaken the latex material.
- During withdrawal, the condom should be held tightly against the base of the penis to keep it from slipping off. Withdrawal needs to be done while the penis is still erect.

A female condom made as a lubricated polyurethane sheath and called Reality is also available. Follow instructions on the product packaging for proper use.

Source: Centers for Disease Control and Prevention. STD Prevention. Available at: www.cdc.gov/std. Accessed April 29, 2005

Is Your Teenager at Risk?
Studies show that if your teenager has one or more of the following characteristics, he or she has an increased chance of getting a sexually transmitted disease:

- Multiple sexual partners
- Sexual contact with one or more individuals with a known STD, either in the present or the past
- Sexual intercourse with a new partner during the past 2 months
- More than 2 sexual partners in the past 12 months
- Symptoms or signs of an STD
- Having been a patient in an STD clinic
- No contraception or the use of non-barrier birth control (eg, birth control pills)
- Male homosexual activity
- Homelessness
- Use of injection drugs (eg, heroin)
- Engaging in "survival sex" (ie, exchanging sex for money, food, drugs, or shelter)
- Having spent time in a detention facility

Source: Health Canada. Available at: www.hc-sc.gc.ca/english. Accessed April 29, 2005

For detailed information about specific STDs, including HIV infection, syphilis, chlamydia, gonorrhea, genital herpes, and human papillomavirus, see the summaries of these infectious diseases in Part 4.

CHAPTER 17

Blood Transfusions

Your child may need a blood transfusion for a number of medical conditions or circumstances. He may have been injured in a serious car accident or burned. He may have had surgery (eg, a heart operation), an organ transplant, severe anemia, cancer, sickle cell disease, or hemophilia (a bleeding disorder).

No matter what the reason, transfusions can be a source of worry for parents. Particularly since the emergence of acquired immunodeficiency syndrome (AIDS) and early news reports of blood contaminated with the AIDS virus, there have been concerns about the safety of blood transfusions. While it's true that all medical procedures have risks, most transfusion-related worries have been eliminated. Routine testing at blood banks make sure that transfused blood is safe to use.

Today, the nation's blood supply is safer than ever before. The risk that your child will contract a disease from a transfusion of blood or blood products is very low. In the United States

- All potential blood donors are interviewed. They are asked about their health history, sexual practices, drug use, and recent travel. Depending on their answers, they may not be allowed to donate blood.
- All donated blood is tested for many germs that could be spread through transfusions. For example, blood is tested for
  — Human immunodeficiency virus (HIV), the virus that causes AIDS
  — Hepatitis B
  — Hepatitis C
  — Syphilis
  — Human T-cell lymphotropic virus (HTLV) types 1 and 2, the viruses that sometimes cause a rare type of leukemia or a neurologic illness
  — Cytomegalovirus (in selected cases)

When a unit of blood is contaminated with any of these infectious germs, the donated blood is safely thrown away and never used for a transfusion. At the same time, the donor is told that he should not donate blood in the future.

Giving Parental Consent

Before your child receives a blood transfusion, you'll be asked to give your permission. Ask questions to help ease any worries that you may have. Make sure you understand your child's disease or medical condition, why he needs the blood, and what will happen if you don't allow the transfusion. Sometimes there may be other options instead of a transfusion. Be sure to discuss the benefits and risks of blood transfusions and how those risks can be kept as low as possible. If necessary, talk to a blood transfusion specialist who can answer all of your questions. This is often a clinical pathologist affiliated with a hospital blood bank.

Blood Transfusion Options

In some cases, you may be able to choose an alternative to a blood transfusion for your child. Here are some choices to discuss with your child's doctor.

- *Autologous transfusion.* A patient can donate his own blood, usually several weeks before surgery, which can then be used during or after the operation if it's needed. Because the individual's own blood is used, this technique significantly reduces the risk of getting a disease or having an allergic reaction to donated blood. However, autologous transfusions are not appropriate for children younger than 9 or 10 years. This type of transfusion also cannot be used in emergency situations because these donations need to be given in advance. Some medical conditions may make it impossible to use this option.
- *Blood recycling.* When blood is lost during surgery, it can be collected, cleaned, and then supplied back into the patient. Because only the patient's own blood is used, there is no risk of transmitting diseases or causing allergic reactions. However, because this recycling approach needs advance planning, it cannot be used for emergency surgery, nor can it be used for certain medical conditions.
- *Directed donation.* If your child needs a transfusion, he may be able to receive the blood of parents, other family members, or other known donors. You may feel your child is safer using the blood of a relative or someone else familiar to you. Keep in mind, however, that this method does not eliminate the risk of disease transmission. Additionally, the donor must have the same or a compatible blood type. Your relatives and friends may have infections that they are unaware of or are uncomfortable discussing, yet they may feel pressured into donating because of the circumstances. Blood from the Red Cross has the benefit of coming from volunteer donors, many of whom are repeat donors, so their blood has been tested in the past and proven to be safe. Finally, some hospitals do not permit directed donations.

In certain cases, children may be candidates for using alternatives to human blood. Youngsters with hemophilia can be given a highly purified clotting factor that is made in the laboratory using recombinant DNA techniques. These manufactured factors are completely free of germs that can be spread to a transfusion recipient. Certain hormones or growth factors are also available that stimulate the body's own production of red blood cells.

CHAPTER 18
Bioterrorism

Terrorism is something that most Americans didn't think about much before September 2001, especially not on US soil. Since then, it is never far from the minds of many people, especially because it is found on the front pages of newspapers across the country. Some people caution that some of the infectious diseases that scientists and doctors are working so hard to remove from the world can actually be used as "weapons." This threat is commonly referred to as *bioterrorism.*

Headlines in recent years have described terrorist threats from anthrax and smallpox. They are only 2 of a number of germs that could be used in acts of bioterrorism. Other possible threats including botulism, plague, tularemia, and the Ebola virus have also been singled out by the Centers for Disease Control and Prevention as being easily spread and potentially causing many deaths as well as social disruption. Other germs including *Salmonella* species, *Staphylococcus* enterotoxin B, *Coxiella burnetii* (Q fever), and chemicals such as ricin toxin are somewhat more difficult to spread and are less serious health risks. However, they could be used as weapons of terrorism. Other organisms including hantavirus and tick-borne encephalitis viruses could be made in laboratories for use by terrorists.

If a bioterrorist attack using weapons like these occurs, the health and well-being of children may be especially at risk. One reason is that children breathe more rapidly than adults. Youngsters are also more likely to have cuts or scrapes that germs can use to enter the body, and their skin itself is penetrated more easily than that of adults. In comparison to their body weight, children have greater skin surface than adults, which could lead to an increased absorption of these germs. To complicate matters, young children in particular may be unable to describe how they're feeling and what symptoms they may be experiencing.

Physical Symptoms of Terrorist Attacks

If bioterrorist weapons are used, common early symptoms in children may include one or more of the following, depending on the particular germ used in the attack:

- Fever
- Headaches
- Vomiting
- Diarrhea
- Abdominal pain

■ Skin ulcers or rash
■ General feelings of discomfort (malaise)

All of these symptoms are common and related to a variety of common infections. If you suspect that your child may have been exposed to terrorist-related germs, contact your pediatrician. It is important that your youngster be evaluated and treated promptly.

Encouraging Communication

Talk with your child about what she knows or has heard about terrorism. Encourage your child to express her concerns and worries. At the same time, reassure her that you, her doctor, and the US government are doing everything possible to protect her from injury and keep her safe. Answer your child's questions honestly, with explanations she can understand. Encourage your child to express herself in ways she feels most comfortable, which for some youngsters may be through play or by writing stories or drawing pictures.

Maintain the family's routines and schedules, which will provide your child with a sense of security and familiarity. Limit her exposure to disturbing news events that can be traumatizing. Do not allow your child to watch these televised reports by herself. Talk with her about what she's seen on TV.

Don't ignore the effect that terrorist events and threats can have on teenagers. Look for warning signs that an teenager is having difficulty coping with the news of the day such as problems sleeping, fatigue, inability to enjoy activities that she used to find enjoyable, and starting to use drugs or alcohol. Younger children may respond to stressful situations with complaints of vague physical symptoms such as aches and pains.

Stay as informed as possible, and keep the lines of communication open at all times. If your child senses that you're not worried, she'll be less frightened and anxious as well.

Preparing Your Family for Possible Bioterrorism

While events like hurricanes or floods provide some advance warning, this isn't the case with terrorism. But you and your family can still do some advance preparation by creating your own Family Disaster Plan. This way you know how to react if such an event occurs and how to keep the risks and disruptions in your lives to a minimum.

Here are some important components of that plan.

- Because family members don't spend 24 hours a day together (eg, work, school, running errands), discuss in advance how your family members will meet up with one another in case of a terrorist attack or other emergency. Select a meeting point where you can find one another, such as a child's school, a neighbor's house, or a public place. Also designate a third party—perhaps an out-of-town relative (it may be easier to call long distance than locally)—as a common contact.
- Share emergency phone numbers—not only 911, but also the numbers at work and school, as well as those of neighbors and local disaster and emergency offices. Keep these phone numbers posted by your phone, as well as in your wallet or purse. Make certain that even your youngest child knows how and when to dial 911.

- Keep bottled water, nonperishable food, and other emergency necessities at home. A typical disaster supply kit should include items such as water (at least 1 gallon per day for each person for 3 to 7 days), food for 3 to 7 days, a first aid kit and medicines, clothing, blankets or pillows, special items needed by babies and the elderly, a battery-operated radio, keys, important documents, pet care items, and tools.
- Decide on the best escape routes from your home. Make sure that your child knows where emergency exits are located in her school.
- Take classes that provide training in cardiopulmonary resuscitation (CPR) and first aid.
- Create a plan for what you will do with your pet in case you need to leave your home and neighborhood.

For More Information

In Part 4 of this book, you can read about some of the specific germs, such as anthrax, smallpox, plague, hantavirus, *Salmonella, Shigella, Vibrio,* and *E coli,* that are of greatest concern in a terrorist attack. Here are some other resources for information.

- American Academy of Pediatrics
  www.aap.org/terrorism
- Centers for Disease Control and Prevention
  www.bt.cdc.gov

Part 3

Understanding the Use of Antibiotics When Your Child Is Sick

CHAPTER 19

Antibiotics: History and Achievements

When a child is sick, parents worry. Even if he has only a mild cold that makes him cranky and restless or an achy ear that only hurts a little, these times can be very stressful. Of course, you want him to get the best possible treatment. For many parents, this means taking him to the pediatrician and leaving the office with a prescription for antibiotics.

But that isn't necessarily what will happen during the doctor's visit. After examining your youngster, your pediatrician may tell you that based on your child's symptoms and perhaps some test results, antibiotics just are not necessary.

Antibiotics: What's in a Name?

The term *antibiotics* literally means "against life"; in this case, against microbes. There are many types of antibiotics—antibacterials, antivirals, antifungals, and antiparasitics. Some drugs are effective against many organisms; these are called *broad-spectrum* antibiotics. Others are effective against just a few organisms and are called *narrow-spectrum* antibiotics. The most commonly used antibiotics are antibacterials. Your child may have received ampicillin for an ear infection or penicillin for a strep throat. Part 4 discusses more about which antibiotics are used for which organisms.

Many parents are surprised by this decision. After all, antibiotics are powerful medicines that have eased human pain and suffering for decades. They have even saved lives. But most doctors aren't as quick to reach for their prescription pads as they once were. In recent years, they're realizing there is a downside to choosing antibiotics—if these medicines are used when they're *not* needed or they're taken incorrectly, they can actually place your child at a *greater* health risk. That's right—antibiotics have to be prescribed and used with care, or their potential benefits will decrease for everyone.

A Look Back

Part 1 of this book describes the great effect immunizations have had on the health of children. Serious diseases that once killed thousands of youngsters each year have been almost eliminated in many parts of the world because of the widespread use of childhood vaccinations.

In much the same way, the discovery of antimicrobial drugs (antibiotics) was one of the most significant medical achievements of the 20th century. There are several types of antimicrobials—antibacterials, antivirals, antifungals, and antiparasitic drugs. (Although antibacterials are often referred to by the general term antibiotics, in this chapter and elsewhere in the book, we will use the more precise term.) Of course, antimicrobials aren't magic bullets that can heal every disease. When used at the right time, they can cure many serious and life-threatening illnesses.

Antibacterials are specifically designed to treat bacterial infections. Billions of microscopic bacteria normally live on the skin, in the gut, and in our mouths and throats. Most are harmless to humans, but some are pathogenic (disease producing) and can cause infections in the ears, throat, skin, and other parts of the body. In the pre-antibiotic era of the early 1900s, people had no medicines against these common germs and as a result, human suffering was enormous. Even though the body's disease-fighting immune system can often successfully fight off bacterial infections, sometimes the germs (microbes) are too strong and your child can get sick. For example,

- Before antibiotics, 90% of children with bacterial meningitis died. Among those children who lived, most had severe and lasting disabilities, from deafness to mental retardation.
- Strep throat was at times a fatal disease, and ear infections sometimes spread from the ear to the brain, causing severe problems.

- Other serious infections, from tuberculosis to pneumonia to whooping cough, were caused by aggressive bacteria that reproduced with extraordinary speed and led to serious illness and sometimes death.

The Emergence of Penicillin

With the discovery of penicillin and the dawning of the antibiotic era, the body's own defenses gained a powerful ally. In the 1920s, British scientist Alexander Fleming was working in his laboratory at St Mary's Hospital in London when almost by accident, he discovered a naturally growing substance that could attack certain bacteria. In one of his experiments in 1928, Fleming observed colonies of the common *Staphylococcus aureus* bacteria that had been worn down or killed by mold growing on the same plate or petri dish. He determined that the mold made a substance that could dissolve the bacteria. He called this substance *penicillin,* named after the *Penicillium* mold that made it. Fleming and others conducted a series of experiments over the next 2 decades using penicillin removed from mold cultures that showed its ability to destroy infectious bacteria.

Before long, other researchers in Europe and the United States started recreating Fleming's experiments. They were able to make enough penicillin to begin testing it in animals and then humans. Starting in 1941, they found that even low levels of penicillin cured very serious infections and saved many lives. For his discoveries, Alexander Fleming won the Nobel Prize in Physiology and Medicine.

Drug companies were very interested in this discovery and started making penicillin for commercial purposes. It was used widely for treating soldiers during World War II, curing battlefield wound infections and pneumonia. By the mid- to late 1940s, it became widely accessible for the general public. Newspaper headlines hailed it as a miracle drug (even though no medicine has ever really fit that description).

With the success of penicillin, the race to produce other antibiotics began. Today, pediatricians and other doctors can choose from dozens of antibiotics now on the market, and they're being prescribed in very high numbers. At least 150 million antibiotic prescriptions are written in the United States each year, many of them for children.

Problems With Antibiotics

The success of antibiotics has been impressive. At the same time, however, excitement about them has been tempered by a phenomenon called *antibiotic resistance*. This is a problem that surfaced not long after the introduction of penicillin and now threatens the usefulness of these important medicines.

Almost from the beginning, doctors noted that in some cases, penicillin was not useful against certain strains of *Staphylococcus aureus* (bacteria that causes skin infections). Since then, this problem of resistance has grown worse, involving other bacteria and antibiotics. This is a public health concern. Increasingly, some serious infections have become more difficult to treat, forcing doctors to prescribe a second or even third antibiotic when the first treatment does not work.

In light of this growing antibiotic resistance, many doctors have become much more careful in the way they prescribe these medicines. They see the importance of giving antibiotics only when they're absolutely necessary. In fact, one recent survey of office-based physicians, published in *JAMA: The Journal of the American Medical Association* in 2002, showed that doctors lowered the number of antibiotic prescriptions they prescribed for children with common respiratory infections by about 40% during the 1990s.

Antibiotics should be used wisely and only as directed by your pediatrician. Following these guidelines, their life-saving properties will be preserved for your child and generations to come.

CHAPTER 20

How Do Antibiotics Work?

Antibacterials aren't the answer for every infection your child gets. In fact, there are 2 major types of germs that cause most infections, viruses and bacteria, and antibacterials are useful only against bacteria.

- *Bacteria* are one-celled organisms that are just a few thousandths of a millimeter in size. They live on our skin, in our digestive system, and in our mouths and throats. In fact, there are one hundred thousand billion bacteria living and thriving on or inside of us. Although most are either harmless or actually serve a positive role in the body (eg, helping to break down the nutrients in our diet), some are dangerous and cause illnesses. They're responsible for many childhood diseases, including most ear infections, strep throat, some sinus infections, and urinary tract infections.

- *Viruses* are even smaller than bacteria. The poliovirus, for example, is only 16 millionths of a millimeter in diameter. Despite their size, viruses can cause mild and serious diseases when they enter healthy cells in the body. They're responsible for the common cold, the flu, and most sore throats and coughs. They also cause smallpox, the measles, the mumps, hepatitis, and acquired immunodeficiency syndrome (AIDS). As powerful as antibacterials are when used in the right situations, they cannot kill viruses and do not work against viral infections. If they're given to your child when she has a viral infection, they can not only cause side effects, but also add to the serious problem of antibiotic resistance. There are drugs called *antivirals* that have been developed to fight viruses (see Chapter 22).

For children, antibiotics are available in a number of forms, including tablets, capsules, liquids, and chewables. Some antibiotics come as ointments and others come as drops (eg, for ear infections). When your pediatrician prescribes an antibiotic, your pediatrician will choose the best one for the specific germ that is making your child sick.

Side Effects of Antibiotics
As powerful and useful as antibiotics can be, they may produce side effects in some people. In children, they can cause stomach discomfort, loose stools, or nausea. Some youngsters have an allergic reaction to penicillin and other antibiotics, producing symptoms such as skin rashes or breathing difficulties. If these allergic symptoms become severe, causing labored breathing, difficulty swallowing because of a tight throat, or wheezing, call your pediatrician and go to the emergency department right away.

The Activity of Antibacterials

Antibacterials fight infectious bacteria in the body. They attack the disease process by destroying the structure of the bacteria or their ability to divide or reproduce. Scientists often categorize antibacterials in the following way:

- Some antibacterials (eg, penicillin, cephalosporin) kill bacteria outright and are called *bactericidal*. They may directly attack the bacterial cell wall, which injures the cell. The bacteria can no longer attack the body, preventing these cells from doing any further damage within the body.
- Other antibacterials (eg, tetracycline, erythromycin) block the bacteria's growth or reproduction. Often called *bacteriostatic* antibiotics, they prevent nutrients from reaching the bacteria, which stops them from dividing and multiplying. Because millions of bacteria are needed to continue the disease process, these antibiotics can stop the infection and give the body's own immune system time to attack.

Some antibacterials are called *broad spectrum* and can fight many types of germs in the body, while others are more specific. If your pediatrician uses blood, urine, or other tests that identify the specific bacteria causing your child's infection, your pediatrician can prescribe an antibacterial that can target those germs.

Remember, if your child has a cold, antibiotics aren't the answer. It's sometimes difficult for parents to determine if their child's illness is caused by viruses or bacteria. For this reason, never try to diagnose and treat your youngster's illness yourself. Contact or visit your pediatrician's office.

Are Antibiotics Ever Used to Prevent Illnesses?
While antimicrobial drugs are mostly used to treat infections that your infant or child may develop, they are sometimes prescribed to prevent an illness from ever occurring. For example, children who have frequent urinary tract infections are sometimes given antibacterials to reduce the likelihood that they'll recur. Medicines can kill the bacteria before they have a chance to cause an infection.

Here are other circumstances in which *prophylactic* (preventive) antibacterial drugs may be prescribed for children.

- Your pediatrician may prescribe penicillin for your child for prevention of acute rheumatic fever.
- Sometimes, a child who has been bitten by a dog, another animal, or even another person will be given medicines to prevent an infection from developing.
- When youngsters are hospitalized for a surgical procedure, they may be given medicines before their operation to prevent an infection from developing at the site of the surgical incision. Typically, these drugs are given to children no more than 30 minutes before the operation. A single dose is often all that's needed.

If your pediatrician believes that your child can benefit from taking medicines as a preventive measure, your pediatrician will choose them carefully and prescribe them for the shortest possible period. This strategy will reduce the chances that use of these drugs will contribute to the problem of antimicrobial resistance.

CHAPTER 21

Appropriate Use of Antibiotics

Each time you take your sick child to the doctor's office, your pediatrician probably thinks, "What is this youngster's diagnosis and what can I do to help him?"

For years, many doctors would, by habit, grab their pens to write a prescription for penicillin, erythromycin, or another antibacterial, even when the patient appeared to have a virus (eg, the common cold) that couldn't be helped by this type of medicine. Some doctors reasoned that even though the antibacterial wouldn't cure the cold, it could attack any bacterial infections that might develop while the body was fighting off the cold. At worst, they thought, it would cost the parents a few dollars to buy the medicine, and it would also bring them peace of mind that at least something was being done. No harm, they believed.

But now we know something quite different. Those antibacterials given for a sniffling or sneezing child were not only ineffective, but they carried a much higher price than just the cost of the medicine. At the Centers for Disease Control and Prevention, studies have shown that about 50 million of the 150 million outpatient antibacterial prescriptions each year are not necessary, with many of them written for viral, not bacterial, infections. In the process, all of those unnecessary prescriptions are contributing to the serious and growing problem of antibiotic resistance.

The Scope of the Problem

As you read in Chapter 19, antibiotics have changed the way that many infections are treated in the United States and around the world. It's important for doctors and parents to remember that antibacterials are the right medicine to use only when treating *bacterial* infections. When they're taken for something else, it increases the chance of antibacterial resistance. Even so, tens of millions of times a year, parents ask their pediatricians for an antibacterial for their children with viral illnesses.

How does this resistance develop? Each time a child or an adult takes antibacterials, these medicines kill sensitive bacteria. At the same time, some of the infectious germs learn to adapt to the antibacterial. The germs actually *mutate* or reshape their cellular structure so that the antibacterials can no longer kill them. When that happens, these resistant organisms can survive and multiply to cause more serious illnesses, more doctors' visits, and more resistance to follow-up treatments with the same antibacterials. Even worse, these resistant bacteria can be passed on to family members, play-mates, and others. The resistant bacteria often stay with the patient for weeks to months. Although they may not cause ongoing illness in the patient, they can still be spread to other people.

These days, antibiotic resistance continues to grow. Each time antibiotics are taken at the wrong time, the risk of resistance increases, threatening the usefulness of these drugs. In fact, no matter what bacterial infection your child may develop, its treatment may be affected by a resistance problem. Even some of the newest antibacterials are showing early signs of resistance.

Consider penicillin, for example. Penicillin was once very effective against common germs such as *Streptococcus pneumoniae,* which causes many cases of pneumonia, meningitis, and ear infections. After being treated with the same antibacterials in case after case, year after year, these bacteria are learning to adapt and have evolved in ways that make them increasingly resistant to penicillin and other antibacterials. When that resistance occurs—and more than 30% of *S pneumoniae* organisms have now been shown to be resistant to penicillin—it makes treatment more difficult because certain antibacterials cannot kill the bacteria. Diseases ranging from middle-ear infections to tuberculosis are harder to manage today because of the growing threat of resistance. At times, your pediatrician may have to turn to newer or more powerful antibacterials, which may be more costly and might cause more side effects.

Picture a scenario in which your child develops a serious bacterial illness. Because of antibiotic resistance, there are now fewer options available to effectively treat it. The illness might last longer and become more severe as your pediatrician tries one medicine and then another to fight it. As unsettling as this picture is, it's not science fiction—it is happening today, and it will get worse unless steps are taken to stop this dangerous trend.

In the laboratories of drug companies, researchers are developing new antibiotics that can hopefully help the growing crisis of resistance. In the meantime, it's important for parents to remember that antibiotics should be used only when absolutely necessary and only as prescribed by your pediatrician.

What You Can Do

As a parent, it's important to talk with your pediatrician about the best treatment options when your child is sick. Ask your pediatrician about the differences between bacterial and viral illnesses. Antibacterials may be useful for some infections, but they're not useful for others. For example,

- *Colds.* Because colds are caused by viruses, they should not be treated with antibacterials.
- *Bronchitis.* Children rarely need antibacterials to treat bronchitis or a cough because most cases are caused by viruses.
- *Ear infections.* Although some ear infections may need treatment with antibacterials, others may clear up without them (see "Ear Infections: Antibacterials or Not?" on page 153).
- *Sore throats.* Because sore throats are usually caused by a virus, they should not be treated with antibacterials. The exception is strep throat, which is caused by bacteria and can only be diagnosed by a throat culture or a rapid office strep test.
- *Sinus infections.* Antibacterials may be the appropriate treatment for some cases of sinusitis, particularly for severe or long-lasting infections.
- *Pneumonia* is usually caused by viruses or bacteria. If your pediatrician determines that your child has viral pneumonia, the best treatment is not antibacterials, but plenty of rest, fluids, and other measures.
- *Meningitis.* The most serious cases of meningitis are caused by bacteria and need prompt antibiotic treatment, often in the hospital. If the infection is shown to have a viral basis, however, it should not be treated with antibacterials.

About three fourths of all prescriptions given to children in doctors' offices are for ear infections, sinus infections, coughs (bronchitis), sore throats, and the common cold, even though antibacterials are often a poor treatment choice for these illnesses. Even so, some parents want their pediatricians to "do something," which often translates to requests for an antibacterial. One study showed that when treating children, doctors prescribe antibacterials in about 65% of cases if they believe parents want them, compared with 12% of cases in which they don't believe parents want them. Keep in mind that taking antibacterials inappropriately can cause much greater harm to your sick child than if he didn't use them at all.

The best advice is to resist the temptation to ask your pediatrician for antibacterial when your child is sick with a cold. Let it run its course, while keeping your child as comfortable as possible. Ask your pediatrician for advice about easing your child's symptoms until the virus clears up. It should get better within a week or so—without antibacterials.

Guidelines for Antibiotic Use

When your child is given a prescription for antibiotics, here are some important guidelines to follow.

- Make sure that you give the medicine exactly as directed. That means having your child take the recommended dose according to the schedule on the label (eg, 1, 2, or 3 times a day).
- Your child needs to take the entire course of antibiotics. This means that if your pediatrician prescribes taking the medicine for 10 days, be sure your child takes it for the full 10 days, even if he's feeling better before then. If he stops taking the medicine early, some of the microbes may stay in your child's body and continue to multiply. This may cause another infection or mutate to a new form that could be resistant to future treatment. With some illnesses, complications can develop if the infection is not completely wiped out.

- *Never* give your child antibiotics that were prescribed for another person or for an earlier illness, including those that you may have in your medicine cabinet. Your leftover antibiotic may be the wrong one for the problem you are treating, it may be outdated, or you may only have enough for an incomplete course of treatment. This can cause growth of resistant microbes and a longer and more serious infection. Throw out any leftover pills—don't save them for future use. (If medicine is taken properly, there should be no leftover pills!)

- Ask your pediatrician whether your child should be seen by the doctor again after all of the prescribed antibiotics are taken. Sometimes, such as with ear infections, your pediatrician may want to recheck your child's ears to make sure that all the fluid is gone.

- If your child hasn't gotten better after taking the full course of antibiotics, be sure to let your pediatrician know. Your youngster's infection may be caused by germs that are resistant to the medicine he has taken. Your doctor could decide to try a different antibiotic instead.

Ear Infections: Antibacterials or Not?

Because of worries about the inappropriate use of antibacterials, a growing number of pediatricians are prescribing antibacterials much less often for middle ear infections, even when caused by bacteria. In some cases, your doctor may recommend a "wait-and-see" approach if your child has an ear infection and his symptoms are mild. The infection may get better on its own without antibacterials. In the meantime, the only treatment that may be necessary is taking care of the symptoms. You can do this by applying a warm pad to the ear or giving acetaminophen or ibuprofen. Antibacterials may be chosen in more serious cases in which the pain is intense or in infants for which the risk for complications is greatest.

In one recent study of nearly 200 children with ear infections, parents were given prescriptions for antibacterials for their youngsters, but were asked to wait 48 hours before filling the prescriptions. In the meantime, they were told to give only pain medicine. Only 31% of the parents actually ended up filling the antibacterial prescription, while the rest said that their child's symptoms had improved on their own before the 48 hours were up.

CHAPTER 22

Medicines for Treating Viruses, Fungi, and Parasites

Every person encounters infectious organisms throughout the day in the air, in soil and water, in foods, and on surfaces everywhere. Fortunately, your child's immune system is capable of resisting most of these organisms, keeping her healthy. When these organisms become a problem and cause an infection, your pediatrician has a number of medicines that can help your child get better.

Antibacterials are the prescription drugs with which parents are probably most familiar. Nearly every parent has had the experience of giving their child a course of antibacterials for an ear infection or strep throat. Most can name some of the most common antibacterials—penicillin, amoxicillin, tetracycline—that have helped their youngster fight off bacterial infections. But as you read in Chapter 19, antibacterials are only one of the medicines that fall under the category of *antibiotics*. Although your child has probably been given antibacterials more often than other types of infection-fighting prescription medicines, drugs are also available to fight certain childhood diseases caused by

- Viruses
- Fungi (yeasts and molds)
- Parasites

Remember, as important as antibacterials are, they are useful only against infections caused by bacteria. For illnesses caused by other kinds of germs, antibacterials simply will not help your child get better. They can actually add risks because of the possible side effects that all medicines have. At the same time, inappropriately used medicines can contribute to the growing problem of antibiotic resistance.

This chapter discusses additional types of drugs that can be helpful for your child when she develops an infection caused by organisms other than bacteria.

Antiviral Medicines

Every child gets a viral illness from time to time. Many viral infections affect the respiratory tract, which includes the nose, throat, and breathing passages where they can cause the common cold, the flu, a sore throat, and sinusitis. Viruses also can cause more serious illnesses such as acquired immunodeficiency syndrome (AIDS), hepatitis, and rabies. Because immunizations are available to protect your child against some viral infections (eg, chickenpox, polio), make sure she is fully protected by all the vaccines recommended by the American Academy of Pediatrics (see page 37).

Antiviral drugs are relatively recent developments, but an increasing number of these virus-fighting drugs are now available. They are made to prevent infection or shorten the duration of infections by preventing the virus from spreading, although they may not kill viruses that already exist. These medicines aren't appropriate for all viral infections—if your child has the common cold, for instance, simply let it run its course. Your pediatrician will be able to tell you when prescription antiviral drugs may be needed.

Unlike broad-spectrum antibiotics, which are often useful against a wide range of bacterial organisms, antiviral medicines tend to be more specific and attack particular viruses. In the disease descriptions in Part 4, you'll find more information on the medicines that are used for managing specific viruses. Here are a few examples of antiviral drugs sometimes prescribed for children.

- *Acyclovir* is a medicine that can be used to treat chickenpox, as well as the symptoms associated with herpes infections that may affect the skin, eyes, mouth, genitals, or brain. Acyclovir can ease the discomfort and speed up the healing of herpes sores, but it will not completely kill the virus. The herpes simplex virus will stay dormant in the body and can cause symptoms again in the future.
- *Amantadine* is among several antiviral medications that can be used to treat and prevent the flu. These medicines are most useful when started soon after your child's flu symptoms begin. In general, the medicine should be started within the first 2 days of the illness. Amantadine is only effective in treating one type of flu virus, influenza A.
- *Ribavirin* and *interferon* are antiviral drugs sometimes prescribed for adults who develop chronic hepatitis. Their use in children has been limited.

Other medicines, called *antiretroviral drugs,* are used to combat infections caused by a particular type of virus called a *retrovirus.* The most widely known retrovirus, human immunodeficiency virus (HIV), is responsible for AIDS.

Keep in mind that even though viral illnesses should not be treated with antibacterials, bacterial infections sometimes occur as a secondary complication of a viral disease. In those cases, antibacterials can be used to treat the bacterial infection.

Antifungal Medicines

Fungal infections are caused by microscopic plants whose spores become airborne and are breathed in by children. They can also enter the body through a cut in the skin. When these spores are inhaled, they may settle in the lungs and begin to multiply and form clusters. Eventually they make their way into the bloodstream and travel throughout the body. Like many infectious organisms, they can cause serious illnesses in children whose immune systems are already weakened by another disease such as cancer or AIDS.

You're probably most familiar with fungi such as mushrooms, yeast, mold, and mildew. Some fungi can live in the body and never cause any sickness. But others cause diseases, including common infections such as ringworm of the skin, hair, and nails; athlete's foot; jock itch; and thrush or yeast infections (candidiasis).

Many drugs can fight these fungal infections. They're often available in a topical form that can be applied directly on the skin. Some are over-the-counter medicines, while others must be prescribed by your doctor.

For serious fungal infections, pediatricians may select a medication called amphotericin B or newer antifungal drugs called azoles. Two of the most widely used azoles are fluconazole and itraconazole. Some prescription antifungal drugs are not licensed for use in children, largely because little research has been done with youngsters. These medicines should be used with care and your pediatrician's guidance because they may have serious side effects.

Although over-the-counter antifungal products are considered safe when used according to the instructions on the label, it's always a good idea to talk with your pediatrician before treating your child with these medicines.

Antiparasitic Medicines

Parasites can cause childhood infections. In some parts of the world, they are a common cause of illness and death. In the Western world, adults and children often contract parasitic diseases while traveling to tropical regions of the world where these illnesses are most prevalent, such as rural Central and South America, Asia, and Africa.

Some parasites are so tiny that they can't be seen except under the microscope, while others are large enough to be viewed very easily with the naked eye. Most live in food, water, and soil. When they're transmitted to your child, often when she consumes contaminated food or water, her immune system can successfully fight off many of them. Other parasites, however, can cause potentially serious infections.

The parasitic infection best known to parents is pinworms, but others include malaria, tapeworms, hookworms, and trichinosis. In the descriptions of these diseases in Part 4, you'll find specific information about the medicines used to treat these infections. Some antibacterials also work against parasites. Metronidazole can block the reproduction cycle of some parasites as well as some bacteria. There are some antiparasitic drugs that are only available directly from the Centers for Disease Control and Prevention (CDC), and your doctor must specifically request them from the CDC.

Resistance is increasingly becoming a problem with some antiparasitic medicines. For example, some drugs used to treat malaria are not as effective as they were in the past because of resistance. As a result, new antimalaria drugs are now in development and being studied in clinical trials.

There are common myths that certain parasitic diseases are caused by poor hygiene and can only be prevented or treated by improving personal cleanliness. These are only myths. Medicines are available to treat parasitic infections. Your child's cleanliness is not going to cure the infection. However, as with many other infectious diseases, including some parasitic illnesses, hand washing is important and a good way to avoid germs that can make your child sick.

Part 4

Getting the Facts About Infectious Diseases

CHAPTER 23

Overview of Infectious Diseases

susceptible

Infectious diseases are illnesses caused by germs (microbes). It is important to realize that not all germs (bacteria, viruses, fungi, and parasites) cause disease. In fact, a host of bacteria normally live on the skin, eyelids, nose, and mouth and in the gut. These bacteria are called *normal flora* and are considered normal inhabitants. These normal flora are helpful to us! The bacteria in our bowels break down foods and form vitamin K, an essential vitamin for all of us. The normal bacteria on our skin and in our mouths protect us by preventing or decreasing the chance that we will become infected with harmful bacteria and fungi.

The World of Microbes

prions. Infectious proteins. The smallest known infectious agents.
viruses. Very small. Viruses take over your cells to reproduce themselves.
bacteria. Two types: free-living, normal inhabitants (normal flora); pathogens that produce disease.
fungi. Molds and yeasts. Fungi colonize (live on or in a child) and are pathogens.
parasites. Forms range from single cells (amoeba, protozoa) to worms.

The normal balance of bacteria can be upset by antibiotics and some illnesses. Viral infections often damage body surfaces and set the stage for infection by harmful bacteria.

Frequently, bacteria are present on a body surface such as the nose or throat or in the bowels, but there is no illness. This is called *carriage* of the bacteria, and the person with the bacteria is called a *carrier.* There is no illness in the carrier, but the carrier sometimes can transmit or spread the bacteria to another person. Many of the bacteria that are carried can cause infection and illness.

It is not always clear why the same strains of bacteria cause carriage in one child, mild illness in another, and serious infection in others. Sometimes it is because of factors in the child or the bacteria, but often doctors don't understand the reasons.

Some important factors in the child include age, immunity, nutrition, genetic makeup, and general health. Newborns are at risk because their protective systems are not yet tested and are not always mature. Infants are at risk because they tend to put everything into their mouths and rarely clean their hands. Older children are less at risk because their hygiene is better and they have become immune through prior infection or carriage of bacteria.

Another important factor for a child is the use of medical devices such as catheters (tubes placed in blood vessels or into the bladder) and other tubes (eg, from the nose to the stomach, from the nose to the lungs). These catheters and tubes provide a direct path for bacteria and fungi to get into the blood, bladder, or lungs. Medicines such as corticosteroids (used in asthma and many other conditions) and cancer chemotherapy can interfere with a child's ability to fight infection. Even antibacterials can be a factor by killing the normal protective flora.

Factors in bacteria, viruses, and fungi include genes that determine how harmful (virulent) the microbe can be. Some germs make toxins that cause illness by themselves or contribute to infections caused by the germ. Examples include enterotoxins, which cause diarrhea; tetanus toxin, which causes lock jaw; and toxic shock toxin, which leads to low blood pressure and collapse (shock).

Germs and Children: Terminology

normal flora. Bacteria that live on or in a child.

pathogen. A germ that can cause a disease.

colonization. Presence of a germ in or on you without disease.

infection. A germ causing an illness. Your body will react by making antibodies.

intoxication. Illness due to a toxin made by a germ.

latent infection. A germ (most often a virus) in a resting state.

reactivation. The latent germ wakes up and reproduces.

carrier. A child who is colonized but not sick.

contagious. Able to spread the illness.

incubation. Time between infection and symptoms.

Infections are a normal part of childhood. Most children will have at least 6 to 8 respiratory (breathing tract) infections each year. These include colds, ear infections, sinus infections, bronchitis, and pneumonia. Infections of the bowels also are common.

When children gather together in child care settings and school, there is the opportunity for infections to spread from one child to another. Chapter 8 reviewed some of the ways in which germs spread and some ways to prevent this spread.

Not all infections are contagious (able to spread from person to person). Ear and bladder infections are not spread from child to child, while diarrhea and colds are easily spread.

The *incubation period* is the time it takes after a child is infected until he becomes ill. Sometimes the incubation is short (eg, a day or so for the flu), while other times it is quite long (eg, 2 weeks for chickenpox and many years for human immunodeficiency virus [HIV]). In some cases, a person is contagious during the incubation period, while in others the person is not contagious until the illness begins. The amount of time a child remains contagious depends on the infection and the child. Young children are often contagious for longer than older children.

Infections are sometimes so mild that there are few or no symptoms. Other infections cause more severe illness. Infections cause harm by damaging a person's body parts (cells and organs) and causing inflammation. Inflammation is one way a child protects himself from infection. Inflammation usually destroys the infecting agent. Unfortunately, inflammation can be harmful to the child as well. Inflammation can harm organs, cause pain, and interfere with normal body functions.

Many infections come and go with no harm to the child. Others cause pain and, sometimes, death. Some infections resolve, but leave a child with organ damage. While many germs come and go, some germs stay with your child even after the illness resolves. For example, herpesviruses (herpes simplex, cytomegalovirus, Epstein Barr virus, varicella, and human herpesvirus 6 and 7) remain in your child for a lifetime. If your child gets chickenpox, that virus stays inside his nerve cells after the rash and illness go away. The virus can reappear later in life as shingles (herpes zoster).

You can read lots more about all these germs in the chapters that follow.

How This Section Is Organized

The chapters in Part 4 are organized by various characteristics *most associated* with each particular organism or illness, though many could be grouped in a number of different chapters. For example, the flu is caused by a virus, but the "Flu (Influenza)" section is included in Chapter 24, "Vaccine-Preventable Illnesses," along with other illnesses that have vaccines that are part of the current child and adolescent immunization schedule. The beginning of each chapter features "Chapter at a Glance," a listing that makes it easy to find various illnesses. You can also locate topics quickly by using the index in the back of this book.

For most of the illnesses covered in these chapters, the following information is provided:

- "Signs and Symptoms"
- "What You Can Do"
- "When to Call Your Pediatrician"
- "How Is the Diagnosis Made?"
- "Treatment"
- "What Is the Prognosis?"
- "Prevention"

Some illnesses that are less common have shorter listings that do not incorporate all 7 of these subheadings. Please note that illnesses in each chapter are organized alphabetically, rather than listing illnesses from common to uncommon. Frequency of illnesses can vary by location and population.

As noted elsewhere in the book, the information provided in the following chapters should not replace the expert advice of your pediatrician. It will provide guidance that will help you understand more about your child's illness, but your pediatrician will use the latest medical information along with an understanding of your child's unique situation to determine the best diagnosis and treatment strategies.

CHAPTER 24

Vaccine-Preventable Illnesses

Chapter at a Glance

 The use of vaccines has led to major improvements in child health over a relatively short period. Many of the infectious illnesses you or your parents had as children, from chickenpox to polio to measles, no longer affect most children today. If you follow the immunization guidelines recommended by the American Academy of Pediatrics (AAP) (see page 37), you can help make your child healthier than was ever possible in earlier generations.

This chapter discusses infectious diseases that can now be prevented by vaccines.

Chickenpox (Varicella)

Chickenpox is a highly contagious disease caused by a virus called varicella zoster. Before the vaccine that protects against chickenpox became available in 1995, it was one of the most common diseases of childhood, affecting almost all children before the age of 9 years.

Signs and Symptoms

Most children with chickenpox have relatively mild symptoms. They commonly develop a very itchy, blister-like rash that appears 10 to 21 days after exposure and infection with the virus. The blisters usually appear first on the torso and scalp, often surrounded by a reddened area. They may spread to other parts of the body, including the face, arms, and legs. In time, the blisters become crusty before finally healing. Most children develop a mild fever during the course of the infection.

What You Can Do

If your child has chickenpox and is feverish or uncomfortable, you may choose to give him appropriate doses of acetaminophen (keep in mind, however, that a fever helps the body fight off an infection). *Never* give aspirin to a child with a fever.

Try to prevent your child from scratching the rash, or the rash itself could become infected with bacteria and may leave small scars. Keep his fingernails trimmed. Bathe him with soap and water or, if you choose, oatmeal baths sold in pharmacies. An antihistamine is useful to decrease itch.

Keep your youngster away from other children who have never had chickenpox or the chickenpox vaccine, especially children with weakened immune systems. The contagious period begins 1 to 2 days prior to the first appearance of the rash and continues for another 5 to 7 days (or 24 hours after the last new blister develops). Children with chickenpox should be kept home from school until the rash has crusted over.

When to Call Your Pediatrician

Most children with chickenpox do not need to be seen by a pediatrician. However, contact your pediatrician if your child has a high fever (temperature greater than 102°F or 38.9°C) or if the fever lasts for more than 4 days. Also, notify your pediatrician if your child has any signs of a bacterial infection, such as part of the rash becoming extremely red, tender, and warm, or if your child's symptoms seem much worse.

Treatment

Your pediatrician can prescribe an antiviral medication called acyclovir that can reduce the symptoms of chickenpox. However, to be most effective, it must be given within 24 hours after the disease begins. This medicine is most often prescribed for teenagers and for children with asthma or a skin condition called eczema rather than otherwise healthy young children.

What Is the Prognosis?

As uncomfortable as chickenpox may be, the disease clears up completely without complications in most children. Bacterial infections do occur in some children. These are usually mild skin infections, but at times the infection can be more severe and involve the tissues under the skin and the muscles. In these cases, antibiotics and surgery are needed to control the bacteria. A few children will have a more severe disease affecting the brain during the rash or a few weeks after the rash. Although most of these children recover, some will be left with damage to the brain.

Prevention

The AAP recommends the chickenpox vaccine at 12 to 18 months of age for all healthy youngsters who have never had the disease. Until your child reaches his first birthday, the best way to protect him from chickenpox is to keep him away from children with the active disease. Keep in mind that an infant will have immunity during the first few months of life if his mother has had chickenpox or the chickenpox vaccine at some point in her life.

Diphtheria

Diphtheria is a disease caused by *Corynebacterium diphtheriae* bacteria. The infection can be spread easily through sneezing and coughing. However, thanks to the widespread use of the vaccine against diphtheria (part of the combination diphtheria-tetanus-acellular pertussis [DTaP] vaccine), there are very few cases of diphtheria in the United States.

Signs and Symptoms

Diphtheria can cause a mild fever, a sore throat, and chills a few days after infection with the bacteria. A nasal discharge, fatigue, and a thick gray membrane covering the throat may develop as well. If not treated promptly, the infection can spread a toxin or poison throughout the body and cause very serious problems, including difficulty swallowing, paralysis, and heart failure.

How Is the Diagnosis Made?

Your child's pediatrician will send samples from your youngster's nose, throat, wound (if there is one), and blood to a laboratory for tests to find the bacteria.

Treatment

Diphtheria must be treated immediately with an antitoxin against the diphtheria toxin. Your pediatrician will also prescribe antibiotics such as erythromycin or penicillin in combination with the antitoxin.

What Is the Prognosis?

Without prompt and proper treatment, some people with diphtheria die from the disease.

Prevention

Your child should be immunized with the DTaP vaccine, receiving a series of 5 shots for full protection from diphtheria. The initial shots should be given when your child is 2, 4, and 6 months old. A fourth shot should be given between 15 and 18 months of age, and the fifth shot at 4 to 6 years of age. Booster doses of tetanus, diphtheria, and pertussis (Tdap) vaccine are now recommended at 11 to 13 years of age. This vaccine was licensed for use in 2005. It allows greater protection for teens (and hopefully someday, adults) from whooping cough (pertussis). Booster doses of tetanus and diphtheria are recommended every 10 years for adults.

Flu (Influenza)

Almost every child has influenza from time to time. Commonly called *the flu,* the high fever and muscle aches caused by influenza are hard to ignore, often forcing the most active youngster into bed for a few days of rest and recovery.

Influenza is a respiratory illness caused by a virus. Flu infections are highly contagious. They spread easily in schools, households, child care settings, the workplace, and any other places where groups of people are together. Your child can catch the flu if someone around her has the infection and sneezes or coughs, sending viral droplets into the air where they can be breathed in by others. She can also get the disease by touching a toy that has been contaminated by someone with the infection and then putting her hand or fingers into her mouth or nose. Children are most contagious during the 24 hours before symptoms begin and the period when their symptoms are at their worst.

Although there are 3 influenza viruses—types A, B, and C—most flu outbreaks are caused by A or B. Epidemics of influenza usually occur during the winter months, often lasting through March.

Signs and Symptoms

When your child gets the flu, she will probably develop a fever (temperature greater than 100°F), usually quite rapidly, often accompanied by the chills, headaches, lack of energy, a dry cough, and muscle aches and pain. As the illness progresses, other symptoms such as a sore throat and runny or stuffy nose may develop and worsen. Some children also have abdominal pain, nausea, and vomiting.

Particularly in infants, influenza can cause ear infections, croup, bronchiolitis (an infection of the lungs' small breathing tubes), or pneumonia.

What You Can Do

You're probably familiar with many of the home treatments for the flu. They've been used by generations of parents, although they are not as useful in getting rid of the virus as some parents think. Your child may benefit from getting plenty of rest, and she should drink liquids to prevent dehydration. To help make your feverish youngster more comfortable and reduce her temperature, some pediatricians recommend giving her acetaminophen (although there's evidence that a fever is the body's way of fighting off the invading infection). However, do *not* give *aspirin* to any child or teenager who has a temperature. The use of aspirin in such circumstances has been associated with a rare but very serious illness called Reye syndrome. Be sure to read the labels on any medicine you plan to give to your child because some medicines contain aspirin (acetylsalicylic acid) as part of their ingredients!

When to Call Your Pediatrician

Contact your pediatrician early if your child has flu symptoms—some antiviral medicines work best if given within the first 48 hours after symptoms begin. In particular, let your doctor know if a fever continues, your child complains of an earache, or she has a cough that does not go away. These are some of the common signs of complications associated with the flu, such as an ear infection, a sinus infection, or pneumonia. Complications are more likely to occur in a child who has an underlying health problem, including heart disease, lung disease, a weakened immune system, or a malignancy.

How Is the Diagnosis Made?

In most cases, your pediatrician will make the diagnosis of influenza by evaluating your child's symptoms. There may also be information from local public health officials about whether a flu epidemic is present in your community. Although doctors can run laboratory tests to confirm an influenza diagnosis or identify the specific viral type (A or B), these tests are not performed routinely. When they are done, they usually involve swabbing your child's nasal passages or throat, then sending the sample or culture to the laboratory for analysis. There are also some rapid tests that doctors can perform in their offices to identify the disease.

Treatment

Because a virus causes the flu, it shouldn't be treated with medicines such as antibacterials. In some children, such as those with a high risk of developing complications, your pediatrician may recommend an antiviral prescription medicine called amantadine to help lower the severity of the disease. (Another antiviral drug, rimantadine, is also available, but it is not approved for use in children.) Amantadine can reduce your child's symptoms, but is effective only against influenza A infections, and only if given within the first 48 hours after the illness begins. Newer antiviral medications zanamivir and oseltamivir are also prescribed in children and can decrease the release of the virus from infected cells. Talk with your doctor about these medicines, which appear safe and effective in shortening the illness. They may allow your child to return to school sooner.

What Is the Prognosis?

The flu can last for a week or sometimes longer, but unless there are complications, the symptoms tend to run their course and disappear on their own. Complications can occur in normal children but are more common and often more severe in children with underlying illnesses. Thousands of people, mostly adults, die each year of complications of influenza. Most deaths are preventable by vaccination.

Prevention

People with the flu are most infectious during a 24-hour period *before* symptoms appear and also during the days when the symptoms are at their worst. Try to keep your child away from others who may have the flu. Do not let her share food, utensils, drinking glasses, toothbrushes, pacifiers, towels, or washcloths. Teach her good hygiene, including regular hand washing.

Before each influenza season, your child can be given the flu vaccine to be protected against this common infection. A new version of the vaccine is made each year to handle the strains of the virus that are expected to circulate in the United States in the upcoming winter. Because of this annual change in the formula of the vaccine, it must be given each year. Your pediatrician will recommend giving the vaccine during the fall months, typically from early October through December, before the start of the flu season.

The AAP recommends a yearly influenza immunization in healthy children 6 to 23 months old. Children in this age group have a higher likelihood of being hospitalized when they contract the flu. The vaccination is not approved for infants younger than 6 months.

Older children and teenagers also can be immunized against the flu virus. It is particularly recommended for children 6 months and older who are considered high risk because they have any of the following conditions:

- Asthma, cystic fibrosis, or other chronic lung disease
- Significant heart disease
- Diabetes or other chronic metabolic disease
- Human immunodeficiency virus (HIV)
- Sickle cell anemia
- Chronic kidney problems
- A disease that requires long-term aspirin therapy (eg, rheumatoid arthritis, Kawasaki disease)

All people in the household of these at-risk children, including other children, parents, and other caregivers, should strongly consider getting the vaccine as well. When a child up to the age of 8 years receives the influenza vaccine for the first time, the AAP recommends 2 doses given at least 4 weeks apart.

The vaccine can and should be given to any child or adult who wishes to lower her chance of getting influenza. Consider having your college-aged teenager immunized because the flu season occurs right in the middle of final examinations.

The influenza vaccine is safe. The vaccine given by injection contains an *inactivated* or killed virus. This means your child cannot catch the flu from it. The side effects associated with this vaccine, such as a fever, occur only rarely. The worst side effect may be a sore arm. Because the flu vaccine is given in the fall and winter when most viral colds occur, it is not unusual for someone to have already been exposed to a cold when she gets the flu vaccine. A day or two after receiving the flu vaccine, the cold symptoms may start, making it easy to mistakenly assume the vaccine caused the cold symptoms.

Because eggs are used in the manufacturing process of the vaccine, children who are allergic to eggs or egg products should not be immunized because of the risk of allergic reactions. Your pediatrician may recommend skin testing before giving the vaccine to a child who may have had an allergic reaction to eggs in the past.

In 2003, a nasal-spray influenza vaccine for the prevention of influenza A and B was approved by the Food and Drug Administration (FDA) for healthy children and teenagers aged 5 to 17 years, as well as healthy adults. Unlike the injected flu vaccine, the nasal spray contains a live, weakened flu virus. It can be given to most children as well as the household contacts of people at risk for the flu, as long as they don't have a weakened immune system. Talk to your pediatrician about whether this spray vaccine is an option for your child and other family members, but remember, it's not yet approved for children younger than 5 years.

In some circumstances, drugs such as amantadine may be used to prevent an influenza A infection in children older than 1 year. Another antiviral drug, oseltamivir, has also been approved for prevention in teenagers who are 13 years or older. It can also be given to members of a household in which someone has already developed the flu. None of these medicines are a substitute for yearly immunizations against influenza.

German Measles (Rubella)

German measles, or rubella, is a disease that has become rare in the United States because of the availability of the vaccine against this infection. The rubella vaccine became available in the late 1960s and since then, no major outbreaks of the disease have occurred. However, the infection has not been wiped out in other parts of the world.

German measles is caused by a virus, but *not* the same virus that causes measles. German measles occurs most often in the winter and spring. The disease is spread through close contact or the air. People with German measles become contagious several days before symptoms begin. The contagious period lasts 5 to 7 days after symptoms appear.

Signs and Symptoms

Children with German measles have a low-grade fever (100°F–102°F or 37.8°C–38.9°C) along with a pink rash and swollen, tender glands at the back of the neck or behind the ears. The appearance of the rash can vary, but it usually begins on the face. Then it spreads to the neck, torso, arms, and legs and fades from the face as it moves to other parts of the body. Teenagers may have aching joints as well. These symptoms develop about 14 to 21 days after a child is infected with the virus.

When to Call Your Pediatrician

If your child has symptoms associated with German measles, such as a rash and fever, call your pediatrician. However, because the symptoms of German measles can be mild in children, parents may not even realize that their child has the infection. In fact, about 25% to 50% of children who have been infected with German measles have no symptoms at all.

Treatment

Make sure your child is kept comfortable. Give him fluids and encourage bed rest if he's feeling tired.

Children with rubella should not attend school or child care for 7 days after their rash first appears.

What Is the Prognosis?

In most cases, German measles is a mild disease. It runs its course and most children make a full recovery. If a pregnant woman develops German measles, the developing baby can be infected and could suffer a severe infection with lasting damage to the eyes, heart, and brain.

Prevention

The rubella immunization should be given to all children as part of the measles-mumps-rubella (MMR) vaccine. It should be given when your child is between 12 and 15 months old. A second shot should also be given when your child enters school at age 4 to 6 years. If he doesn't receive the second dose at that time, it needs to be given as soon as possible, and no later than 11 to 12 years of age.

German measles is a much more serious concern when it occurs in a pregnant woman in her first trimester, when it can cause a miscarriage or severe birth defects from deafness to mental retardation in her fetus. For this reason, women of childbearing age, particularly those planning to become pregnant, should be properly vaccinated against rubella. (Although it has not been shown to cause fetal problems, the immunization should not be given to a woman who is already pregnant.)

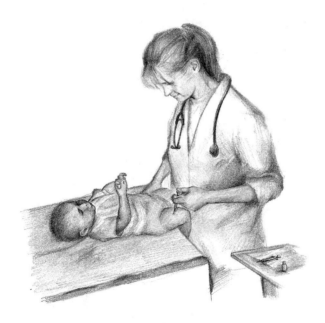

Haemophilus influenzae type b Infections

If you're like many parents, you may have been unfamiliar with *Haemophilus influenzae* type b (Hib) infections until your pediatrician recommended a vaccine to protect your child against them. These Hib diseases are potentially serious. Thanks to the vaccine, they are preventable.

Bacterial infections caused by Hib are usually spread by sneezing and coughing and are responsible for childhood illnesses such as meningitis and epiglottitis (swelling of the epiglottis in the back of the throat). They can also cause some cases of pneumonia and ear infections. Despite the name of these bacteria, they are not responsible for the flu or influenza.

Signs and Symptoms

The symptoms of Hib depend on the specific disease that it causes. For instance

- *Meningitis* is an inflammation and swelling of the tissues that cover the brain and spinal cord. Until a vaccine became available, Hib was the most common cause of bacterial meningitis in the United States. It occurs most often in children between the ages of 6 months and 5 years. Symptoms include a fever, a decrease in appetite, an increase in crying or irritability, seizures, excessive sleepiness, and vomiting. In children older than 2 years, there may be additional symptoms such as a headache, a stiff neck, and back pain.
- *Epiglottitis* is a rare but serious inflammation in the throat, affecting the epiglottis (a flap of tissue at the back of the throat) and occurring most often in children 2 to 4 years of age. Your child's first symptoms will probably be a severe sore throat and fever (typically a temperature greater than 101°F [38.3°C]), followed by a raspy or harsh sound called stridor during breathing. As the epiglottis becomes swollen, it can make swallowing difficult, trigger drooling, and may block normal breathing. Some children with epiglottitis have choked to death. Prompt treatment usually can prevent this.
- *Other Hib infections.* This bacteria causes infection in the joints (arthritis), bones (osteomyelitis), skin of the face (cheek or around the eye), lungs (pneumonia), and even the heart (pericarditis). Signs of infections in these areas include fever, swelling, pain, and redness along with a drastic decrease in energy and activity.

When to Call Your Pediatrician

Because timely treatment is important for Hib infections, contact your pediatrician immediately if you notice that your child has any of the symptoms that have been described.

How Is the Diagnosis Made?

To diagnose meningitis, your pediatrician will perform blood tests and order a spinal tap or lumbar puncture (inserting a special needle in the lower back to obtain some spinal fluid for laboratory analysis). Epiglottitis is often initially diagnosed based on symptoms. Your pediatrician may send you directly to an emergency department where an ear, nose, and throat specialist (otolaryngologist) will examine your child to confirm the diagnosis and begin treatment immediately.

Treatment

If your child has meningitis, she will be hospitalized and receive intravenous antibiotics and nourishment. She'll also be observed carefully for potentially serious complications.

To treat epiglottitis, your child will be given an anesthetic, and then a tube will be placed through the nose or throat into the trachea, which will help her breathe more easily. In the most severe cases, a tracheostomy is performed, in which a breathing tube is inserted through a small incision in the neck. Antibiotics are prescribed as well.

What Is the Prognosis?

If treated early and appropriately, children are likely to recover fully from Hib epiglottitis, pneumonia, and skin infections. Infections in the joints and around the brain are more likely to cause permanent damage. Meningitis, for example, can lead to hearing loss and brain injury.

Prevention

Make sure your child is immunized with the Hib conjugate vaccine. It will dramatically lower her chances of getting Hib diseases during the early years of life when she is most vulnerable to Hib infections. The first Hib vaccine should be given at 2 months of age, with additional doses at 4 months and then between 12 and 15 months. Depending on which type of vaccine is used, an additional shot may be recommended at 6 months of age.

Hepatitis B

Hepatitis B is a liver disease caused by a virus. It is spread via infected blood and body fluids, although there is also an extremely small risk of contracting it through blood transfusions. Sexually active teenagers may be at particular risk for the disease, as are users of non-sterilized needles and syringes.

To prevent hepatitis B, make certain that your child receives the series of immunizations recommended by the AAP.

- The first hepatitis B shot should be administered shortly after birth and prior to the time the newborn is discharged from the hospital.
- A second dose is recommended at least 4 weeks after the first.
- A third dose should be given at least 16 weeks after the first dose and at least 8 weeks after the second dose.

Follow your pediatrician's guidance on the best time for these vaccinations. For more detailed information about hepatitis B and other types of hepatitis, see page 207 in Chapter 25, "Organisms Associated With Infections of the Gastrointestinal Tract."

Measles

Measles was once a common disease among preschool and school-aged children and almost an expected part of growing up. This is no longer true. Measles has not been completely eliminated as a childhood illness in the United States, but most cases now occur in children who were infected in other parts of the world where immunizations are not as widely used. These infected children can and do bring measles into the country, so the disease is just a plane ride away.

Children and adults still get the infection, although in much smaller numbers than in the past. Since the measles vaccine became available in 1963, there has been a more than 99% decline in the number of measles cases in the United States.

Measles is caused by a virus that can spread easily through the air when an infected person sneezes or coughs and someone nearby inhales the infected droplets. It can also be transmitted by direct contact with fluids from the nose or mouth of an infected person.

Signs and Symptoms

Prior to the approval of the measles vaccine, measles epidemics usually took place during the late winter and spring. The most recognizable symptom of measles is an extensive red or brownish blotchy rash, although this is not the only symptom.

Once a child is exposed to and infected with the measles virus, his first symptoms will not appear for 8 to 12 days (the *incubation* period). Infected children tend to be contagious for 1 to 2 days before symptoms finally emerge and 3 to 5 days before the rash breaks out. This contagious period continues for 4 days after the rash appears.

Prior to the appearance of the rash, children with measles develop cold-like symptoms, including a cough, runny nose, fever, and inflamed eye or *pinkeye* (conjunctivitis). These symptoms tend to get worse during the first 1 to 3 days of the illness. In some children, the cough can become quite severe.

After a child has been ill for about 2 to 3 days, the rash will finally become visible, first as tiny red bumps that form larger patches of red. The rash usually begins on the face and neck and then spreads to the torso, arms, and legs. It lasts for 5 to 8 days before it begins to go away.

Young children with measles may develop other symptoms, including an ear infection, pneumonia, croup, and diarrhea.

What You Can Do

If your child has contracted the measles, keep him home from school or child care. In particular, be sure he stays away from others who may not have been immunized against the disease.

As part of your home care, give your child plenty of liquids to drink. Some pediatricians recommend that you treat him with over-the-counter acetaminophen if a fever is making him uncomfortable.

When to Call Your Pediatrician

If your child develops symptoms commonly associated with measles, contact your pediatrician right away. The doctor will want to examine your youngster to diagnose the illness. Discuss with your pediatrician the best way to keep your child from infecting other children and adults that he may encounter in your doctor's waiting room or elsewhere. If your pediatrician diagnoses measles, your pediatrician will call the local health department, which will take steps to prevent the spread of measles in the community.

How Is the Diagnosis Made?

Your pediatrician will make the diagnosis by examining your child and looking for the characteristic rash and other symptoms. The doctor may also choose to give your child a blood test that can detect antibodies to the measles virus or perform a culture of nasal discharge or cough material to grow the virus.

Treatment

There is no antiviral medication that can be used to treat the measles. Some children will benefit from a dose of vitamin A. Your pediatrician will decide if this will be helpful for your child. Follow the home care recommendations described in "What You Can Do."

What Is the Prognosis?

Measles runs its course within 10 to 14 days in most children, and they make a full and complete recovery. In a small number of cases, complications may develop. Very young children are most likely to have breathing and neurologic problems that can be life threatening. Bacterial infections such as otitis media and pneumonia may also develop as a complication of the measles. In rare instances, a swelling of the brain (encephalitis) occurs and results in permanent brain damage. Death occurs in about 1 to 3 of every 1,000 cases of measles.

Prevention

Measles is a preventable disease. To protect your child, make sure he is immunized according to the schedule recommended by the AAP.

- The first dose of the measles vaccine, given as part of the MMR vaccine, should be given when your child is 12 to 15 months old.
- The second dose is usually administered at 4 to 6 years of age.

In almost every instance, children who receive 2 doses of the MMR vaccine after their first birthdays are protected against the measles for the rest of their lives.

If your young child is exposed to a person with the measles before he receives the MMR vaccine, talk with your pediatrician about what you can do to keep your youngster healthy. If he's younger than 1 year, your pediatrician may recommend giving him immune globulin for up to 6 days following exposure, which may provide temporary protection against measles.

If you plan to take your infant to a part of the world where measles is common, contact your pediatrician to see if your child would benefit from earlier immunization or immune globulin use.

Meningococcal Infections

Neisseria meningitidis is a type of bacteria that can cause serious, life-threatening infections such as meningococcemia and meningitis.

These infections are often spread through sneezing, coughing, sharing glasses or utensils, close physical contact, or touching an unwashed hand.

Signs and Symptoms

The signs and symptoms of meningococcemia are fever, aches, loss of appetite, and development of a rash. The rash starts as small red dots and progresses to large bruises. Within hours, a child can be overcome by the infections and develop shock and organ failure.

Signs and symptoms of meningococcal meningitis are similar to meningitis caused by other bacteria—fever, decreased appetite, irritability, excessive sleepiness, vomiting, headache, stiff neck, and back pain.

When to Call Your Pediatrician

Because timely treatment is important for meningococcal infections, contact your pediatrician immediately if you notice that your child has any of the symptoms that have been described.

How Is the Diagnosis Made?

Your pediatrician will perform blood tests and order a spinal tap or lumbar puncture if meningitis is suspected.

Treatment

Your pediatrician will prescribe antibacterials and send you directly to an emergency department or hospital for admission and further treatment. For more information on treatments, see the sections in the book that describe meningitis and sepsis.

What Is the Prognosis?

Meningococcal infections can be life threatening in normal children as well as children who have other illnesses or conditions affecting the immune system. About 10% to 15% of children with meningococcal infection will die. Some survivors are left with limb damage and amputations because of gangrene, and some are left with deafness or brain damage because of infection around the brain.

Prevention

In early 2005, the FDA licensed a new conjugate meningococcal vaccine for use in children and adults aged 11 to 55 years. It protects a person against

4 of the 5 serotypes of meningococcus that cause disease in children and adults. At this time, the vaccine is being recommended for all children aged 11 to 12 years, children entering high school, college freshman living in dormitories, children who have no spleen or a damaged spleen, and children with immune problems that increase their risk for developing meningococcal infections. You can find updates about this and other new vaccines at the AAP Web site, www.aap.org.

Mumps

If you grew up before the mumps vaccine became available, you might remember your experience with the disease, particularly the uncomfortable swelling on the side of one or both cheeks. These swollen salivary glands are the most characteristic sign of mumps, which is caused by a virus and usually spread through coughing. It occurs most often in children and teenagers 5 to 14 years old, but like so many diseases described in this chapter, a vaccine has turned it into a very uncommon infection. There are now less than 500 reported cases in the United States each year.

Signs and Symptoms

Most often, mumps affects the parotid glands, which are located between the jaw and ear. In addition to swelling, the region can become painful when touched or while chewing, especially when consuming foods that stimulate the release of salivary juices or drinking orange juice or other juices that are acidic. Other symptoms may include

- Fever lasting 3 to 5 days
- Headache
- Nausea
- Occasional vomiting
- Weakness
- A decrease in appetite
- Swelling and pain in the joints (and in boys, of the testes)

A child with mumps will become contagious beginning a day or two before the swelling begins, and the contagious period will continue for about 5 days after the swelling has started. (It's interesting to note that approximately one third of those infected with mumps do not show obvious swelling.) As a general guideline, keep your child with mumps away from school and child care for 9 days after the gland swelling has begun.

What You Can Do

Here are some home care steps to keep in mind for a child with mumps.

- Make sure she gets plenty of rest.
- Feed her soft, non-citrus foods that can be easily chewed and swallowed.
- Encourage her to drink extra fluids to prevent dehydration.

How Is the Diagnosis Made?

Because mumps is so uncommon today, your pediatrician may take a sample from your child's throat or urine and test it in the laboratory for the presence of the mumps virus. This test can help to diagnose or rule out mumps or identify another infectious organism that may be causing the swelling.

Treatment

Your pediatrician won't recommend any specific treatment for mumps, other than steps to keep your child comfortable. Because mumps is caused by a virus, antibacterials will not help.

Notify your doctor if your child's condition becomes worse, especially if she develops abdominal pain, shows an unusual lack of energy, or (for boys) his testicles become painful.

What Is the Prognosis?

Most children do not have serious complications after a bout with mumps. A complication for some boys, usually after puberty, is *orchitis* (a swelling of the testicles). Meningitis and deafness can also be among the complications resulting from mumps.

Prevention

The MMR vaccine can protect your child against mumps and should be given when she is between 12 and 15 months of age, with an additional dose at 4 to 6 years of age.

Pneumococcal Infections

Pneumococcus *(Streptococcus pneumoniae)* is a type of bacteria that can cause infections, some serious, in many parts of the body. Pneumococcus is responsible for many cases of

- Brain and spinal cord infection (meningitis)
- Lung infection (pneumonia)

- Infection of the bloodstream (bacteremia)
- Joint infection (arthritis)
- Ear infection (otitis media)
- Infection of the sinus membranes (sinusitis)
- Eye infection (conjunctivitis)

These infections are often spread through sneezing, coughing, or touching an unwashed hand.

Signs and Symptoms
The signs and symptoms of pneumococcal infections depend on the site of the infection. Typical signs and symptoms for meningitis are fever, headache, lethargy, vomiting, seizures, and stiff neck; for pneumonia, fever, cough, and difficulty breathing; for bacteremia, fever and less energy; for ear infections, fever and ear pain; and for sinusitis, fever and pain in the face.

Treatment
Your pediatrician will prescribe antibacterials for treating pneumococcal infections. For more information on treatments, see the sections in the book that describe the particular pneumococcal illness that your child has, such as pneumonia and sinusitis.

What Is the Prognosis?
Pneumococcal infections can be serious and may pose greater health risks in very young children whose immune systems are still developing. Some of these diseases are life threatening in normal children as well as children who have other illnesses or health conditions such as HIV infection, certain cancers (eg, leukemia, lymphoma), sickle cell disease, diabetes, and chronic heart, lung, or kidney disease.

Prevention
A vaccine can protect your child against pneumococcal infections and has been most effective against diseases such as meningitis, pneumonia, and bacteremia. It is not as useful in preventing ear infections and sinusitis. The newest generation of this vaccine, called the pneumococcal conjugate vaccine, is recommended for all children aged 2 to 23 months and certain children aged 24 to 59 months. The vaccine should be given at 2 months, 4 months, and 6 months and then at 12 to 15 months.

Polio

For parents of an earlier era, polio was one of the most feared infectious diseases. Many were worried about letting their children swim in public swimming pools or get together at neighborhood movie theaters because they were afraid that their youngsters might become the next victims of polio. After the polio vaccine became widely available in the mid-1950s, the world saw a dramatic decline in this disease.

Polio is caused by a virus that affects infants and young children more often than other age groups. It is spread through close person-to-person contact and can produce paralysis of the muscles. Some cases are mild, but others are much more severe, leaving people physically impaired for the rest of their lives. Thanks to the polio vaccine, the wild poliovirus has been virtually eliminated from the United States and much of the rest of the world.

Signs and Symptoms

For most people, polio may cause no symptoms at all. At times, however, it can impair and paralyze the arms and legs. It causes death in some people, most often when the muscles involved in breathing become paralyzed.

When symptoms occur, they may begin with a low-grade fever and a sore throat, beginning about 6 to 20 days after exposure to the poliovirus. Some children may also have pain or stiffness in the back, neck, and legs, although these symptoms may not last long. When polio results in paralysis, the muscle pain can be severe.

The most contagious period for polio is 7 to 10 days before the appearance of symptoms. It can continue for another 7 to 10 days after symptoms surface.

Treatment

No treatment is available for polio.

What Is the Prognosis?

Some children fully recover from polio, but others are disabled for a lifetime or may die from the disease.

Prevention

To protect your child from polio, make sure that he is properly immunized against the disease. All youngsters require 4 doses of the polio vaccine before they start school. These shots should be given at 2 months and 4 months of age, then between 6 to 18 months of age. A booster dose is needed between 4 and 6 years of age.

Today, children are given the inactivated polio vaccine (IPV) as shots in the arm or leg. The oral polio vaccine (OPV) is no longer recommended. This oral preparation came in the form of liquid drops and was swallowed, but it carried a very small risk (1 in 2.4 million people) of actually causing polio (vaccine-associated paralytic polio). Since 2000, only IPV is used in the United States, and there is no risk of IPV causing the disease.

Tetanus

Tetanus, also known as lockjaw (which comes from the locking or tightening of the muscles around the jaw, which prevents a child from opening her mouth or swallowing), is a serious and potentially fatal infection caused by a poison (toxin) made by the bacteria *Clostridium tetani*. This germ is present in soil and can contaminate a wound. In fact, any open wound or cut, no matter how small, is a possible site of a tetanus infection. However, an infection is more likely to occur in deep puncture wounds and those contaminated with dirt, feces, or soil. A child who is injured by a dirty garden tool or a rock thrown up by a lawn mower may develop tetanus if she has not been properly immunized. A newborn can get the infection if the umbilical cord gets contaminated.

Tetanus is not contagious and cannot be spread from person to person.

Because of the common use of tetanus immunizations, tetanus is very rare in the United States. There are only a few dozen cases each year, usually in unimmunized people or people who have not kept up with the recommended booster every 10 years.

Signs and Symptoms

Symptoms usually develop gradually in the first 1 to 2 weeks after a wound has been contaminated with tetanus bacteria. The affected child experiences spasms of the jaw muscles, a headache, and irritability. Next, she experiences muscle tightening, pain, and spasms spread to other parts of the body including the neck, shoulders, and back with increasing intensity. The disease is fatal in some cases.

How Is the Diagnosis Made?

To make the diagnosis, your pediatrician will rule out other possible causes of the symptoms your child has. If muscle spasms occur in a child who has had a recent puncture wound, the pediatrician will culture and test the bacteria to prove the diagnosis. Your pediatrician will start therapy unless there is another cause of the spasms.

Treatment

Successful treatment is possible if the disease is diagnosed and managed promptly. Your child will be hospitalized immediately and probably placed in an intensive care unit. Your doctor may prescribe an antibiotic medicine such as metronidazole or penicillin and an antitoxin drug.

It is also important to have the wound cleaned and debrided, removing all dirt and dead tissue, although extensive debriding is not necessary for puncture wounds. Supportive care is given to help breathing and control the spasms.

Prevention

Tetanus is preventable if your child has received the appropriate vaccinations that protect against it. Your child should start receiving a series of tetanus shots as part of the DTaP vaccine at 2, 4, and 6 months of age, with a fourth shot between 15 and 18 months of age and a fifth shot at 4 to 6 years of age. Booster doses of Tdap are given at 11 to 13 years of age, and booster doses of Td are given every 10 years after that.

If your child has a wound that may have been contaminated with soil, contact your pediatrician as soon as possible, especially if you're unsure of your youngster's immunization status. Your doctor will examine the youngster's medical records to make sure she has received the recommended tetanus shots and is protected from a tetanus infection. Your pediatrician may decide to give your child a tetanus vaccine if she is not up to date with these immunizations or an extra shot if the last dose of vaccine was more than 5 years ago. If your child has not received any vaccine, your doctor may prescribe a single dose of a medicine called human tetanus immune globulin (TIG).

Whooping Cough (Pertussis)

About 4,000 new cases of whooping cough (pertussis) occur in the United States each year. That's significantly less than the 183,000 cases reported to the Centers for Disease Control and Prevention in 1940 before the wide availability of the pertussis vaccine. Whooping cough is caused by *Bordetella pertussis* bacteria, which affect the linings of the airways, causing swelling and narrowing of the breathing passages. It is suspected that whooping cough is more common than we think, especially in teenagers, so vaccination remains important.

Signs and Symptoms

A severe, violent, and rapid cough is the most common symptom of whooping cough. The respiratory secretions that are expelled during these coughing episodes can spread the disease to other people. When a child develops whooping cough, he has bursts of coughing that result in shortness of breath. After a coughing spell, he breathes in deeply. This breathing pattern often makes a whooping sound as the child breathes in, only to be followed by the next coughing spell.

Before a child develops the characteristic cough of pertussis, his illness will begin with symptoms that might be mistaken for the common cold (eg, runny nose, nasal congestion, sneezing, low-grade fever). As the cough and the whooping sound develop and worsen, his lips and fingertips may take on a dark or bluish color because of a lack of oxygen during the coughing spells. Other symptoms may include

- Drooling
- Tearing
- Vomiting
- Exhaustion related to the cough

These children also become more vulnerable to other infections, including pneumonia, as well as complications such as seizures. For children younger than 1 year, whooping cough leads to pneumonia about 20% of the time. In general, the disease is most severe in babies in the first 6 months of life, particularly in those who were born prematurely (preterm). In all ages, the cough lasts for months—this illness has been called the *100-day cough*.

Once a child has been infected with pertussis bacteria, symptoms may occur 7 to 10 days later, although this incubation period can last from 6 to 21 days.

When to Call Your Pediatrician

Contact your doctor if cold-like symptoms are followed by symptoms that could indicate the presence of whooping cough. These include a cough that worsens, becoming much more violent and frequent, and a darkening of the fingertips and lips during the cough. Your child may vomit at the end of a coughing spasm. He may also be extremely tired from the severe coughing and may have difficulty eating and drinking.

How Is the Diagnosis Made?

The distinctive pertussis cough is a key to making the diagnosis. Your pediatrician may also take a culture of your child's nasal and throat secretions, which will be tested in the laboratory for the presence of pertussis bacteria.

Treatment

Infants younger than 6 months and some older children with whooping cough will be hospitalized at the beginning of treatment. Antibiotics will be given for about 2 weeks and should be started as early in the disease process as possible. These medicines are important in keeping the infection from spreading to others. While at the hospital, children may need to be given oxygen to help them breathe, and the thick secretions in their breathing passages may need to be suctioned.

What Is the Prognosis?

Some children with whooping cough die from the disease. In most cases, however, the recovery process begins several weeks after the infection develops, although the cough itself lasts for months.

Prevention

Your child should receive the DTaP vaccine. It should be given in 5 doses—at 2, 4, and 6 months of age, with booster shots at 12 to 18 months of age and again before entering school.

The current version of this vaccine carries a much lower risk of side effects than earlier formulations. Concerns about side effects should not be a reason to keep your child from getting this important immunization.

A version of the vaccine has just been licensed for use in older children. This vaccine, called Tdap, has less diptheria and acellular pertussis. It will be used routinely for children aged 11 to 12 years. Stay tuned because this vaccine may be recommended for adults in the future.

See Also

CHAPTER 25

Organisms Associated With Infections of the Gastrointestinal Tract

Chapter at a Glance

This chapter describes infections that commonly lead to problems in the gastrointestinal (GI) tract, which ranges from the mouth to the anus and includes the throat, stomach, and intestines.

Anaerobic Infections

Some infections are caused by bacteria that cannot survive or multiply when oxygen is present. These bacteria, called anaerobes, normally live in the GI tract, where there is only a limited amount of oxygen. By definition, the term *anaerobic* means "life without air."

Here are brief descriptions of anaerobic infections that sometimes affect children.

- *Actinomycosis* (lumpy jaw disease) is caused most often by a species of bacteria called *Actinomyces*. This infection usually occurs on the face and neck, sometimes after a dental infection or procedure such as a tooth extraction or oral surgery or after trauma to the face. It can also affect other parts of the body, including the abdomen, where it may be related to a perforation of the intestine or trauma in the region. Abscesses (collections of pus) may form when these infections are present. Actinomycosis rarely develops in infants and children.

  Laboratory tests can confirm the presence of *Actinomyces* bacteria. When actinomycosis is diagnosed, your doctor may treat it with intravenous antibiotics (eg, penicillin, ampicillin) for 4 to 6 weeks, followed by high doses of antibiotics taken by mouth for months.

- Bacteroides *and* Prevotella *infections.* Bacterial organisms from species called *Bacteroides* and *Prevotella* are anaerobic. They are common organisms in the mouth, GI tract, and female genital tract. They can cause infections in various parts of the body in children and adults of all ages. The most common are dental infections, inflammation of the abdominal lining (peritonitis), and abscesses within the abdomen, uterus, or tubes. In other regions of the body, these bacteria have been associated with conditions like chronic ear infections, deep skin infections, and lung abscesses.

  Cultures can be collected and sent to the laboratory to identify and confirm the organisms responsible for the infection, determining whether *Bacteroides* or *Prevotella* species are involved. These infections are treated with antibiotics such as clindamycin or metronidazole. In most cases, the bacteria are resistant to penicillin drugs. If an abscess has formed, it may need to be drained using a needle or by surgery.

Campylobacter Infections

Campylobacter are a type of bacteria that produce infections in the GI tract. They are a major bacterial cause of diarrheal sickness among children in the United States. You may hear your pediatrician use the names *Campylobacter jejuni* or *Campylobacter coli,* which are the most common *Campylobacter* species associated with diarrhea. Common ways that a child can get the infection are from contaminated food, especially undercooked chicken; unpasteurized milk; and household pets. Infection can also spread by person-to-person contact. The incubation period is usually 2 to 7 days.

Signs and Symptoms

Illness caused by *Campylobacter* infections includes diarrhea, stomach pain, and fever. Blood may be present in the stools. In young infants, bloody diarrhea may be the only sign that an infection is present. Severe diarrhea can cause dehydration, with symptoms such as excessive thirst and a decline in the frequency of urination. *Campylobacter* can also enter the blood stream and infect other organs, though this is not common.

Signs of Dehydration	
Increased thirst	Sleepy
Decreased urine	Irritable
Dry mouth	Doughy feel to skin
Dry eyes	Thready pulse
Sunken eyes	Cold, clammy skin
Sunken soft spot in infants	Shock

In rare cases, complications caused by the body's immune system may develop. The antibodies made against *Campylobacter* can react against the child's body, causing an uncommon form of arthritis called reactive arthritis, a skin sore called erythema nodosum, and a serious condition of the nerves called Guillain-Barré syndrome. With Guillain-Barré syndrome, the child develops weakness that usually starts in the legs and moves up the body.

What You Can Do

If your child has blood in his diarrhea or stools, you should call your pediatrician. Children with *Campylobacter* infections tend to get better on their own without any particular treatment. Until your child's diarrhea goes away, make sure he drinks lots of fluids. Rehydration fluids are sold in stores, but can also be made at home. Talk to your pediatrician about how to include the proper amount of salt and sugar.

How Is the Diagnosis Made?

The blood and feces can be tested in the laboratory for the presence of *Campylobacter* bacteria. This will help your pediatrician give you an exact diagnosis of the cause of your child's diarrhea.

Treatment

Sometimes, particularly when a *Campylobacter* infection is severe, antibiotics may be given. If taken early in the course of the illness, antibiotics such as erythromycin and azithromycin can eliminate the bacteria from the stool in 2 to 3 days and shorten the length of the illness. When your pediatrician gives these medicines, make sure your child takes them as instructed. Over-the-counter antidiarrheal medicines may make your child sicker and should not be taken if there is blood in the stools.

What Is the Prognosis?

If your child has a mild *Campylobacter* infection, the illness may last only for a day or two. In other cases, youngsters may recover within a week, although about 20% have a relapse or a prolonged or severe illness.

Prevention

Many cases of *Campylobacter* infections are connected with touching or eating undercooked poultry. Therefore, proper food handling and preparation are important.

To prevent these infections in your family

- Wash your hands thoroughly after handling raw poultry. Also, wash cutting boards and utensils with soap and water after they've been in contact with raw poultry. It is important to cook poultry thoroughly before eating.
- Drink only milk that has been pasteurized.
- Because pets can be carriers of *Campylobacter* bacteria, members of your family should wash their hands thoroughly after having contact with the feces of dogs, cats, hamsters, and birds.

- Wash your hands carefully after touching the underclothes or diapers of young children and infants with diarrhea.
- Children should always wash their hands before eating.
- If a child that attends child care has diarrhea, you should tell the caregivers right away.

Preventing Gastroenteritis

Wash your hands.

Don't share utensils.

Wash and/or peel raw fruits and vegetables.

Cook meats thoroughly.

Avoid contaminating foods eaten raw (eg, fruit, salad) with foods that get cooked (eg, chicken, turkey, beef, pork).

Clostridium difficile

Clostridium difficile is a cause of diarrhea in children. It is also responsible for producing a serious form of colitis (inflammation of the colon) called pseudomembranous colitis. These infections are often contracted in the hospital while a child is receiving antibiotic treatment, although illness may develop days or weeks after leaving the hospital. These anaerobic bacteria are often found normally in the gut of newborns and young children. The disease is caused when the bacteria produce a toxin (poison) that damages the lining of the gut. This happens most often when your child is taking antibiotics that kill other bacteria in the gut, permitting *C difficile* to multiply to very high numbers. The incubation period for this illness is not known. The bacteria can live in the gut for long periods without causing illness.

Signs and Symptoms
C difficile causes diarrhea with stomach cramps or tenderness, fever, and blood and mucus in the stools.

How Is the Diagnosis Made?
To make a proper diagnosis, your child's stool can be tested for the presence of toxins produced by *C difficile*.

Treatment

Because antibiotic use and overuse is associated with *C difficile* infections, children on antibiotics should be taken off these medicines as soon as possible. In mild cases, children may get better once they stop taking the antibiotics. Some children, however, may need to be given particular medicines such as metronidazole or vancomycin that fight the bacteria. Most children make a full recovery. If a relapse of the illness occurs, which happens in up to 10% to 20% of patients, the same treatment is often repeated.

Prevention

It may be possible to prevent or reduce the risk of *C difficile* disease through proper hand washing, as well as the proper handling of dirty diapers and other waste matter. Also, the use of antibiotics should be limited to only those circumstances in which it is absolutely necessary.

Escherichia coli Diarrhea

In recent years, you may have seen the term *E coli* in the newspaper, most often in describing food-borne infections. *E coli* is short for *Escherichia coli.* It has been in the newspaper headlines when both children and adults have become ill from eating *E coli*–contaminated undercooked ground beef, mostly at fast-food restaurants.

There are many strains of *E coli* bacteria, most of which are harmless and normal inhabitants of the gut. However, at least 5 types of diarrhea-producing *E coli* have been identified, some of which are a common cause of traveler's diarrhea. An especially nasty strain that doctors have labeled *E coli* O157:H7 can produce toxins or poisons that have caused many cases of severe illness and even death.

According to the Centers for Disease Control and Prevention, about 73,000 cases of *E coli* O157:H7 infections occur each year in the United States. These bacteria live in the gut of cows. They are present in cow manure and unpasteurized milk. Most cases in people are caused by eating contaminated undercooked ground beef. It can also be transmitted by water or juices made from fruits that are contaminated with cow manure. Person-to-person transmission occurs in child care settings.

Signs and Symptoms

Depending on the strain of *E coli* he has, your child may have watery diarrhea, diarrhea with blood and mucus, or a combination of both. Severe abdominal cramps and fever may be present. With certain strains of *E coli*, especially those that cause traveler's diarrhea, the diarrhea tends to be watery and can lead to dehydration.

In a small number of cases, a serious complication called hemolytic uremic syndrome (HUS) can develop in children usually younger than 5 years, frequently about 2 weeks after the diarrhea has begun. In the United States, most cases of HUS are associated with the *E coli* O157:H7 strain. Children with HUS have low red blood cell and platelet counts (red blood cells carry oxygen and platelets help with blood clotting) and may develop kidney failure.

How Is the Diagnosis Made?

An *E coli* infection is diagnosed by testing the stool for the presence of the bacteria.

Treatment

A child's symptoms will usually last for about a week before he gets better. Always try to prevent dehydration by giving your child plenty of fluids whenever he has diarrhea. On your doctor's recommendation you can give him oral rehydration solutions available over the counter or made at home. Older children with watery diarrhea may benefit from antidiarrheal medicines, but *only* under the advice of your pediatrician.

When HUS is present, a child will have to be hospitalized to receive treatment, which could include blood transfusions and kidney dialysis.

What Is the Prognosis?

Most children will recover fully without treatment. Children with HUS usually recover completely, but a few will have lasting damage to the kidneys.

Prevention

To keep your child from being exposed to *E coli* O157:H7, cook ground beef thoroughly to kill bacteria. Make sure there is no pink meat left and the juices are clear. Your youngster should also avoid raw or unpasteurized milk and drink only pasteurized apple juice. He should wash his hands with soap and warm water before eating.

When traveling abroad, take precautions such as making sure your food is thoroughly cooked and the water is boiled. Avoid salads, raw vegetables, fruits that have already been peeled, and food from street vendors. Consume safe beverages such as carbonated drinks with no ice and tea and coffee prepared with boiled water. If your child visits a petting zoo, be sure he thoroughly washes his hands after contact with the animals and of course, before eating.

Giardia lamblia Infections

Giardiasis is the name doctors give to infections caused by a microscopic parasite called *Giardia lamblia.* This organism may be found in the stools of an infected person. It can be transmitted by person-to-person contact in places like child care centers and among family members who have not properly washed their hands after using the bathroom or changing diapers. *Giardia* may also be present in contaminated food and water and is a risk for campers drinking untreated water from mountain streams, which can be contaminated by stool from infected animals and campers.

Signs and Symptoms

Most children with a *G lamblia* infection have no symptoms at all. A few have abdominal pain and watery, foul-smelling diarrhea that can lead to dehydration. They may also have excessive gas and bloating and could have a poor appetite, leading to weight loss. Fever is uncommon. Most often, symptoms begin 7 to 14 days after exposure to the *Giardia* parasite and can last, without treatment, for about 4 to 6 weeks.

How Is the Diagnosis Made?

A stool sample from your child will be examined for the presence of *G lamblia.*

Treatment

To keep your child well hydrated, she should drink plenty of liquids recommended by your pediatrician, such as over-the-counter or homemade oral rehydrating solutions. Your doctor may also prescribe prescription medicines (most commonly, metronidazole, furazolidone, or nitazoxanide) that cure most cases after 5 to 7 days of treatment.

If your child has *Giardia* organisms in the stool but does not have symptoms, no treatment is needed.

Prevention

When a child attends a child care center, parents should make sure the staff members practice good hygiene and encourage children to wash their hands frequently with soap and warm water. Toys that a child puts in her mouth should be washed and disinfected before another youngster plays with them.

It is a good idea to wash and peel raw fruits and vegetables before they are eaten.

Children should avoid drinking untreated water from streams, lakes, rivers, and ponds. Take bottled water on camping trips or boil, filter, and treat your drinking water with chemical tablets before drinking it.

Other Parasites That Live in the Gut

Many diseases associated with parasites rarely occur in the United States, Canada, and Europe. Nevertheless, a number of parasitic diseases that cause diarrhea are sometimes seen in the United States, brought into the country by tourists and immigrants. In Chapter 35, you'll find descriptions of diseases associated with parasites, as well as a table describing some of these infections. Here are brief descriptions of a few other parasitic diseases that specifically cause diarrhea.

Clonorchiasis

This disease, caused by a parasite called *Clonorchis sinensis,* is most common in the Far East and Southeast Asia and infects the bile ducts of humans. Most often, humans become ill after eating uncooked, infected freshwater fish. Most infections cause no illness. In some, the early stages of the infection cause not only diarrhea, but also abdominal pain, particularly over the liver in the right upper abdomen, and nausea. In later stages, clonorchiasis can cause infection or swelling of the bile ducts and pancreas, as well as the formation of stones in the gallbladder.

Fascioliasis

Caused by the *Fasciola hepatica* parasite, this infection develops when humans eat uncooked infected plants such as watercress. It is common worldwide throughout the tropics and temperate regions, including the British Isles and southern France. The symptoms of fascioliasis can last for months and include diarrhea, abdominal pain, fever, vomiting, itchy skin patches (urticaria), and liver enlargement and tenderness.

Fasciolopsiasis

This infection is associated with the parasite *Fasciolopsis buski* and is most prevalent in the Far East and Southeast Asia. Humans contract it after eating uncooked contaminated freshwater plants such as water chestnuts. Most infections do not cause symptoms, but in more serious cases, diarrhea may occur, along with vomiting, abdominal pain, fever, bloating (fluid retention), and a blockage of the intestines.

Intestinal Capillariasis

When humans eat uncooked and infected fish, they may get this disease, which occurs most often in Southeast Asia, especially the Philippines and Thailand. Caused by the parasite *Capillaria philippinensis,* it can cause diarrhea and abdominal pain, which can become more severe over time. In some cases, it can cause bloating, malnutrition, and death.

Opisthorchiasis

Two parasites, *Opisthorchis viverrini* and *Opisthorchis felineus,* can cause opisthorchiasis in humans who eat infected and uncooked freshwater fish. One species, *O viverrini,* is most prevalent in Southeast Asia, particularly Thailand. The other parasite, *O felineus,* is common in Eastern Europe and Siberia. Most people with *Opisthorchis* infections do not have symptoms, but in some cases, it can cause diarrhea, indigestion, abdominal pain, or constipation. In chronic cases, it can lead to infection or enlargement of the liver and malnutrition.

Diagnosis of these diseases is made through examination of the stool for the eggs of the parasite and usually requires the aid of a specialist in parasitic diseases. Several drugs can treat parasitic diseases, although some of them are available only from the Centers for Disease Control and Prevention when a doctor makes a special request for them.

Helicobacter pylori Infections

Most people, including doctors, used to believe that ulcers (sores) in the stomach or duodenum (the first section of the small intestine) were caused by stress, alcohol, or spicy foods. Now we know that this isn't the case. In fact, these ulcers, called *peptic ulcers,* are most often (although not always) caused by bacteria—specifically, an organism called *Helicobacter pylori.*

   H pylori infections occur at a low rate in children in the United States, but may infect more than 75% of children in developing countries. Although infections increase in frequency as people get older, most children and adults with *H pylori* will never develop an infection. No one is certain how *H pylori* is contracted, but person-to-person contact could play a role, as could transmission through contaminated food and water. The incubation period is also unknown.

Signs and Symptoms

When *H pylori* causes an ulcer, the intensity of the symptoms can vary. In some cases, there will be no symptoms at all. Ulcers can cause a burning or gnawing pain in the stomach that may come and go, often happening a few hours after eating, as well as during the night, and then actually subsiding while eating food and drinking water.

Other symptoms may include

- Bloating
- Burping
- Nausea and vomiting
- Loss of appetite
- Weight loss
- Bloody vomit and dark stools from bleeding in the stomach or duodenum

What You Can Do

In the past, doctors treated peptic ulcers by recommending a bland diet as well as bed rest. But today, these lifestyle strategies appear to be inappropriate approaches to managing ulcers.

When to Call Your Pediatrician

Contact your pediatrician if your child

- Has burning stomach pain that is worse between meals and in the early morning hours and feels better when he eats

- Has persistent abdominal pain, vomiting, loss of appetite, or weight loss
- Has bloody stools or bloody vomit

How Is the Diagnosis Made?

Your pediatrician will take a medical history of your child and may perform some simple tests. Your pediatrician may sometimes refer your child to a specialist to conduct the more complicated and invasive tests needed to make the diagnosis of an *H pylori* infection. These tests include analyzing a small piece of tissue (a biopsy) obtained through a device called an endoscope, which is threaded down the throat to the stomach. The tissue is then examined under the microscope and tested for evidence of *H pylori* infection. Your pediatrician can also look at the esophagus, stomach, and duodenum with x-ray film (an *upper GI series*). There are noninvasive tests that can determine whether bacteria are present by analyzing a child's blood, stool, or breath. The breath test can detect carbon dioxide released by a product made by *H pylori.*

Treatment

Doctors only prescribe treatment for *H pylori* infections if they have progressed to an actual ulcer. Combinations of antibiotics such as amoxicillin, clarithromycin, and metronidazole can be taken by your child to kill the bacteria. Make sure he takes the full course of these antibiotics as directed by your pediatrician. They are usually prescribed in combination with drugs called proton pump inhibitors or histamine receptor blockers that interfere with the production of acid in the stomach.

What Is the Prognosis?

An *H pylori* infection increases the risk of developing stomach cancer later in life.

Prevention

There is no known way to prevent *H pylori* infections. However, a vaccine that could someday prevent the infection is currently being researched.

Hepatitis

Hepatitis means "inflammation of the liver." This inflammation can be caused by a wide variety of toxins, drugs, and metabolic diseases, as well as infection. There are at least 5 hepatitis viruses.

- *Hepatitis A* is contracted when a child eats food or drinks water that is contaminated with the virus or has close contact with a person who is infected with the virus. Hepatitis A is present in the stool as early as 1 to 2 weeks before a person develops the illness. The infection can be spread in child care settings when caregivers do not wash their hands after changing the diaper of an infected baby or from infant to infant because most very young infants do not wash their hands or have their hands washed for them. This virus also can be spread during male homosexual activity. The incubation period is 2 to 6 weeks.

- *Hepatitis B* is spread through the blood and body fluids of an infected person, including through saliva or semen. (Because of the routine screening of donated blood, it is very unlikely that your child will get hepatitis B via a blood transfusion.) The virus can be spread through intimate sexual contact with an infected person or by using non-sterilized needles or syringes for drug use, tattoos, or body piercing. An infected pregnant woman can give the virus to her newborn during the delivery. Person-to-person transmission is uncommon and generally limited to long-term close contact with people with chronic hepatitis B infection. The incubation period is 2 to 5 months.

- *Hepatitis C* infections are most often acquired from transfusions of contaminated blood, although your child's risk of contracting the virus by this route is very low because of routine testing of donated blood. Sexual transmission and transmission among family members through close contact is uncommon. When hepatitis C infections occur in children and teenagers, doctors frequently can't determine how the virus was acquired. The incubation period is 2 weeks to 6 months.

- *Hepatitis D* can be contracted in ways similar to hepatitis B, including through blood, sexual contact, and the use of non-sterilized needles or syringes. Unlike the hepatitis B virus, transmission of hepatitis D from mother to newborn is uncommon. The hepatitis D virus causes hepatitis only in people who already have a hepatitis B infection.

- *Hepatitis E* is rare in the United States. When it has occurred abroad, it has been associated with drinking contaminated water.

Signs and Symptoms

Hepatitis symptoms tend to be similar from one virus type to another. Many of these symptoms are flu like, such as fever, nausea, vomiting, loss of appetite, and tiredness, sometimes with pain or tenderness of the liver in the right upper abdomen. A hepatitis infection is also associated with *jaundice,* a yellow discoloration of the skin and a yellowish color to the whites of the eyes. This is caused by inflammation and swelling of the liver with blockage

Hepatitis Viruses

Type	Transmission	Prognosis
A	Fecal-oral (stool to mouth), contaminated food and water	Expect full recovery.
B	Blood, needles, sexual	10% of older children develop chronic infection. 90% of newborns develop chronic infection.
C	Blood, needles; often unclear	Expect chronic infection.
D	Blood, needles, sexual	Makes hepatitis B infection more severe.
E	Traveler: fecal-oral, contaminated food and water	Expect recovery, although pregnant women are at risk for severe disease.
Others	A variety of viruses can affect the liver.	

and backup of bile (bilirubin) into the blood. This backup also usually causes the urine to turn dark orange and stools light yellow or clay colored.

However, many children infected with the hepatitis virus have few if any symptoms, meaning you might not even know that your child is sick. In fact, the younger the child, the more likely she is to be symptom free. For example, among children infected with hepatitis A, only about 30% younger than 6 years have symptoms, and most of them are mild. Symptoms are more common in older children with hepatitis A, and they tend to last for several weeks.

Children infected with the hepatitis B and C viruses are often free of symptoms or have only a very mild illness.

When to Call Your Pediatrician
If your youngster has developed any of the symptoms associated with hepatitis, including jaundice, or if she has had contact with someone who has hepatitis (eg, in a child care center), call your pediatrician.

How Is the Diagnosis Made?
If your pediatrician suspects that your child has hepatitis, your pediatrician will conduct a physical examination and take a thorough medical history to determine whether your child may be at risk of getting the infection. Your doctor may also order a simple blood test that can determine whether your child is infected with the hepatitis virus and if so, which type.

Treatment

In most cases, no specific therapy is given for acute hepatitis. The child's own immune system will fight and overcome the infecting virus. Your pediatrician will recommend supportive care for your child, which can include rest, a well-balanced diet, and lots of fluids. Do not give your child acetaminophen without talking to your pediatrician first—there is a risk of toxicity because her liver may not be fully functioning. Your pediatrician may also want to reevaluate the dosages of any other medicines your child is taking. They may have to be adjusted because of changes in the liver's ability to manage the current dosages.

If a child develops chronic hepatitis B or C, your pediatrician will probably send her to a specialist in gastroenterology or, in some instances, a liver specialist (hepatologist). Medicines such as interferon and ribavirin are used in adults with chronic hepatitis, but there are limited studies of these drugs in children. Your doctor may recommend enrolling your child in a study using these medicines or others.

What Is the Prognosis?

Most children with hepatitis fully recover. The mild symptoms of hepatitis A, for example, tend to resolve on their own within a month or less, and your child will be back to normal. Chronic infections are extremely rare.

Some children with acute hepatitis B, particularly those who have contracted it before 5 years of age, develop a chronic infection. These children can become lifetime carriers of the virus. In certain cases, the chronic liver infection causes progressive damage, leading to scarring (cirrhosis) and liver cancer.

Hepatitis C infections become long lasting in at least half of the children who develop this infection. In adults, chronic hepatitis leads to cirrhosis in 60% to 70% of patients, while in children this is unusual (less than 5%).

Prevention

Vaccines are available to protect children from hepatitis A and B. The hepatitis A vaccine is approved only for youngsters 2 years and older. The hepatitis A vaccines, however, are not recommended for everyone, but should be given to children living in US communities with consistently high hepatitis A rates. Other groups considered high risk, including certain travelers, should also be vaccinated for hepatitis A. When immediate protection is needed following close contact with a person with hepatitis A, your doctor may recommend an injection of immune (gamma) globulin.

The hepatitis B vaccine is part of the recommended series of immunizations given to children beginning at birth. Your child should receive a total of 3 doses of the hepatitis B vaccine, according to the schedule on page 37.

Although there is no vaccine specifically for hepatitis D, the hepatitis B vaccine should protect against hepatitis D. Hepatitis D cannot develop unless a hepatitis B infection is already present.

To further lower your youngster's risk of hepatitis, she should practice good hygiene and avoid contaminated food and water. Encourage your child to wash her hands before eating and after going to the bathroom. If she spends time in a child care setting, make sure the staff practices good hand washing behaviors, especially after changing diapers and when preparing and serving food to children.

Before traveling with your child to foreign countries, ask your pediatrician about the risk of exposure to hepatitis and any precautions that your family needs to take. In some cases, your pediatrician may recommend that your child receive the hepatitis A vaccine or an injection of gamma globulin, or both, before traveling abroad. General food precautions for travelers should be observed. (See "Keeping Safe While Traveling" on page 293 in Chapter 30.)

Rotavirus and Other Viruses Causing Gastrointestinal Illness

Several viruses are responsible for viral gastroenteritis, an intestinal infection that causes vomiting, diarrhea, and related symptoms in children. These viruses, which injure the cells that line the small intestine, tend to be quite contagious. Outbreaks can occur in child care centers or after the ingestion of contaminated food such as shellfish, salads, or ice. Often, the food is contaminated by infected food handlers.

Here are 3 of the most prevalent of these viruses.

- *Rotaviruses* are the most common cause of severe diarrhea in children younger than 2 years. In fact, virtually all children are infected with this virus by 3 years of age. Infections occur most commonly from November through March. Rotavirus infection was once called the "winter vomiting disease."

- *Astroviruses* lead to infections that occur mostly in infants and children younger than 4 years. They occur most often during the winter months.
- *Caliciviruses* can cause infections that are often spread through contact with an infected child or adult, although a route of transmission frequently cannot be determined. Illnesses caused by these viruses occur year-round. Caliciviruses, including the Norwalk-like virus (norovirus), have gotten plenty of attention in recent years, in large part because of outbreaks of Norwalk-like viruses on cruise ships.

Signs and Symptoms

In most cases, viral GI illnesses are not serious, but children can feel quite sick. Youngsters with a rotavirus infection have watery diarrhea, vomiting, a fever, and abdominal pain. These symptoms begin 1 to 2 days after exposure to the virus and usually last for 3 to 8 days. In severe cases, children may become dehydrated.

An astrovirus infection produces abdominal pain, diarrhea, vomiting, nausea, fever, and an overall feeling of malaise. In most cases, the symptoms begin 1 to 4 days after the child has been exposed to the virus and last 5 to 6 days.

Calicivirus infections are characterized by diarrhea, vomiting, fever, headache, abdominal cramps, and muscle aches. These symptoms begin 1 to 3 days after exposure to the virus and last from 1 day to 2 weeks. In severe cases, your child may need to go to the hospital.

Prolonged or severe diarrhea, particularly when accompanied by vomiting, can lead to dehydration. Signs of dehydration include increased thirst, less urine, dry mouth, fewer tears, and weight loss. As dehydration becomes more severe, your child will become cranky and irritable, his eyes will appear sunken, and he may have a faster heart and breathing rate. If dehydration continues, the kidneys will stop working and the heart will not have enough fluid to pump. The blood pressure will drop and your child will go into shock.

How Is the Diagnosis Made?

Pediatricians usually diagnose viral gastroenteritis by examining the child and evaluating his symptoms. In some cases, your pediatrician may test a stool sample or conduct blood tests, which can eliminate other possible causes of your youngster's illness. Viral gastroenteritis rarely causes blood to appear in the stools. If you see diarrhea with streaks of blood, you should call your pediatrician.

Treatment

These viral illnesses resolve on their own with time and without any specific treatment. Make your child as comfortable as possible and take steps to prevent dehydration. Encourage him to rest, drink extra fluids, and continue to eat his regular diet. It is important that the fluids contain salt because salts are lost in the diarrhea. Rehydration fluids are sold over the counter, but you can also make these at home. Talk to your pediatrician to be sure you have the correct amount of salt and water. In severe cases, intravenous fluids may be required. If your child is vomiting, continue to offer fluids but give small amounts and more frequent feedings. Be careful with apple juice because too much apple juice is a common cause of diarrhea, even in healthy children.

Because these are viral illnesses, the use of antibacterials is not appropriate and may, in fact, make the diarrhea worse. Older children may benefit from antidiarrheal medicines, but only under the advice of your pediatrician.

Prevention

Vaccines to protect children against all of these viral infections are not currently available. The best way to avoid these illnesses is to keep your child away from people with the infection. Do not allow him to share food and eating utensils. Make sure your child washes his hands before eating and after using the bathroom.

In 1998, a vaccine for rotavirus was licensed and used for a short time. The vaccine was withdrawn from the market because of a rare side effect. Other rotavirus vaccines are being studied and hopefully will be approved for use in the United States in the near future.

Shigella Infections

Shigella bacteria cause a diarrheal illness that can occur in children. Four species of *Shigella* bacteria *(S boydii, S dysenteriae, S flexneri,* and *S sonnei)* have been identified as infecting the lining of the intestines.

These bacterial illnesses are highly contagious. They are spread through the feces of people with the infection, particularly in close contact environments such as within families and in child care centers. They can also be contracted by consuming contaminated food or water or by touching an object on which the bacteria may be present. Children aged 2 to 4 years are particularly vulnerable to developing the disease. The incubation period is usually 2 to 4 days.

Signs and Symptoms

A *Shigella* infection can cause mild watery or loose stools with no other symptoms, or it can be more serious, with fever, abdominal cramps or tenderness, crampy rectal pain (tenesmus), and mucous-filled and sometimes bloody stools.

When to Call Your Pediatrician

Call your pediatrician if you notice blood in your child's stool, there's no improvement in her diarrhea, or she is showing signs of dehydration.

How Is the Diagnosis Made?

A pediatrician may order laboratory tests in which a culture of the child's feces is examined for evidence of *Shigella* bacteria.

Treatment

If your child's symptoms are mild, your pediatrician may decide that it's not necessary to prescribe medicine to treat the infection. These children generally get better rapidly without any medicine. However, antibiotics such as cefixime, ampicillin, or trimethoprim sulfamethoxazole may be prescribed in more severe cases. These drugs can kill *Shigella* bacteria in the child's stools, shorten the duration of the diarrhea, and lower the chances of spreading the illness.

If your child is having lots of watery diarrhea, be sure to give her extra fluids to avoid dehydration. It is important that the fluids contain salt because salts are lost in the diarrhea. Rehydration fluids are sold over the counter, but you can also make these at home. Talk to your pediatrician to be sure you have the correct amount of salt and water. In severe cases, intravenous fluids may be required.

Do not self-prescribe antidiarrheal medicines, which can actually make your child worse.

What Is the Prognosis?

In most cases, *Shigella* infections run their course in 2 to 3 days. Occasionally, complications may develop, including bacteremia (bacteria in the blood), hemolytic uremic syndrome (a disorder characterized by kidney failure and anemia), and Reiter syndrome (painful urination, joint achiness).

Prevention

If your child attends a child care facility, make sure staff members practice good hygiene, including frequent hand washing, particularly before food preparation and after diaper changes, and regularly disinfect toys. At home as well as at these child care settings, food should be stored, handled, and prepared according to good sanitation guidelines. People with a diarrheal illness should not be involved in preparing food for others.

Vibrio Infections (Cholera and Noncholera)

Cholera is an infection of the intestines caused by bacteria called *Vibrio cholerae*. It causes a watery diarrhea that can range from mild to extremely severe.

Your child may contract cholera by drinking water or, less commonly, eating food such as raw or undercooked shellfish contaminated with *V cholerae*. Cholera has occurred in children who have visited Latin America or Asia or consumed food imported from that part of the world. Contaminated crabs, oysters, and other shellfish from the Gulf of Mexico have also caused cholera. It is probably not spread through person-to-person contact.

There are some species of *Vibrio* that do not cause cholera, although they can produce diarrhea and may be responsible for blood and wound infections. They are associated with preparing or eating raw or undercooked seafood, particularly oysters, shrimp, and crabs.

Signs and Symptoms

In some cases of *Vibrio* infection, no symptoms are present. In most cases, however, there is mild to moderate diarrhea. In a relatively small number of cases, the watery diarrhea becomes severe. Fever, abdominal cramps, and blood in the stools should not accompany cholera-associated diarrhea, although dehydration can occur. Vomiting, sometimes severe, is common.

Early signs of dehydration include thirst, dry mouth, sunken eyes, and decreased urination. In the most severe cases, especially when lost fluids are not replaced, very serious complications can develop, including seizures, shock, and coma.

In noncholera *Vibrio* infections, the most common symptom is diarrhea, with watery stools accompanied by abdominal cramps. Other symptoms may include headaches, chills, a low-grade fever, and vomiting. Diarrhea caused by these *Vibrio* infections can be bloody with mucus.

Skin infections typically are very painful with redness and swelling. Fever is often present. Large blisters may form in more serious infections. When the bacteria gets into the bloodstream, the child will become very ill. There may be bleeding into the skin, low blood pressure, and sometimes shock.

How Is the Diagnosis Made?
Laboratory tests can detect the presence of *Vibrio* bacteria in the child's feces, wounds, or blood.

Treatment
Children with cholera need to be rehydrated right away. This can usually be done with oral solutions made specifically for this purpose and available over the counter. For youngsters who are moderately to severely ill, intravenous fluids may be necessary. They also may be given antibiotics such as trimethoprim sulfamethoxazole, doxycycline, or tetracycline to get rid of the bacteria and shorten the duration of the diarrhea. Antidiarrheal medicines can make the illness worse, particularly in young children, and should not be used.

Noncholera *Vibrio* infections causing diarrhea usually get better without treatment in 2 to 3 days, but it is important to make sure your child remains well hydrated. Antibiotics may be prescribed for severe infections.

For skin infections, your child will need antibiotics. If the infection is mild, an oral antibiotic will be given. More serious skin infections and bacteria in the blood are treated in the hospital with intravenous antibiotics. In some cases, your child may require surgery to drain pus and damaged tissues.

Prevention
V cholerae can be killed by boiling, filtering, or treating water with chemicals such as chlorine or iodine. Adequately cooking food that may contain the organism will also destroy bacteria. Leftover cooked seafood should be refrigerated as soon as possible.

When traveling abroad, take precautions such as making sure your food is thoroughly cooked and the water is boiled. Avoid salads, raw vegetables, fruits that have already been peeled, and food from street vendors. Consume safe beverages such as carbonated drinks with no ice and tea and coffee prepared with boiled water. When taking measures like these, the risk of contracting cholera is low.

Although 2 cholera vaccines have been made, they are of only limited effectiveness and not available in the United States.

Yersinia enterocolitica and *Yersinia pseudotuberculosis* Infections

Yersinia enterocolitica and *Yersinia pseudotuberculosis* are bacterial infections that are uncommon, but can cause problems when they occur. *Y enterocolitica* causes a condition called enterocolitis, which is an inflammation of the small intestine and colon that occurs, and often recurs, mostly in young children.

These infections appear to be acquired by eating contaminated food, particularly raw or inadequately cooked pork products, and drinking unpasteurized milk. They might also be contracted by touching an infected animal, drinking contaminated well water, or on rare occasions, from contaminated transfusions. The infections are increasing in frequency among children whose immune system is weakened. The incubation period is around 4 to 6 days.

Signs and Symptoms

When a *Y enterocolitica* infection is present, it not only causes an inflamed small intestine and colon, but also symptoms such as diarrhea and a fever. A child with this infection may have stools that contain blood and mucus. These symptoms may last for 1 to 3 weeks, sometimes longer.

Along with these more common symptoms, very young children who have too much iron stored in their bodies, such as those who receive blood transfusions, or whose immune system is already suppressed or weakened because of another illness, may be susceptible to bacteremia (the spread of bacteria to the blood). Older youngsters may also have symptoms that mimic appendicitis (a pseudoappendicitis syndrome), with right-sided abdominal pain and tenderness. On rare occasions, this infection may be associated with conditions such as a sore throat, eye inflammation, meningitis, and pneumonia. In older youngsters, joint pain or a red skin lump (erythema nodosum) on the lower legs may develop after the infection itself has gone away.

Children with *Y pseudotuberculosis* will likely develop a fever, a rash, and abdominal pain, including the pseudoappendicitis syndrome. Some children may also have diarrhea, a rash, and excess fluid in the chest region or spaces around the joints.

When to Call Your Pediatrician

Contact your pediatrician if your child's stool is streaked with blood. Look for signs of dehydration that could be caused by your youngster's diarrhea, including dry mouth, unusual thirst, and a decline in the frequency of urination.

How Is the Diagnosis Made?

Your pediatrician can order tests to detect the presence of *Yersinia* organisms in your child's stool. Evidence of the infection may also be seen by taking throat swabs and evaluating them in the laboratory, examining the urine, or testing the blood for antibodies to the bacteria.

Because these are relatively rare infections, most laboratories do not routinely perform tests looking for *Yersinia* organisms in feces.

Treatment

In most children, the infection will go away on its own. In some cases, *Yersinia* infections need to be treated with antibiotics. As with all cases of diarrhea, fluids are given to prevent or treat dehydration.

Prevention

Make sure your child does not consume raw or undercooked pork, unpasteurized milk, and contaminated water. Wash your hands thoroughly with soap and water after handling raw pork intestines (chitterlings).

No vaccine is available to prevent *Yersinia* infections.

Also See

CHAPTER 26

Organisms Causing or Associated With Lung Diseases

Chapter at a Glance

Healthy lungs are crucial to your child's well-being. Oxygen enters the body through the lungs and goes into the bloodstream, where it is transported throughout the body. At the same time, the lungs pull carbon dioxide out from the blood and make sure that it leaves the body each time your child breathes out.

The lungs can get infections that, when serious, can cause chronic and sometimes life-threatening illnesses. Infection in the lungs is called pneumonia. Infections of the breathing tubes include laryngitis, tracheitis, bronchitis, and bronchiolitis. This chapter describes common organisms that can cause lung infections and sometimes make breathing more difficult.

Symptoms of Respiratory Infections
Cough
Fever
Difficulty breathing
Rapid breathing
Wheezing
Sputum production

Chlamydia (Chlamydophila) pneumoniae Infections

When you hear the word *chlamydia,* you might think of the sexually trans-mitted disease (STD) by that name. The STD is caused by *Chlamydia trachomatis,* one species of *Chlamydia* bacteria. Another species, called *Chlamydia* (or *Chlamydophila*) *pneumoniae,* causes respiratory illnesses. These lung infections are spread in the same way as many other respira-tory diseases. They are passed from person to person directly through coughs or sneezes and indirectly from germs on hands or other objects. The number of these infections peaks in school-aged children between 5 and 15 years of age.

Signs and Symptoms

Illnesses caused by *C pneumoniae* can cause a prolonged cough, bronchi-tis, and pneumonia as well as a sore throat, laryngitis, ear infections, and sinusitis. They usually start gradually with a sore throat that is followed by a cough about a week or more later. The cough may last for 2 to 6 weeks. In some cases, the child may get bronchitis or a mild case of pneumonia. While some infected children have only mild to moderate symptoms or no symptoms at all, the infection may be more severe in others.

How Is the Diagnosis Made?

Many cases of *C pneumoniae* are diagnosed by a pediatrician after doing a physical examination of the child and looking at his symptoms. The doctor can also order blood tests that detect antibodies to the bacteria. However, it can take a week or more for the antibodies to show up in the blood. Al-though there are special laboratories that can evaluate swab specimens from the nose or throat, there are no reliable commercially available studies at this time.

Treatment

Recovery from a *Chlamydia* respiratory infection may be slow. Your pedia-trician can prescribe antibiotics such as erythromycin or tetracycline to clear up the infection and help your child get better faster.

Prevention

To lower the chances of your child getting a *C pneumoniae* infection, he should practice good hygiene, including frequent hand washing.

Hantavirus Pulmonary Syndrome

Hantavirus pulmonary syndrome (HPS) was first identified in 1993 when an outbreak of this infectious lung disease took place in the southwestern United States. The viruses that cause HPS come from a group of organisms known as hantaviruses. These germs are carried by particular kinds of mice. People get the infection by direct contact with infected rodents or their droppings, urine, or saliva or breathing in air contaminated with the virus. On rare occasions, the infection is passed to humans by a mouse bite. There is no evidence that it can be spread from person to person. The incubation period (the time after contact with an infected mouse to the beginning of symptoms) may be 1 to 6 weeks, though that period has not been established definitively.

The majority of cases of HPS occur during the spring and summer, mostly in rural areas. Although it is a relatively uncommon infection, it can be deadly.

Signs and Symptoms
In the first 3 to 7 days of HPS, many of its symptoms resemble those of a severe cold, the flu, or a gastrointestinal disease.

- Fever
- Chills
- Headaches
- Nausea
- Vomiting
- Diarrhea
- Dizziness
- Fatigue
- Muscle aches in the large muscle groups (ie, back, thighs, shoulders)

After the first few days, respiratory difficulties begin abruptly and can progress rapidly. People with the infection will develop a condition called adult respiratory distress syndrome (ARDS), in which the lungs lose their ability to move oxygen to the blood. Patients may develop a cough and shortness of the breath. Very quickly every organ of the body is affected.

When to Call Your Pediatrician

If your child has the symptoms of a severe cold or the flu and then develops shortness of breath or other respiratory problems, contact your doctor at once or take your youngster to the emergency department.

How Is the Diagnosis Made?

Blood tests can be done at specialized laboratories to identify the hantavirus.

Treatment

No specific therapy is available to directly treat HPS. There are studies taking place on an antiviral medication called ribavirin. This drug may someday be an effective treatment for HPS.

    Children with HPS need to be hospitalized in an intensive care unit. They may require oxygen therapy and get help breathing with a ventilator for about 2 to 4 days to combat ARDS.

What Is the Prognosis?

About 45% of patients with HPS die from the infection. However, early identification and supportive care in the hospital will help the majority of infected people recover from this dangerous syndrome.

Prevention

Take steps to reduce the likelihood of rodents in your home and other areas where your child spends time. Seal all holes through which rodents may enter your home. Exterminate rodents in the area with spring-loaded traps and other measures. Wear rubber gloves when touching dead rodents, and disinfect the gloves after you use them.

    Remove brush and grass away from your home's foundation to prevent rodents from nesting. When entering an area where rodents may have lived, avoid stirring up or breathing potentially contaminated dust. Consider using a mask when cleaning areas contaminated with rodent droppings. Use tight-fitting lids on garbage cans to prevent rodents from getting into the trash.

Legionnaires Disease

Legionnaires disease, also called *legionellosis,* is caused by *Legionella pneumophila* bacteria and related species. These organisms have been found in water delivery systems. The infection can be caught by inhaling mists from water contaminated with the germs. Outbreaks have been traced to exposure from contaminated whirlpool spas, humidifiers, and air conditioning cooling towers and have occurred in hospitals, hotels, and cruise ships. The incubation period for legionnaires disease is 2 to 10 days.

The disease and the organism that causes legionnaires disease were identified and got their names from the first known outbreak, at an American Legion convention held at a Philadelphia, PA, hotel in 1976.

A related disease called Pontiac fever is caused by the same *Legionella* species. It is a milder, less serious infection with an incubation period of 1 to 2 days.

Signs and Symptoms

The symptoms of legionnaires disease can range from mild to severe. A form of pneumonia is a key component of the disease and may have symptoms that include

- Fever
- Cough
- Chills
- Muscle aches
- Progressive breathing difficulties

These symptoms can get worse for the first few days of the infection before the patient begins to get better. People at greatest risk of contracting legionnaires disease are the elderly and those with suppressed immune systems. Children rarely get the infection and when they do, their illness is usually mild or they may have no symptoms at all.

Pontiac fever causes flu-like symptoms such as muscle aches and a fever, but there are no signs of pneumonia.

When to Call Your Pediatrician

Call your pediatrician if your child develops breathing problems.

How Is the Diagnosis Made?

Your pediatrician can collect a sample of the secretions from your child's respiratory tract and send it to the laboratory for analysis. Urine tests can also be performed to look for the bacteria, as well as antibody tests that can be conducted on blood samples.

Treatment

Antibiotics are used to treat legionnaires disease. Azithromycin should be given intravenously to children with this infection. As their condition improves, they can be switched to oral medicines. Other drugs are sometimes used in combination with azithromycin.

No treatment is needed for Pontiac fever, which goes away on its own in 2 to 5 days.

What Is the Prognosis?
The most serious cases of legionnaires disease lead to respiratory failure and death, especially in the elderly or people with weak immune systems. These deaths occur in 5% to 15% of cases.

Mycoplasma pneumoniae Infections
Some lung infections, including many cases of mild pneumonia (also referred to as *walking* pneumonia), are caused by an organism called *Mycoplasma pneumoniae*. It is spread from person to person in secretions such as phlegm from the respiratory passages and has an incubation period of 2 to 3 weeks. Transmission of this organism usually takes place through close contact. Outbreaks have occurred and are common in summer camps and colleges, as well as within households among family members.

While *M pneumoniae* infections are uncommon in children younger than 5 years, they are a leading cause of pneumonia in school-aged children and young adults. Community-wide epidemics of this illness occur every 4 to 7 years.

Signs and Symptoms
M pneumoniae infections cause symptoms that are usually mild. They can get worse over time in some children. The most common symptoms are

- Bronchitis
- Upper respiratory tract infections, including sore throats and, at times, ear infections

Children with this infection may also have a high fever, long-lasting weakness, and in some cases, headaches and a rash. Their cough can change from a dry cough to a phlegmy one. On rare occasions, youngsters may develop croup and a sinus infection (sinusitis).

When to Call Your Pediatrician
If these symptoms, including a fever, last for more than a few days, contact your pediatrician.

How Is the Diagnosis Made?
Your pediatrician will give your child a physical examination. The doctor may order blood tests for antibodies to *M pneumoniae* or *cold agglutinins,*

which are a special type of antibody. Special tests are being developed to identify the organism in throat and respiratory samples, but these are not generally available yet.

Treatment
In most cases, the bronchitis and upper respiratory tract illnesses associated with *M pneumoniae* infections are mild and get better on their own without antibiotic treatment. However, antibiotics such as erythromycin, azithromycin, or doxycycline may be given for more serious symptoms associated with pneumonia and ear infections.

What Is the Prognosis?
This infection often causes wheezing in children with asthma or reactive airways. Most people fully recover from this infection, even when antibiotics are not used. The death rate is quite low.

Parainfluenza Viral Infections
Human parainfluenza viruses (HPIVs) are a group of organisms, types 1 through 4, that cause several different respiratory infections. For example, they are the major cause of croup, which is an inflammation of the voice box (larynx) and windpipe (trachea) that makes breathing more difficult. They also cause some cases of lower respiratory tract diseases, including pneumonia (a lung infection) and bronchiolitis (an infection of the lung's small breathing tubes). They can make the symptoms of chronic lung disease worse in children.

Parainfluenza viruses have an incubation period of 2 to 6 days. They are spread from person to person by direct contact or exposure to contaminated secretions from the nose or throat. Children are usually exposed to most types of parainfluenza by 5 years of age.

Signs and Symptoms
The following symptoms occur in many types of parainfluenza infections, although they may be different from child to child or one kind of infection to another:

- A rough, barking cough
- Rapid, noisy, or labored breathing
- Hoarseness and wheezing
- Redness of the eye
- A runny nose

- Cough
- Fever
- A decline in appetite
- Vomiting
- Diarrhea

How Is the Diagnosis Made?

The diagnosis of HPIVs may be made by testing the secretions collected from a sick child's nose and throat. Viral cultures or tests are taken to look for parts of the virus. An increase in antibodies to parainfluenza may be found in the blood of infected children. As with most infections, it can take several weeks for the antibodies to appear.

Treatment

The treatment of viral illnesses, including those caused by parainfluenza viruses, should not involve the use of antibacterials, which are not effective against viruses. Most parainfluenza infections do not require specific treatment other than soothing the symptoms and making your child more comfortable until she feels better. The illness goes away on its own. Antibacterials should only be used if a secondary bacterial infection develops.

Talk to your pediatrician about whether your child with a fever should be given acetaminophen to lower her body temperature. Make sure she drinks lots of liquids.

Some supportive therapies are unique to the specific infection that is present. For croup, which is characterized by a barking cough, your child may feel better if you take her into the bathroom, turn on the hot water in the shower, and let the bathroom fill with steam. The warm, moist air should allow her to breathe easier. Breathing in steam is usually helpful, but if it isn't, take your child outdoors for a few minutes. Inhaling the moist, cool night air may loosen up her airway, and she will be able to breathe easier.

Your pediatrician may prescribe a dose of corticosteroids for croup. Usually a single dose is all that is needed.

Prevention

In the first few months of life, infants have protection against some parainfluenza types because of antibodies from their mothers.

Keep your child away from youngsters who have viral infections, particularly in the early and most contagious stages. Regular and thorough hand washing is an important way to lower the chances of spreading most viral infections. Your child should not share eating utensils and glasses with a sick youngster.

A vaccine against parainfluenza viruses is not available, although vaccines against viral types 1 and 3 are in development.

Respiratory Syncytial Virus

The respiratory syncytial virus (RSV) is the major cause of infections of the breathing passages and lungs in infants and young children. In addition to causing pneumonia, it is the leading cause of bronchiolitis (an infection of the bronchioles, the small breathing tubes of the lungs). Some cases of bronchiolitis, however, are caused by the flu, parainfluenza virus, adenovirus, or measles.

Respiratory syncytial virus is transmitted from an infected child by secretions from the nose or mouth by direct contact or airborne droplets. The period of greatest contagiousness is in the first 2 to 4 days of the infection. The incubation period ranges from 2 to 8 days, commonly 4 to 6 days. Annual epidemics take place during the winter and early spring.

Signs and Symptoms
Many children with RSV infections have only mild symptoms, typically similar to the symptoms of a common cold. In children younger than 2 years, the infection may progress to symptoms more commonly found in bronchiolitis.

- Initially, the child will have a runny nose, mild cough, and in some cases, a fever.
- Within 1 to 2 days, the cough will get worse.
- At the same time, the youngster's breathing will become more rapid and difficult. He may wheeze each time he breathes out.
- Your child will have a hard time drinking because he is using so much energy breathing. Even swallowing becomes very difficult for these youngsters.
- His fingertips and the area around his lips may turn a bluish color, a sign that his strained breathing is not delivering enough oxygen to his bloodstream.

What You Can Do
In the early stages of an RSV infection, help ease your child's cold-like symptoms. Gentle suctioning of the nose may be useful to clear the nostrils. Mist has not been shown to be useful. Hot-air vaporizers should be avoided because of the risk for scald burns, and cool-mist vaporizers are often contaminated with molds. Make sure your child drinks enough liquid to prevent dehydration.

When to Call Your Pediatrician
Contact your pediatrician immediately if your baby or child

- Has breathing difficulties
- Is younger than 2 or 3 months and has a fever
- Shows signs of dehydration, such as a dry mouth, crying without tears, and urinating less often

How Is the Diagnosis Made?
Your pediatrician may order laboratory tests of specimens taken from your child's nose and throat to see if RSV is present. The virus can be grown in special cultures, or parts of the virus can be identified by rapid tests.

Treatment
If your child is having difficulty breathing or has asthma or a tendency for reactive airways, your doctor may try a medicine called a *bronchodilator* to help open his airways. Bronchodilators won't help many infants with this viral infection. Some youngsters with bronchiolitis may have to be hospitalized for treatment with oxygen. If your child is unable to drink because of rapid breathing, he may need to receive intravenous fluids. On rare occasions, infected babies will need a respirator to help them breathe.

Antibacterials are not used for treating viral infections, including those caused by RSV.

What Is the Prognosis?
Most children with RSV infections are well on their way to recovery in about a week, and almost all fully recover. Nearly all children are infected with RSV at least once by 2 years of age, and a recurrence of the infection throughout life is common. As the child grows, RSV infections become less serious than when they were infants and are usually hard to distinguish from a cold.

These infections can make asthma and other chronic breathing conditions worse. Infants with congenital heart disease may have a more severe case of RSV. Some children will require hospitalization, and a few will need intensive care.

Prevention

Your child should avoid close contact with other children and adults who are infected with RSV or other viruses that cause bronchiolitis. In child care centers, good hygiene practices should be used by the staff and the youngsters, including frequent and thorough hand washing.

Vaccines are being developed for RSV, but none are currently licensed for use. Palivizumab is an antibody that has been made to prevent RSV infection. It is given as an intramuscular shot once a month to children who are at increased risk for serious diseases caused by RSV. These include premature babies, babies with chronic lung disease, and some babies with immunodeficiencies.

Severe Acute Respiratory Syndrome and Other Coronaviruses

In late 2002 and early 2003, reports of a new disease called severe acute respiratory syndrome (SARS) emerged from parts of Asia. Since then, the illness has been found in other parts of the world, including Europe and North and South America. During the initial 2003 outbreak, only 8 people in the United States were diagnosed with SARS. All of them had traveled to parts of the world where there were people infected with SARS. In all of those areas, SARS was uncommon in children.

Severe acute respiratory syndrome is caused by a specific virus from a family of organisms called coronaviruses. They received their name because when examined under the microscope, they look something like a halo or crown. Other coronaviruses are a common cause of mild to moderate upper respiratory tract infections in children and adults. The incubation period is 2 to 7 days.

Signs and Symptoms

In many places, SARS has been a very contagious disease. In most cases, it starts with a high fever. People with the infection may then develop other symptoms, including

- Body aches
- Headaches
- Vague feelings of illness (malaise)

- Mild respiratory problems (shortness of breath)
- Diarrhea

A dry cough tends to occur after several days. Pneumonia then develops in most people.

What You Can Do
Before traveling to Asia and other areas where cases of SARS have been most prevalent, seek the advice of your pediatrician and keep up-to-date on travel advisories from the Centers for Disease Control and Prevention (www.cdc.gov/travel).

When to Call Your Pediatrician
If your child develops these symptoms, particularly breathing difficulties that might indicate the development of SARS or other pneumonia-like infections, contact your pediatrician. Also contact your pediatrician if your child develops any respiratory symptoms after traveling to an area with a known SARS outbreak or being in contact with anyone known or suspected of having SARS.

How Is the Diagnosis Made?
Because the symptoms of SARS are similar to those of other respiratory infections, your pediatrician will conduct a physical examination and perform tests that may rule out other conditions. Diagnostic tests specifically for coronaviruses are generally unavailable.

Treatment
The treatment of SARS is similar to that given to patients with viral pneumonia and is generally supportive. It may include giving oxygen during hospitalization (in some cases, a ventilator or breathing device will be used). A number of antiviral medications are being tested for use in SARS, but no specific medication has been proven to be effective.

What Is the Prognosis?
Most people recover from SARS. However, in the initial outbreaks of 2002 and 2003, there were 774 deaths among the more than 8,000 cases that were identified.

At this time, the risk of SARS in children and adults in the United States is thought to be relatively low. Public health officials continue to monitor the worldwide patterns of the disease.

Prevention

Severe acute respiratory syndrome is spread during close contact with a person who has the infection, usually during sneezing or coughing. A child can also pick up the virus if she touches a toy or other object or surface that has been contaminated with the virus.

To reduce the risk of SARS, make sure your child washes her hands frequently with soap and hot water. No vaccination is available to prevent SARS.

Tuberculosis

Tuberculosis (TB) is a chronic airborne infection that affects the lungs. It is caused by bacteria called *Mycobacterium tuberculosis*. Most cases are spread when a person with the infection who has the active lung disease coughs or sneezes, shooting droplets of the bacteria into the air where they can be inhaled by others. Adults with active TB disease often have hollow spaces (cavities) in their lungs that are filled with TB bacteria. Children with TB rarely develop lung cavities and are rarely contagious.

When a person inhales the bacteria, infection in the lung and lymph nodes follows. This type of infection causes no symptoms (a *latent* infection). During the latent infection, a person will develop a positive tuberculin skin test reaction (formerly called Mantoux or purified protein derivative test). It takes about 8 to 10 weeks before an infected person will have a positive tuberculin skin test. This is considered the incubation period. A person with a positive tuberculin skin test should be tested for active lung disease.

Some infected people will go on to get the disease, which is called TB. If an older child or adult is infected, he has about a 10% chance of progressing to disease. In young infants, the risk is much higher—40%. Younger children are more likely to get infections in other parts of the body in addition to the lungs.

Children at the highest risk of developing TB include those living in a household with an adult with active TB, infected with human immunodeficiency virus (HIV) (the virus that causes acquired immunodeficiency syndrome [AIDS]), and living in communities in which adults have TB.

Signs and Symptoms

In children and teenagers, latent infections do not cause symptoms. However, when the TB disease occurs, symptoms are present and may include

- Fever
- Persistent cough
- Chills
- Night sweats
- Weight loss
- Delay in growth
- Rapid and heavy breathing
- Fatigue
- Irritability

Other parts of the body may be involved in addition to the lungs and respiratory system if the infection spreads through the bloodstream. It may lead to a serious condition called TB meningitis, which affects the brain and central nervous system. Other organs that can get infected include the bones and joints, lymph nodes, kidneys, and lining of the bowel.

When to Call Your Pediatrician
If your child has been in contact with anyone with a TB infection or develops some of the symptoms, including a fever, a persistent cough, and night sweats, contact your pediatrician.

How Is the Diagnosis Made?
Because many children with TB have minimal or no symptoms, tests must be conducted to confirm the presence of the bacteria. Your pediatrician can give a tuberculin skin test. To perform this test, the doctor will inject an inactive portion of TB bacteria into the skin. If your child has been infected with the bacteria, his skin will become red and swollen where the shot was given about 48 hours after the test.

When the skin test is positive, your child should have a chest x-ray film to look for signs of TB disease. Your doctor may also send secretions from your child's cough or his stomach contents to the laboratory to determine if TB bacteria are present.

Treatment
All children who have been infected with this bacteria should get treatment. If your child is symptom free and has a normal chest x-ray film, the infection is in the latent state. Treatment can keep the infection from becoming active and causing TB. Your pediatrician will recommend a medicine called isoniazid, which must be taken each day for many months.

If your child has active TB, he will need to take a combination of 3 or 4 drugs to kill the bacteria. It is important that your child take these drugs exactly as prescribed to control the disease and make certain that drug-resistant strains of the bacteria do not emerge.

What Is the Prognosis?

Your child must take the prescribed medicine for 6 months to 1 year to kill all the TB bacteria. With proper drug treatment, your youngster has an excellent chance of getting well.

Prevention

If your child is diagnosed with either latent infection or TB disease, try to find out who may have given him this infection. Tuberculin skin tests can be given to people who your youngster has come in contact with, including family members, child care workers, babysitters, and housekeepers. If any of these people has a positive test, they should be seen by their own physicians for further diagnostic testing and treatment.

It is very important to identify adults with TB because they are often contagious. This means that there are enough organisms in their lungs and coughs to spread the disease to others. These adults may not know that they have an infection and think that their chronic cough is from smoking or other conditions. If an adult is diagnosed with active TB, everyone in the household should be tested. If tuberculin skin tests are positive, additional studies should be performed. If tuberculin skin tests are negative, people exposed to the active TB case should be treated with isoniazid as a preventive measure. The tuberculin skin tests are repeated in 3 months (this is the incubation time). If they are still negative, the isoniazid should be stopped. If the tuberculin skin tests have turned positive, isoniazid is continued for a full 9 months to prevent TB disease.

In the past, tuberculin skin testing was done on all children. In many cases, the skin test was positive because of infection with other mycobacteria. (There are many of these bacteria in the soil and water.) Now, tuberculin skin testing is recommended only for children at high risk for TB, such as those with recent exposure to people with TB, immigrants from areas of the world where TB remains common, travelers who have been exposed, and health care workers. Consult with your pediatrician to see if your child should be tested for TB.

See Also

CHAPTER 27

Organisms Spread by or Related to Insects or Animals

Chapter at a Glance

When parents think of infections spread by animals, many probably first think about rabies. However, as serious as rabies is, it has become a rare disease in the United States. Many other types of infections associated with animals and insects can also affect children. When they occur, they need a pediatrician's attention. This chapter describes the most common of these infections and steps you can take to prevent or manage them.

Cat-scratch Disease

You may find it hard to believe that a small household pet like a cat can cause your child to become ill for a long period of time. A common bacterial infection called cat-scratch disease (CSD) can make your youngster sick for weeks or even months, all because, as the name suggests, a cat has bitten or scratched him. Most cases occur in people younger than 20 years.

Cat-scratch disease is caused by an organism called *Bartonella henselae,* which is transmitted to humans by cats (usually kittens) that appear healthy, but are infected with this bacteria. The disease spreads from cat to cat by fleas, but cannot be transmitted from person to person.

It takes a week or more from the time a person is scratched for the first symptoms to appear, sometimes as long as a month and a half.

Signs and Symptoms

The most common sign of CSD is one or more swollen lymph nodes or glands, a condition called lymphadenopathy. The affected lymph nodes may be in your child's armpit, on his neck, or in the area of the groin. In most cases, children have a bump on the skin where the cat scratch or bite occurred. This bump usually appears 1 to 2 weeks before the lymph nodes become swollen and can last for many weeks.

The skin over the swollen lymph nodes is warm, reddened, hardened, and tender to the touch. Children may also have a fever, headaches, tiredness, and a decreased appetite.

In a small number of cases, children with CSD—typically those who also have a weak immune system because of cancer, human immunodeficiency virus (HIV), or an organ transplantation—may develop infections in other parts of the body. Some children with normal immune systems develop infections in the liver and spleen. These children have prolonged fever, which is called fever of unknown origin. Rarely, a child with CSD develops brain inflammation (encephalitis), inflammation of the retina of the eye, a bone infection, pneumonia, or tender purple-red bumps on the skin (erythema nodosum).

An unusual complication called Parinaud oculoglandular syndrome occurs when the bacteria enters the body through the eyelid. In this case, the eyelid, the white of the eye (conjunctiva), or both are red. The lymph node in front of the ear on the same side of the infected eye will be swollen.

What You Can Do

If a cat scratches or bites your child, immediately wash the area with soap and water.

When to Call Your Pediatrician

Contact your pediatrician if your child develops swollen lymph nodes. This swelling can have a number of causes, including CSD.

How Is the Diagnosis Made?

Your pediatrician will ask whether your child has had exposure to cats and kittens. The pediatrician will look for a bump where the cat scratch has occurred and evaluate any swollen lymph nodes that may be present.

Laboratory tests are available to detect antibodies in the blood related to CSD, but many commercial tests are considered unreliable. In most cases, your pediatrician will not use this test.

Treatment

Your pediatrician may recommend treatments aimed at easing the symptoms of CSD in your child. For example, if your youngster has a painful, pus-filled lymph node, the doctor may drain the pus with a needle to make your child more comfortable.

Antibiotics may speed recovery.

What Is the Prognosis?

Cat-scratch disease is self-limited, meaning that the infection and the lymph node swelling will usually go away on their own in 2 to 4 months, even without treatment.

Prevention

Do not allow your child to play roughly with cats and kittens. This kind of play can increase the chances of a scratch or bite. Teach your child how to interact with animals. A child should never try to take food away from a cat and should avoid teasing, petting, or trying to capture stray cats.

If your child has an open wound or broken skin, do not permit cats to lick it.

Leptospirosis

Leptospirosis is a bacterial infection caused by species of *Leptospira* organisms that can infect domestic and wild animals. The bacteria is excreted in the animal's urine and can survive in the soil or water for weeks or months. Humans can then become infected from the contaminated soil or water, often during activities like swimming or canoeing in lakes or rivers. The bacteria enter the body through cuts in the skin; through the nose, eyes, or mouth (mucosal membranes); or by swallowing contaminated water. It is very rare for the infection to spread from person to person. The time from exposure to the bacteria until beginning of illness is about a week, but sometimes can take as long as a month.

Leptospirosis is an uncommon disease. The Centers for Disease Control and Prevention estimates that about 100 to 200 cases are identified each year in the United States, with about half of those cases occurring in Hawaii. It is more common in other parts of the world.

Signs and Symptoms

Illness seen with leptospirosis includes

- Fever and chills
- Headaches
- Muscle soreness in the calves and back
- Redness of the eyes (conjunctivitis)
- Abdominal pain, nausea, and vomiting
- Skin rash over the shins (pretibial)

These symptoms may initially last for 3 to 7 days. Then there may be a short period (for 1 to 3 days) during which the fever goes away, followed by a second phase in which the fever returns, with any of the previously described symptoms as well as increased inflammation of the eye (uveitis, iritis), covering of the brain (meningitis), liver (hepatitis), and lymph nodes. The rash may become worse.

At times, leptospirosis can be life threatening (Weil syndrome). When the infection goes untreated, liver infection (hepatitis) with yellowing of the skin and eyes (jaundice), bleeding, kidney failure, irregular heart rhythms, inflammation of the lining of the brain and spinal cord (meningitis), and a form of pneumonia called hemorrhagic pneumonitis may develop.

When to Call Your Pediatrician

Contact your pediatrician if your child has symptoms that suggest the presence of leptospirosis.

How Is the Diagnosis Made?

Most often, leptospirosis is diagnosed with antibody testing of blood samples.

Treatment

Your pediatrician will prescribe antibiotics to treat leptospirosis. Children with a mild infection can be treated with oral amoxicillin if they are younger than 8 years. Oral doxycycline is used for children 8 years and older. (In young children, tetracyclines such as doxycycline can cause staining of the teeth.)

Some patients with leptospirosis become very ill and should be hospitalized to receive penicillin intravenously.

What Is the Prognosis?

This disease can last from a few days to several weeks, but most children fully recover. Even so, some of the serious complications such as brain or spinal cord inflammation or kidney damage can cause lasting health problems. On rare occasions, death may occur.

Prevention
Make sure your child follows good hygiene habits. She should wash her hands frequently and avoid direct contact with the urine of pets and other animals. Your child should not play in and around dirty puddles of standing water in the outdoors.

Although there is a vaccine to protect pets from leptospirosis, there is no vaccine approved for use in people.

Lice
Despite myths to the contrary, the presence of head lice in a child's hair is not an indication of poor hygiene. Lice are not affected by length of hair or how often hair is shampooed or brushed. Rather, head lice are transmitted by direct contact with the hair of people infested with lice. Some experts feel that lice can sometimes be spread through contact with personal items like hairbrushes, combs, and hats. This is uncommon because lice that fall off the hair are usually damaged and unable to infect another person. Cases of lice are occurring at earlier ages as more children are attending preschool and child care centers. Lice now occurs most commonly in children aged 3 to 12 years. They are uncommon in African American children.

Head lice are actually tiny parasitic, wingless insects that can live on the head and scalp. Also called *Pediculus humanus capitis,* they can survive only 1 to 2 days away from the scalp.

In addition to head lice, there are other common lice infestations.

- Body lice *(Pediculus humanus corporis)* and their eggs live in the seams of clothing, but rarely are seen feeding on the skin. These are spread from person to person by direct contact with skin or infested clothing. Body lice are rare in the United States and are associated with poor hygiene. Unlike head and pubic lice, body lice can carry other infections.
- Pubic lice *(Phthirus pubis),* sometimes called crabs because of their appearance, occur most commonly in teenagers and young adults. They are almost always spread through sexual contact. They also can be spread by towels. Pubic lice can infest any coarse hairy area of the body, including the eyelashes and eyebrows.

The time between laying of the egg and hatching is about a week. Adult lice appear 2 to 3 weeks later.

Signs and Symptoms

Although most children with head lice have no symptoms, some experience itching. The itch is an allergic reaction to the bite of the lice and can continue for weeks after the lice are gone. When you look at the hair of a child with head lice, you may see the adult lice, which are white or light brown and move quickly. The eggs or *nits* are attached onto hairs. They are usually located in hair behind the ears and near the base of the neck. The lice deposit their eggs on a shaft of hair close to the scalp. Many of the eggs never hatch. If the nit is located more than an inch from the scalp, it is likely to be either empty or dead. Remember, it is very easy to confuse dandruff, lint, or pollen in the hair with nits.

Children with body lice tend to experience intense itching, especially at night. Body lice can transmit other infections such as typhus and trench fever.

Severe itching in the genital area is common with pubic lice.

What You Can Do

Over-the-counter treatments for head lice are available. Before you use these, be sure your child really has lice. Don't mistake dandruff, pollen, or lint for nits. After treatment, it is not necessary to manually remove nits. Even so, combing the hair with a fine-tooth comb can be useful in removing nits that may have survived treatment.

American Academy of Pediatrics (AAP) policy states that it is not necessary to keep a healthy child home because of head lice.

When to Call Your Pediatrician

Before using home treatments, be sure your child actually has head lice. If you are in doubt, call or visit your pediatrician. If you use nonprescription home treatments and your child still has lice infestation, contact your pediatrician. The doctor may recommend the use of a prescription product. Remember that the itching caused by head lice can last for weeks, even after the lice are gone.

How Is the Diagnosis Made?

Your pediatrician can see and identify lice or nits with the naked eye and may confirm the diagnosis using a hand lens or microscope.

Treatment

Several treatments are available for head lice.

- Permethrin 1% is available without a prescription in the form of a cream rinse. It is currently the AAP-recommended treatment for head lice. After shampooing with a nonconditioning shampoo and then towel drying, apply permethrin to your child's scalp and hair for 10 minutes before rinsing. It has low toxicity and does not cause allergic reactions in children with plant allergies. A second treatment should be applied 7 to 10 days later to kill newly hatched lice.
- Pyrethrin-based products can be purchased without a prescription and should be used in a 10-minute–long shampoo. Treatment can be repeated 7 to 10 days later if needed.
- Products intended to block lice breathing, such as mayonnaise, petroleum jelly, mineral oil, or olive oil massaged into the hair and left on overnight, are of uncertain value.
- If these treatments are ineffective, your pediatrician may wish to use a prescription hair treatment such as malathion (0.5%), permethrin (5%), or pills such as trimethoprim sulfamethoxazole or ivermectin.

Keep in mind that some of these products are potentially dangerous insecticides and should be used only according to the instructions on the package or those provided by your pediatrician. Some have also been shown to be useful for treating pubic lice.

Body lice live primarily in clothing. Therefore, infestations should be managed by wearing clean clothes, bathing regularly, and changing bed linens often. If your teenager has pubic lice, you should have him examined for other sexually transmitted diseases.

Lice do not survive away from the body for more than 2 or 3 days. It is not necessary to throw away brushes, combs, clothes, or hats. Routine washing in hot water (130°F) of these items, bedding, or clothing or simply keeping them in a bag for a few days will kill any lice. Bagging items for 2 weeks will ensure that any eggs will also be killed.

What Is the Prognosis?

Lice can usually be eliminated with the treatments described here. Reinfestations can occur.

Prevention

To prevent body lice, change your child's clothes regularly and wash them thoroughly in hot water at temperatures exceeding 130°F (53.5°C). Bedding should be changed and washed routinely as well.

Your child should try to avoid head-to-head contact with other youngsters.

Lyme Disease

Lyme disease is a tick-borne disease caused by bacteria called *Borrelia burgdorferi*. It was initially identified in the 1970s in Lyme, CT, and neighboring areas. Although Lyme disease can occur in people of all ages, the incidence is highest in children aged 5 to 9 years, as well as middle-aged adults 45 to 54 years old.

The bacteria that cause Lyme disease are transmitted by the bites of deer ticks that carry the bacteria. Deer ticks are no bigger than a poppy seed. The infections frequently occur in people who are camping, hiking, or participating in other outdoor activities in the summer and fall.

In the United States, most cases of Lyme disease have occurred in the northeast part of the country, from southern Maine to northern Virginia. Lower numbers have been reported in the upper Midwest, particularly Wisconsin and Minnesota, as well as on the West Coast, especially northern California. Tick-infested areas include wooded regions, marshes, high grasses, gardens, and beach areas.

Signs and Symptoms

In the early stages of Lyme disease, your child may develop a distinctive circular red rash called *erythema migrans* at the site where the tick has bitten her. This rash will appear after an incubation period of 7 to 14 days. The rash tends to be surrounded by a light ring or halo. Some people have described it as having a bull's-eye–like appearance. It can be warm to the touch and in some people, it may itch or burn. Most people, however, will not feel anything out of the ordinary. The rash may grow in size over a period of days or weeks.

Along with the rash, your child can develop other symptoms, many of them flu like, that may include

- Fever
- Fatigue

- Headaches
- Mild neck stiffness
- Muscle and joint aches

In some youngsters, the disease is more widespread throughout the body, and multiple rashes can develop in addition to these symptoms. Some children experience involvement of the nervous system, including meningitis and temporary paralysis of the facial muscles (Bell palsy).

Fortunately, if children are treated effectively in the disease's early stages, it is unlikely that it will progress to a later stage. In the late stage, children can develop a form of arthritis called Lyme arthritis that affects the knees and other large joints, a type of meningitis, infection of the brain, or infection of the heart that can lead to an abnormal heart rhythm.

What You Can Do
If you find a tick on your child's skin or clothing, remove it promptly and carefully. Ticks must be attached to the skin for at least 36 hours before they can transmit the Lyme disease bacteria.

- Use a cotton ball soaked in alcohol to gently clean the area of the skin around the tick bite.
- Next, grab the tick with fine tweezers as close to the skin as possible and slowly pull it straight out. Do not use a twisting motion and try not to squeeze the tick's body. If you use your fingers to get rid of the tick, protect them with a tissue, cloth, or gloves and then wash your hands once the tick is removed.
- Cleanse your child's bitten area with alcohol or another first-aid ointment. Be sure the tick is dead before you dispose of it.

When to Call Your Pediatrician
Contact your pediatrician if you suspect that your child has been bitten by a tick and she develops the rash or other findings associated with Lyme disease.

How Is the Diagnosis Made?
Your pediatrician will diagnose Lyme disease by recognizing its rash, as well as by identifying the other common symptoms. The doctor will also take into consideration whether your child lives in or has traveled to a region where Lyme disease is common.

Although a biopsy of the rash can be performed, there is no commercially available test to identify the Lyme disease organism. Blood tests for

Lyme disease are not usually performed or recommended immediately after a tick bite. This is because the body's immune system hasn't produced enough antibodies against the infecting bacteria to make them detectable in the first few weeks of the infection.

Treatment

Your pediatrician will prescribe oral antibiotics if your child has Lyme disease. The most common medication used in children aged 8 years and older is doxycycline. Children younger than 8 years are usually prescribed amoxicillin instead. If your child is allergic to drugs in the penicillin family, alternative medications such as cefuroxime and erythromycin will be chosen. All of these drugs are typically prescribed for a course of 14 to 21 days.

Antibiotics are also recommended for the later stages of the disease to manage symptoms such as Lyme arthritis and facial nerve palsy. Infections involving the central nervous system (the brain and its covering) are treated with intravenous antibiotics.

What Is the Prognosis?

With prompt and proper treatment of Lyme disease in its early stages, your child will have a very good chance of making a full recovery. Even with the best treatment, however, her symptoms may last for several weeks, although the rash itself might disappear in a few days.

Prevention

If you live in a part of the country where cases of Lyme disease have been reported or visit such a region, keep your child away from tick-infested areas as much as possible. When she's outdoors, she should stay on cleared trails and away from overgrown grass and brush.

In high-risk areas, take the following precautions:

- Your child should dress in a long-sleeved shirt and long pants to cover her arms, legs, and other exposed areas as much as possible. Her pants should be tucked into socks or boots, and long-sleeved shirts should be buttoned at the cuff. Have her wear a hat and closed-toe shoes, especially in densely wooded areas.
- You can spray a chemical called permethrin onto your child's clothing. It can kill ticks on contact. Do *not* spray permethrin directly on the skin.
- A number of other tick and insect repellents available can be applied directly to your child's skin. Choose a product that contains a substance

called DEET (diethyltoluamide). Apply it every 1 to 2 hours for maximum protection. Follow the instructions on the label, and use the product lightly on your child's face and hands. Do not use the repellent on any irritated skin or open sores.

- Once your child has come indoors, wash her skin with soap and water to remove the repellent. At the same time, take a couple of minutes to inspect her body and clothing for the presence of ticks. They may hide behind her ears or attach themselves to the hair on her head and the back of her neck. If she is wearing light-colored clothing, it will be easier to spot any ticks that may be present.
- Pets may bring ticks into the house and should be inspected if they have been outdoors in tick-infested areas. Treatments to prevent ticks on pets can be obtained from your veterinarian.
- Giving antibiotics to prevent Lyme disease in a child who is well but on whom a tick was found is not recommended.

A vaccine for Lyme disease was approved in the United States in 1998, but it has been unavailable since 2002 because of low demand. There is a version of the vaccine for pets.

Lymphocytic Choriomeningitis

Lymphocytic choriomeningitis is a viral infection of the brain or the membranes around the brain and spinal cord. It mostly affects young adults, though it is uncommon. It is caused by the lymphocytic choriomeningitis (LCM) virus.

The LCM organism is carried by common house mice or pet hamsters. Humans become infected by breathing in dried particles of the animal's urine, feces, or saliva that have become airborne or ingesting food or dust contaminated by the rodent's urine.

The incubation time is around a week, but can take as long as 3 weeks.

Signs and Symptoms

Once infected, some children remain symptom free, but many others may have a flu-like illness with

- Fever
- Headaches
- Cough
- Nausea and vomiting

- Muscle aches
- Joint pain
- Chest pain

After a few days of this initial phase of the infection, symptoms may go away, only to be followed by the appearance of additional symptoms associated with meningitis or encephalitis, including a stiff neck, drowsiness, and confusion.

When to Call Your Pediatrician
If your child has a persistent and severe flu-like illness following contact with a mouse or hamster, its cage, or its urine or feces, you should call your pediatrician for advice.

How Is the Diagnosis Made?
The infection can be diagnosed by blood tests for antibodies to the LCM virus.

Treatment
Although there is no antiviral medication with proven effectiveness for this condition, some patients will need supportive care. Patients with more severe cases may need to be hospitalized.

What Is the Prognosis?
Most children with LCM infections recover completely.

Prevention
To prevent this disease, keep your child from having direct contact with mice or hamsters and their feces. Cages should be cleaned regularly to prevent a buildup of dried feces, which can be blown into the air. Prevent rodent infestation, especially in areas where food is stored. If you notice rodent droppings, use a liquid disinfectant to clean the area.

Pasteurella Infections
Bacterial organisms from the *Pasteurella* species live in the mouths of most cats, as well as a significant number of dogs and other animals. If your child is bitten or scratched by an animal that carries *Pasteurella* organisms such as *Pasteurella multocida,* these bacteria can enter the body through the break in the skin. They most often cause a potentially serious infection of the skin called cellulitis. On occasion, these bacteria can be spread to humans from an animal's saliva or nose mucus.

Signs and Symptoms

Symptoms of cellulitis usually begin after a very short incubation period, typically within 24 hours after your child has been bitten or scratched. He may develop swelling, redness, warmth, and tenderness of the skin, sometimes with discharge of pus. In some children, lymph nodes in the area of the infected skin may become enlarged and chills and fever can occur.

Complications may be present in some children, including an infection of the joints (arthritis), bones (osteomyelitis), and tendons (tenosynovitis). Less frequently, youngsters may have pneumonia, urinary tract infections, meningitis, blood infections (septicemia), or eye infections.

What You Can Do

If your child is bitten or scratched by an animal, wash the wound thoroughly with soap and water.

When to Call Your Pediatrician

If your child is bitten or scratched by a pet, wild animal, or any animal unknown to you, call your pediatrician for advice after promptly washing the wound. Also contact your doctor if you notice that an area of your child's skin has become red, warm, and tender.

How Is the Diagnosis Made?

Your pediatrician will examine the area of your child's skin that has been bitten or scratched. The doctor can order tests such as cultures and smears of the drainage from the wound to help identify the infectious organism.

Treatment

Your pediatrician will prescribe antibacterial treatment as soon as cellulitis is found. In most cases, children are treated with oral amoxicillin clavulanate because the exact cause of the cellulitis may not be known. If a culture shows the infection is caused by *Pasteurella,* oral penicillin can be used. Most infections require a 7- to 10-day dose of antibacterials, occasionally longer. Your pediatrician also may drain and clean the wound. If your child is very ill, the infection involves the hands, or it is spreading rapidly, your pediatrician will suggest hospital admission and use of intravenous antibacterials. Intravenous antibacterials are used for infections involving the blood, bone, joints, and brain.

Following an animal bite, especially one involving the hands, your doctor may prescribe a preventive antibacterial medicine to stop an infection from occurring. The pediatrician will also make sure that your child has an up-to-date tetanus vaccine.

What Is the Prognosis?

When appropriately treated with antibacterials, *Pasteurella*-related cellulitis usually clears up in about a week. Make sure your child takes the complete course of antibacterials, even if symptoms go away before all the pills are gone.

Prevention

Pets should not be allowed to lick very young infants. Teach your child not to approach or touch unfamiliar pets or other animals. *Pasteurella* organisms are not contagious, so there's no need to isolate your youngster from another child who has this illness.

Psittacosis

You may not be familiar with a disease called psittacosis. If you have pet birds such as parrot-like birds, you should know something about it. Psittacosis, or ornithosis, is a respiratory tract infection caused by the *Chlamydia* (or *Chlamydophila) psittaci* organism.

The sources of psittacosis include parakeets, parrots, macaws, and cockatiels, especially those that may have been smuggled into the country. Pigeons and turkeys are other sources of the disease. In most cases, this disease is spread to humans when they breathe in airborne dust particles from dried bird feces. Birds do not have to be sick to transmit the disease. Transmission from person to person is very uncommon. Fortunately, this infection occurs rarely in children.

The incubation period is a week or two but may be longer.

Signs and Symptoms

Children with psittacosis have mild flu-like symptoms that often include

- Fever
- A nonproductive cough
- Headaches
- A general sense of not feeling well and tiredness

Some patients also develop interstitial pneumonia, which involves the connective tissue of the lung. On rare occasions, complications such as inflammation of the heart (myocarditis), lining of the heart (pericarditis), liver (hepatitis), and brain (encephalopathy) may occur.

When to Call Your Pediatrician

If your child has symptoms associated with psittacosis that don't improve over several days and has been around pet birds, call your pediatrician.

How Is the Diagnosis Made?

Psittacosis is usually diagnosed by taking a medical history of the child, inquiring about exposure to birds, and evaluating the youngster's symptoms. The diagnosis can be confirmed by blood tests that detect increases of antibodies to the bacteria.

Treatment

Children with psittacosis are usually treated with erythromycin if they are younger than 8 years, and tetracycline if they are older.

What Is the Prognosis?

With proper treatment, the overwhelming majority of children recover fully from the infection.

Prevention

If you have birds as pets, clean their cages frequently so their feces do not build up and become airborne. Only purchase birds from a trustworthy breeder or importer. Birds that are believed to be the source of a human infection need to be evaluated and treated by a veterinarian and may need antibiotics. Cages, food bowls, and water bowls that may be contaminated should be disinfected thoroughly, using a household disinfectant such as a 1:100 dilution of bleach or detergent, before they are used again.

Rabies

Children are the victims of about 60% of all dog bites in the United States. Fortunately, a relatively small number of these bites spread the very serious rabies infection. Rabies has become a very rare disease, averaging no more than 5 cases a year in the United States and 1 to 2 deaths annually.

Rabies is caused by a virus that is present in an infected animal and spread to humans via bites or scratches. The greatest risk comes from wild animals, especially bats, but also raccoons, skunks, foxes, and coyotes. Domestic pets such as dogs and cats are usually immunized against rabies. The incubation period averages 4 to 6 weeks, although it can be shorter with bites on the face or much longer in some cases of bites on the feet or legs (extending more than a year on occasion).

Signs and Symptoms

When the rabies virus enters the body, it can move along the nerve pathways to the brain. It causes serious symptoms beginning with pain, tingling, and numbness at the site of the bite or scratch and progresses rapidly to

- Anxiety, restlessness, and aggressiveness
- Swallowing difficulties, particularly water (hydrophobia)
- Muscle spasms
- Drooling
- Seizures
- Paralysis
- Coma and death

What You Can Do

If your child has been bitten by an animal, thoroughly flush the wound with water and wash it with soap and water.

If possible, it is important that the animal be captured so it can be evaluated by a veterinarian for the presence of a rabies infection. Unless proper equipment is available, however, capturing a possibly rabid animal should not be attempted. Captured animals are killed and their brains are examined for rabies immediately. Pets who appear well and have been immunized can be watched for symptoms of the disease. This observation period should extend for 10 days. If the animal develops symptoms, it must be killed and the brain examined.

When to Call Your Pediatrician

Any time that your child is bitten by an animal, contact your pediatrician. All animal bites should be reported to health officials who will be able to tell you whether the bite presents a risk of rabies. *Any bite by a wild animal should be considered a risk for rabies until proven otherwise.* Exceptions to this include rabbits, hares, squirrels, rats, mice, and other small rodents. If a bat is found in a room where your child has been sleeping or playing, you should report it immediately to your pediatrician, even if you don't find a bite mark.

How Is the Diagnosis Made?

Your pediatrician will examine your child. If rabies is suspected, a skin biopsy may be done to look for evidence of the virus. If your child develops encephalitis and lapses into a coma, a brain biopsy may be needed to confirm the diagnosis.

Treatment

There is no specific treatment for rabies once the infection develops in a child. There have been very few survivors of the infection. Therefore, prevention is extremely important.

What Is the Prognosis?

Rabies is almost always a fatal infection. Death is usually caused by respiratory or heart failure within days after the appearance of symptoms. However, prompt and proper treatment of bites can prevent or control the infection before it involves the brain and produces the serious symptoms.

Prevention

Following a bite, if your pediatrician determines that the animal has a high risk of having rabies, the doctor will immediately immunize your child with rabies immune globulin, a type of passive immunization. The globulin, disease-battling antibodies, is injected into the skin around the bite. At the same time, your pediatrician will give your child injections of the rabies vaccine, which stimulates the body to make its own antibodies against the infection. Your child will be given a series of 5 inoculations over a period of 4 weeks.

If the animal is a domestic and healthy pet, your pediatrician will ask you to observe your child. The pediatrician will start the shots only if the animal shows signs of rabies.

Teach your child to avoid contact with any stray or wild animals. Your child should not tease or bother an animal and shouldn't examine or play with a dead animal that she may find.

You can reduce the presence of wild animals in the area of your home by tightly closing garbage can lids. Chimney covers can prevent bats from getting into the home.

Make sure your own family pet receives animal rabies shots according to your veterinarian's recommendations.

Rat-bite Fever

Rat-bite fever is a disease that occurs in humans who have been bitten by an infected rat or, in some cases, squirrels, mice, cats, and weasels. On occasion, the disease can also be spread by ingestion of contaminated food or milk products (Haverhill fever). Most cases in the United States are caused by bacteria called *Streptobacillus moniliformis.* Another form of rat-bite fever, caused by *Spirillum minus,* is almost always caused by a rat bite. It cannot be caught from food or milk and is rarely seen in the United States. Person-to-person transmission does not occur. The incubation period is 3 to 10 days in most cases of *S moniliformis* and 7 to 21 days in cases of *S minus.*

Signs and Symptoms
Rat-bite fever symptoms can vary depending on which organism is responsible for the disease. When the disease is caused by *S moniliformis,* the bite, which usually heals quickly, is followed 3 to 10 days later by

- Fever and chills
- Headache
- Skin rash (mostly on the arms and leg)
- Muscle pain
- Arthritis (particularly in the knees)
- Vomiting and diarrhea
- Complications (eg, abscesses, pneumonia, meningitis, heart inflammation)

With infections caused by *S minus,* the site of the bite may appear to heal initially, but 7 to 21 days later, the following symptoms may surface:

- Fever and chills
- Headache
- Ulceration at the site of the bite with red streaks
- Swelling of the lymph nodes
- A skin rash with reddish-brown or purple plaques
- Muscle pain and arthritis (rare)
- Vomiting and sore throat (Haverhill fever)
- Complications (eg, infection of the heart, pneumonia, meningitis, hepatitis)

Both forms of rat-bite fever may result in recurrent fevers, sometimes for months or years.

How Is the Diagnosis Made?
Your pediatrician can conduct tests such as cultures or smears of the blood or fluids from the site of the infection (eg, bite, lymph glands, joints) to find the bacteria responsible for rat-bite fever.

Treatment

To treat rat-bite fever, the doctor will give your child penicillin G by injection or intravenously for 7 to 10 days. Alternative drugs include ampicillin, cefuroxime, and cefotaxime.

What Is the Prognosis?

With prompt treatment, most children with rat-bite fever recover completely.

Prevention

Any animal bite should be cleaned well with soap and water. Treatment for 2 or 3 days with amoxicillin clavulanate by mouth may be helpful in preventing infection.

The need for a tetanus vaccine should be reviewed.

Tularemia

Sometimes called rabbit fever, tularemia is caused by the *Francisella tularensis* bacteria. It is spread to humans through the bites of infected insects—most often, ticks, mosquitoes, and deerflies. It can also be passed to people by direct contact with infected animals, including rabbits, cats, hares, and muskrats. Your child can get tularemia by consuming contaminated food or water, eating inadequately cooked meat, or breathing in the bacteria. It cannot be transmitted from person to person.

Symptoms generally begin after an incubation period of usually 3 to 5 days, but possibly as long as 21 days.

According to the Centers for Disease Control and Prevention, there are about 200 human cases of tularemia reported per year in the United States, mostly in rural regions. Most cases occur during the summer months, similar to tick season.

Signs and Symptoms

Tularemia can cause illnesses that vary depending on how the infection was spread. Most commonly, a painful ulcer develops in the skin at the site of the insect bite, with tender enlarged lymph glands in the groin or armpits. Sometimes the glands may enlarge with no apparent bite.

Infection from food or water begins in the mouth with a severe sore throat, mouth sores, and enlargement of the neck lymph glands. With this form of the illness, your child may develop vomiting, diarrhea, and abdominal pain.

Illness from inhalation of the bacteria mainly results in fever, chills, muscle aches, and a dry cough. When the infection enters through the eyes, it results in swollen and red eyes with tender lymph glands in front of the ears. In many cases, tularemia is seen as a combination of several of these symptoms.

When to Call Your Pediatrician
Call your pediatrician immediately if your child develops an illness that could be a sign of tularemia, especially if he has a high fever, chills, a skin ulcer, or enlarged lymph glands. Prompt treatment is very important with this infection.

How Is the Diagnosis Made?
Your pediatrician will take samples of your child's blood and have them tested in the laboratory for antibodies to tularemia. Sometimes the bacteria can be grown from the blood or infected sites.

Treatment
The doctor will treat your child with an antibiotic such as streptomycin or gentamicin. Treatment usually lasts for a 10-day period, although sometimes longer for more serious cases. Early treatment of the infection is important.

What Is the Prognosis?
When children are treated with the appropriate antibiotics, their infection will quickly clear up, although relapses occasionally occur. If the infection goes completely untreated, however, it can be life threatening in some cases.

Prevention
You can protect your child from the bites that cause tularemia by making sure he wears protective clothing. (See "Lyme Disease" on page 246 in this chapter.) Also, inspect your child frequently for ticks and remove any that may have attached themselves to his skin or scalp. The use of insect repellents, particularly those that contain the chemical DEET, is also recommended. Use gloves, masks, and goggles when skinning or dressing wild animals.

Other preventive measures include

- Instruct your child not to handle sick or dead animals.
- Make sure all meat is cooked thoroughly before feeding it to your youngster.
- Ensure that drinking water comes from an uncontaminated source.

A vaccine is not available to protect against tularemia, although interest in vaccine development has been growing since concerns have been raised about the use of the *F tularensis* bacteria as a bioterrorist weapon. This organism could be spread through an airborne route, at which point it could be breathed in and would need to be treated quickly with antibiotics.

See Also

CHAPTER 28

Organisms Causing or Associated With Skin Infections

Chapter at a Glance

Some skin infections are serious. Others may simply be embarrassing. Skin infections are usually very noticeable to parents. You'll be able to see signs of infection on your child, whether it's a rash, swelling, or other symptoms.

In this chapter, you'll find descriptions of many common skin infections and how they can be identified and treated. With this information, you'll be able to care for your child's symptoms more knowledgeably and with your pediatrician's help, treat the skin condition more effectively.

Symptoms of Skin Infections

Rash	Swelling
Redness	Warmth
Pain	

Terms Used to Describe Skin Rashes

macule. Flat mark.

papule. Raised mark.

erythema and **erythematous.** Red.

purpura. Purple, blue bruise caused by bleeding into the skin.

petechiae. Small red dot caused by bleeding into the skin.

vesicle. Small fluid-filled bump, like a dew drop on a rose petal (eg, chickenpox).

bulla. Blister; thin skin stretched over clear fluid.

urticaria. Hives, raised itchy patches.

multiforme. Rash with many forms.

bull's-eye or **target.** Circular rash with clearing in the center.

Gas Gangrene

Gangrene describes the death of infected tissue. This tissue damage may be caused by the *Clostridium* bacterium—most commonly, *Clostridium perfringens.* When this is the case, the disease is called gas gangrene or clostridial myonecrosis (*myo* refers to muscle, and *necrosis* to death). It is a rare but life-threatening infection that occurs when these bacteria produce toxins or gas that gets trapped in the infected tissue, causing the tissue injury. This condition is frequently associated with a recent surgical wound or trauma.

Signs and Symptoms

If gas gangrene develops in your child, it will probably begin with pain at the site of the existing wound. Next, your youngster may experience fluid buildup (edema), tenderness, and a worsening of the pain. Her heart rate may increase (tachycardia), along with rapid breathing, sweating, paleness, and fever. If untreated, her condition can get worse and lead to a lowering of blood pressure to dangerous levels (hypotension), kidney failure, an impairment of her mental status, and shock.

The incubation period from the time of infection to the appearance of symptoms can be as short as 6 hours and as long as 3 weeks. In most cases, the period is 2 to 4 days.

When to Call Your Pediatrician

If there are signs of infection, particularly if associated with a skin wound, contact your pediatrician immediately.

How Is the Diagnosis Made?

Your doctor will diagnose gas gangrene based on your child's symptoms, along with laboratory tests to find *Clostridium* bacteria such as cultures and smears of a blood sample and secretions from the infected area.

Treatment

Gas gangrene must be treated immediately by

- Surgically removing the dead and infected tissue
- Administering penicillin intravenously
- Managing shock and other complications
- Possibly treating the patient in a high-pressure oxygen chamber, although the effectiveness of this approach has not been proven

What Is the Prognosis?

Unless properly treated, gas gangrene can become progressively worse, leading to the spread of the infection throughout the body (sepsis) and often death within hours.

Prevention

If your child has a skin injury, wash the area with soap and water and keep it clean. If the wound becomes seriously contaminated, visit your pediatrician or an emergency department, where they likely will flush it with water and start antibiotics such as penicillin or clindamycin.

Leprosy

Leprosy is a chronic disease that involves not only the skin, but also the nerves in the extremities. Also known as Hansen disease, leprosy is caused by *Mycobacterium leprae* bacteria.

Children are more likely to develop leprosy than adults. The disease is not easily transmitted. It is usually spread from person to person in the nasal secretions from an individual with untreated leprosy. Contaminated soil or insects may be other avenues of transmission.

This infection is extremely rare in the United States. About 90% of patients with leprosy in the United States are immigrants and refugees from parts of the world where the disease is most common, such as Mexico and Southeast Asia.

Signs and Symptoms

Children with leprosy develop skin lesions that, in the most severe cases, are large and disfiguring. The infected areas of the skin may be lighter in color than the child's normal skin. Youngsters also can develop nerve damage in the hands and feet, as well as muscle weakness and a decline in skin sensation to touch or pain. Leprosy also causes muscle weakness that may produce footdrop, in which the toe drops when the foot is lifted while walking.

The incubation period from the time of infection to the beginning of symptoms is lengthy, usually 3 to 5 years.

When to Call Your Pediatrician

Contact your pediatrician if your child develops any of these symptoms or if you think he has been exposed to leprosy.

How Is the Diagnosis Made?

Your pediatrician will take a scraping or biopsy of the affected skin for analysis to detect the presence of *M leprae*.

Treatment

A number of medicines can be used in treating leprosy, including dapsone, rifampin, and clofazimine. More than one medicine is given at the same time in all treated patients. In addition to these drugs, corticosteroids are sometimes used to reduce the inflammation that can occur during the treatment process.

Therapy may continue for 1 to 2 years or more, depending on the medicines used. Hospitalization is unnecessary in most cases.

What Is the Prognosis?

If leprosy is diagnosed and treated early, the damage caused by the disease can be limited and the child can return to a normal everyday life. Once a child has started treatment and been taking medicine for a number of weeks, he can no longer infect others.

Prevention

If your child has close contact with a person with untreated leprosy, he should wash his hands with soap and water frequently. If someone in your home has leprosy, uninfected children in the same household should be examined annually for at least 5 years to make sure they haven't contracted the disease.

Although a leprosy vaccine has been developed, it is not available in the United States.

Molluscum Contagiosum

Molluscum contagiosum is a common skin infection in children that is caused by poxviruses. It produces harmless, noncancerous growths in the skin's top layers. The disease is spread by direct contact with the skin of an infected person or sharing towels with someone who has the disease. Outbreaks have occasionally been reported in child care centers.

Signs and Symptoms

Molluscum contagiosum causes a small number, usually between 2 and 20, of raised, dome-shaped bumps or nodules on the skin. They tend to be very small and flesh-colored or pinkish, with a shiny appearance and an indentation or dimple in their center. They are found most often on the face, trunk, and extremities, but may develop anywhere on the body except the palms of the hands and soles of the feet. They are painless and may last for several months to a few years.

The incubation period varies between 2 and 7 weeks, although it is sometimes much longer (up to 6 months).

When to Call Your Pediatrician

If you notice bumps or nodules on your child that fit this description, contact your pediatrician.

How Is the Diagnosis Made?

Your pediatrician can make the diagnosis by visual examination of the bumps. If the diagnosis is unclear, the doctor can perform a skin biopsy or send you to a dermatologist for a biopsy.

Treatment

Most often, molluscum nodules go away on their own without treatment. This means that children with just one or a few widely scattered lesions do not need any special care. However, if you and your child choose, these lumps can be removed by a scraping procedure with a sharp instrument (curette) or by using peeling agents or freezing techniques (with liquid nitrogen). These methods are painful and in very rare situations, there may be scarring after the infection has healed.

What Is the Prognosis?

A molluscum contagiosum infection tends to go away over a period of several months to years. In children who have suppressed immune systems, the infection can remain or even spread to another part of the body.

Prevention

Keep your youngster from having skin-to-skin contact with another child or adult with molluscum contagiosum lesions.

Scabies

Scabies is a very itchy, contagious skin infection caused by microscopic mites that burrow into the skin's upper layers and cause a rash. It is an infection that occurs not only in children, but in people of all ages.

Signs and Symptoms

Scabies causes a rash that appears 2 to 4 weeks after the mites enter the skin. The rash is actually the body's reaction to the proteins, eggs, and excretions of the mites. It can be extremely itchy and become worse at night. Along with a rash, the burrowing mites can also form threadlike gray or white lines on the skin that resemble irregular pencil marks.

In children younger than 2 years, the rash appears most commonly on the palms, soles of the feet, head, and neck. In older children, the rash is found between the fingers or in the folds and creases of the wrist and elbows, as well as at the waistline, thighs, buttocks, and genitals.

The incubation period for scabies is usually 4 to 6 weeks. If your child has had a previous scabies infection, symptoms can occur 1 to 4 days after being exposed again to the mites.

What You Can Do

If your child develops scabies, she will probably scratch the scabies rash, which will increase the likelihood of the skin developing a secondary bacterial infection. To lower this risk, keep your child's fingernails trimmed during a scabies infection.

When to Call Your Pediatrician

If you notice that your child has an itchy rash, contact your pediatrician. The doctor will look at the rash, make the diagnosis, and recommend a treatment.

How Is the Diagnosis Made?

Pediatricians can often diagnose a scabies infection by examining the rash and asking relevant questions (eg, the intensity of the rash's itchiness). Because children tend to scratch the rash repeatedly, the scratch marks and crusting of the rash sometimes make this infection hard to identify.

Your pediatrician may decide to confirm the diagnosis of scabies by gently taking a scraping from the rash or a burrow and having it examined under a microscope to identify the mite or its eggs.

Treatment

Children with a scabies rash should be cared for with one of several lotions or creams used for treating this infection. Most often, pediatricians choose a permethrin 5% cream. It should be applied over the entire body from the neck to the toes. In infants and young children, it should also be placed on the head, scalp, and neck because the rash can affect these parts of the body in this age group. About 8 to 14 hours after applying permethrin, bathe your child to remove the cream.

Other lotions and creams can also be used, such as crotamiton 10%. Ask your pediatrician whether the cream or lotion should be reapplied (often about a week after the first use).

Even after scabies has been treated effectively, the itching associated with it can continue for several weeks and even months. This persistent itching does not mean that your child is still infested with scabies. To soothe the itching, ask your pediatrician about giving your child an oral antihistamine or topical corticosteroid.

What Is the Prognosis?

Despite the itchiness and discomfort of a scabies infection, it is a mild and highly treatable condition. You can send your child back to child care or school after completing the treatment for scabies.

Prevention

A scabies infestation is easily spread from person to person through close contact, particularly skin to skin. If someone in your family has scabies, ask your doctor whether others in the household such as family members or live-in help should be tested or treated for scabies.

To reduce the chances of spreading the infection, many doctors recommend washing clothing and bedding in hot water and then drying them in a hot cycle. Even so, because the scabies-related mites live in the human skin, there is debate about whether the infection can actually be spread through contact with clothing or linen.

Tinea Infections (Ringworm, Athlete's Foot, Jock Itch)

Doctors use the word tinea to describe a group of contagious skin infections caused by a few different types of fungi. They can affect many areas of the skin and depending on their location and fungal type, the infection has different names.

- Tinea capitis is a skin infection or ringworm of the scalp caused by a fungus called dermatophytes (*capitis* comes from the Latin word for head). It mostly affects children.
- Tinea corporis is ringworm of the body (*corporis* means body in Latin). In wrestlers this is often called tinea gladiatorum.
- Tinea pedis or athlete's foot is an infection that occurs on the feet, particularly between the toes (*pedis* is the Latin word for foot).
- Tinea cruris or jock itch tends to create a rash in the moist, warm areas of the groin (*cruris* means leg in Latin). It most often occurs in boys when they wear athletic gear.
- Tinea versicolor or pityriasis versicolor is a common skin infection caused by a slow-growing fungus (*Pityrosporum orbiculare*) that is a type of yeast. It is a mild infection that can occur on many parts of the body.

Although the name ringworm is attached to some of these conditions, worms are not involved in any of them. The infections are caused by fungi.

Signs and Symptoms

In many cases of ringworm and other tinea infections, circular, ring-shaped sores are formed, which is why the term ringworm is used. On the body, these lesions or patches may be slightly red and often have a scaly border. They may grow to about 1 inch in diameter. While some children have just one patch, others may have several of them. They tend to be itchy and uncomfortable.

- In ringworm of the scalp, itching may develop on the head, along with round and raised lesions. Hair loss can occur in patches. Some cases of scalp ringworm do not produce obvious rings and can be confused with dandruff or cradle cap. In a few cases, the child will have a reaction to the fungus and develop a large boggy area called a kerion. This looks like a pus-filled sore (abscess), but it is really an allergic reaction to the fungus. The infected area will heal once the fungus is treated. Steroids are often given to speed healing. Sometimes, bacteria can infect the area later. If this occurs, your pediatrician may advise the use of antibacterials.
- When fungi cause athlete's foot, the skin can become itchy and red with cracking and flaking between the toes. This is most common in adolescents.

Tinea infections are spread by skin-to-skin contact, most often when a child touches another person who is already infected. The fungi thrive in warm, damp environments and at times can be spread in moist surfaces, such as the floors of locker rooms or public showers. When a child sweats during physical activity, the moisture on the skin can increase the chances of a fungal infection.

The incubation period for these infections is not known.

When to Call Your Pediatrician

Contact your pediatrician if your child has symptoms of a tinea infection.

How Is the Diagnosis Made?

Most tinea infections can be diagnosed by your pediatrician on visual examination of the affected area. The diagnosis can be confirmed by taking

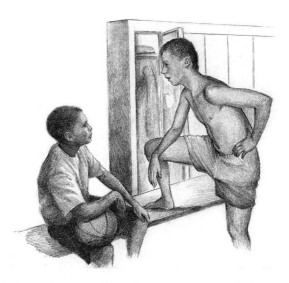

skin scrapings at the site of the infection—for example, by gently scraping a damp area of the scalp with a blunt scalpel or toothbrush—and testing the collected cells in the laboratory. Also, when one type of fungal infection is looked at in a dark room using a special blue light called a Wood's lamp, it will have a fluorescent appearance. Not all of the fungi are fluorescent, so this test can't be used to rule out the possibility of a fungal skin or scalp infection.

Treatment

Antifungal medications applied directly on the head are ineffective for treating ringworm of the scalp. Instead, your pediatrician may recommend giving your child antifungal medications by mouth, most often a medicine called griseofulvin, that should be taken for an average of 4 to 6 weeks. A variety of other medicines can be used. Washing your child's hair with selenium sulfide shampoo can decrease shedding that could spread the infection to others.

Over-the-counter antifungal or drying powders and creams are effective for other types of tinea infections, including athlete's foot and tinea corporis. Your pediatrician may prescribe a cream for treating the rash associated with jock itch. Topical medications including clotrimazole and ketoconazole are used to treat ringworm of the body as well as tinea versicolor.

What Is the Prognosis?

Ringworm infections usually respond well to treatment within a few weeks, although they can sometimes come back.

Prevention

Good hygiene is important for preventing many tinea infections. For example, to avoid ringworm of the scalp, make sure your child shampoos often, and encourage him to avoid sharing hairbrushes, combs, hats, hair ribbons, and hair clips with other children. He should keep his skin and feet clean and dry, especially between the toes. Have your child wear sandals in locker rooms or at public showers or swimming pools. Give your youngster clean socks and underwear every day.

Warts

Warts are tiny, firm bumps on the skin caused by viruses from the human papillomavirus (HPV) family. Warts are contagious and commonly found in school-aged children. They rarely occur in children younger than 2 years.

Signs and Symptoms

Skin warts are dome shaped with a rough appearance and a yellow, tan, black, brown, or gray coloring. They can appear anywhere on the body, but most often they are found on the hands, including near or under the fingernails; toes; face; and around the knees.

Warts also can occur on the soles of the feet, where they are often flat and painful. Your child may say she feels like she is walking on a pebble. Doctors refer to these manifestations as plantar warts. They may have tiny black dots on them, which are actually tiny, clotted blood vessels.

Human papillomaviruses are spread by close physical contact. The virus often gets into the body through breaks in the skin. Swimming in public pools may increase your child's risk of developing plantar warts.

When warts occur on the genitals, they are considered a sexually transmitted disease caused by a type of HPV. They are spread during genital, oral, and anal sex with a partner who is infected.

When to Call Your Pediatrician

Let your pediatrician know if your child develops a wart on her face or genitals. If warts persist or spread or if they are painful, ask your pediatrician for medical advice.

How Is the Diagnosis Made?

Most warts, including genital warts, are diagnosed by their appearance. Genital warts can be identified by performing a biopsy that is sent to the laboratory for confirmation of an HPV infection.

Treatment

While warts will go away on their own without treatment, they can become painful if they are bumped, and some children are embarrassed by them. Your pediatrician may suggest applying an over-the-counter medicine containing salicylic acid to the warts. Prescription-strength chemicals are also available for removing them. Recently, duct tape has been shown to work against warts!

If your child has multiple warts or they keep coming back, your doctor may recommend removing them surgically by scraping, cauterizing (cutting away the warts), or freezing them (with liquid nitrogen). There is a good success rate with the use of surgery, but it sometimes leaves scars. If your teenaged girl has genital warts, she should have a Pap smear to be sure there are no changes in the cells of the cervix. There is a link between genital warts and cancer of the cervix. Warts in the airways are also difficult to treat and often require referral to a specialist.

What Is the Prognosis?

Many warts last for months or years and then go away on their own or in response to treatment. The earlier the treatment is given, the greater the chances are of completely getting rid of the warts.

Prevention

There is no way to effectively prevent warts.

Germs That Can Cause Skin Infections

Bacteria: *Staphylococcus aureus, Streptococcus pyogenes* (group A strep), *Clostridium perfringens, Mycobacterium leprae*

Viruses: Coxsackieviruses, echoviruses, molluscum, chickenpox, measles, rubella

Fungi: *Trichophyton tonsurans, Microsporum canis, Microsporum audouinii, Trichophyton mentagrophytes, Trichophyton rubrum, Epidermophyton floccosum* (the causes of ringworm)

Lice and scabies: *Pediculus humanus capitis, Pediculus humanus corporis, Phthirus pubis, Sarcoptes scabiei*

See Also

CHAPTER 29

Organisms Commonly Acquired Through Sexual Interactions

Chapter at a Glance

Sexually transmitted diseases (STDs) are occurring in high numbers among teenagers. Parents need to know the signs and symptoms associated with these diseases, as well as how they are treated.

Parents should also know how to advise teenagers on preventing these infections by practicing safer sex. Encourage them to be celibate or wait to have their first sexual experience as long as possible. If they are sexually active, they should have as few sexual partners as possible. They should learn to use barrier methods of contraception (ie, male or female latex condoms) correctly and every time they have sex. Finally, they should be made aware of the strong association between drug and alcohol use and failure to use condoms.

Some Safe Sex Tips

■ Be celibate (abstain from having sex).

If your child is already sexually active

■ Use male or female latex condoms during every sexual interaction.
■ Learn to use male or female latex condoms correctly.
■ Limit the number of sexual partners.
■ Beware of drug and alcohol use, which can affect judgment and lead to unsafe sex.

As you'll learn in this chapter, some infections can be spread from mothers to newborns during and sometimes even before birth. Some of these babies have symptoms, but many do not. In some cases, the signs of infection don't show up until the child is months or years old.

Symptoms of Sexually Transmitted Diseases
None (Note well—this is the most common!)
Discharge from the vagina or penis
Sores in the genital area
Pain in the pelvis
Pain with urination or sexual activity
Rash, especially if on the palms and soles

When sexually transmitted diseases occur in young children, it may be a sign of sexual abuse. Feel free to discuss these issues with your pediatrician.

Bacterial Vaginosis

Bacterial vaginosis (BV) is the most common vaginal infection in sexually active teenaged girls. It appears to be caused by a bacterial imbalance or overgrowth in the vagina, resulting in an increase in harmful bacteria. The actual organism responsible for vaginosis hasn't been clearly identified. Bacterial vaginosis in a girl who has not yet reached puberty is not evidence of sexual abuse, but does require follow-up by your pediatrician.

Signs and Symptoms

In many cases, BV does not cause any signs or symptoms. At other times, BV may cause

- A white vaginal discharge that coats the walls of the vagina
- Vaginal discharge with an unpleasant or fishlike odor
- Vaginal pain or itching
- Burning during urination

Doctors are unsure of the incubation period for bacterial vaginosis.

How Is the Diagnosis Made?

Your child's pediatrician can make the diagnosis of BV during a physical examination by looking for the signs associated with the infection. The doctor can also order a laboratory analysis using a sample of vaginal secretions to detect bacteria associated with the infection.

If BV is diagnosed in a sexually active teenager, she should be tested for other STDs such as syphilis, gonorrhea, chlamydia, hepatitis B, and human immunodeficiency virus (HIV).

Treatment
Treatment is recommended for all teenaged girls and adult women who have signs and symptoms of BV. Common treatments include an oral or gel formulation of metronidazole or, in some cases, clindamycin in a cream preparation.

What Is the Prognosis?
Proper treatment can resolve a BV infection.

Teenaged girls and women with BV may have an increased risk of developing pelvic inflammatory disease (PID) (see page 285). If BV is present in a pregnant woman, it can increase the likelihood of premature delivery or endometriosis.

Prevention
While acknowledging that the best preventive steps are unknown, the Centers for Disease Control and Prevention has noted that the risk of BV may be reduced by limiting the number of sexual partners and not using douches, which can upset the natural balance of bacteria in the vagina. It is not necessary to treat the male partner of a patient with BV.

Chlamydia

Chlamydia is the most commonly reported STD. Caused by *Chlamydia trachomatis* bacteria, it occurs at high rates in sexually active teenagers.

A genital *Chlamydia* infection can be spread between sexual partners during vaginal, oral, or anal sexual contact. An infected mother can pass it on to her newborn child. In fact, about 50% of infants delivered vaginally to infected mothers get chlamydia. A smaller number delivered by cesarean birth also get the disease.

If present beyond the newborn period in a child who has not yet reached puberty, a chlamydial infection may be a sign of sexual abuse.

Signs and Symptoms
Chlamydial infection is often called a "silent disease" because so many infected people have no symptoms. This is the case with about three fourths of infected females and about half of infected males. As a result, many infections go unrecognized.

When symptoms are present, females may have

- An abnormal vaginal discharge
- A burning sensation during urination
- Lower abdominal pain
- Low back pain
- Fever
- Nausea
- Bleeding between periods
- Painful sexual intercourse

Males may have

- An abnormal discharge from the penis
- Itching or burning around the tip of the penis
- A burning sensation while urinating
- Tenderness or pain of the testicles

Males and females may develop Reiter syndrome with arthritis, burning during urination, and inflammation with redness of the eyes. When newborns get a chlamydial infection from their mothers, they may develop eye inflammation with redness, swelling, and discharge, with or without pneumonia. The pneumonia may cause a cough and rapid breathing.

If illness is present, it typically begins after an incubation period of 1 to 3 weeks. Pneumonia may occur up to several months after birth in newborns.

What You Can Do
Any sexually active male or female can be infected with *C trachomatis*. Make sure your teenaged son or daughter knows about the risks of a sexually active lifestyle and how to practice safe sex (see beginning of this chapter).

When to Call Your Pediatrician
Call your pediatrician if your child complains of symptoms listed here. If your newborn has an eye discharge or cough, you should call your pediatrician.

How Is the Diagnosis Made?
Your doctor can collect a specimen (eg, of pus) from the cervix or penis and have it tested in the laboratory for evidence of chlamydial infection. A urine sample can also be tested.

If a chlamydial infection is diagnosed in a sexually active teenager, he should be tested for other STDs, including syphilis, HIV, gonorrhea, and hepatitis B. Gonorrhea and chlamydial infection often occur together. His sexual partner(s) should also be notified and tested.

Treatment

To treat chlamydia, your pediatrician will prescribe antibiotics such as oral doxycycline or azithromycin.

A child with chlamydial pneumonia or conjunctivitis should be treated with oral medications like erythromycin. Topical treatment of the eye infection, such as with eyedrops, is ineffective and unnecessary.

What Is the Prognosis?

Prompt treatment should resolve a chlamydial infection and prevent complications.

If the infection is not treated, serious complications can develop, including PID (infection of the uterus, fallopian tubes, or ovaries) in girls and women that can lead to chronic pelvic pain, infertility, and ectopic pregnancies (pregnancy outside the uterus). A person with a chlamydial infection is also more likely to contract an HIV infection. Complications are less common in teenaged boys and men, but may include inflammation of the epididymis (the coiled tube that runs along the back of the testicles).

Prevention

Your teenager can avoid getting chlamydia by practicing safe sex. If your teenaged daughter is sexually active, she should be screened or tested for a *C trachomatis* infection routinely during each gynecological examination, even if she doesn't have symptoms.

Gonorrhea

Gonorrhea is an STD caused by *Neisseria gonorrhoeae* bacteria. It occurs most often in teenagers aged 15 to 19 years. The infection is spread through intimate contact, including sexual interactions. When it is present in a child after the newborn period and before puberty, this infection may be a sign of sexual abuse.

Gonorrhea can also be spread from a mother to her baby during delivery.

Signs and Symptoms

Gonorrhea of the genital tract typically causes symptoms in males, but is often symptom free in females.

In boys and men, symptoms most often include

- A pus-like discharge from the penis
- Pain in the penis
- Burning during urination

If symptoms occur in women, they may include

- Pain or burning during urination
- Bleeding connected with sexual intercourse
- A yellow or bloody discharge from the vagina

Even a symptom-free infection in women can lead to complications such as PID, which affects the uterus, ovaries, and fallopian tubes and can lead to infertility or ectopic pregnancies. In males, the most common complication is called epididymitis, an inflammation of the coiled tube that runs along the back of the testicles.

When the infection occurs in a newborn, it most commonly causes severe eye infections.

When to Call Your Pediatrician

Contact your pediatrician if your teenager has symptoms like those described here. Gonorrhea has symptoms similar to other STDs, so an accurate diagnosis is important. If a newborn has eye discharge, you should call your pediatrician right away.

How Is the Diagnosis Made?

A number of laboratory tests can be performed to diagnose gonorrhea. Your pediatrician may take a sample of the discharge from the cervix or the penis and have it tested in the laboratory. Urine tests can also be conducted. If a newborn has discharge from the eye, it is tested by microscopic examination and culture.

When gonorrhea is diagnosed, the patient should be tested for other STDs such as syphilis, HIV, chlamydial infection, or hepatitis B. In fact, gonorrhea and chlamydial infections often occur at the same time. The sexual partners of the infected person should also be tested for STDs.

Treatment

Gonorrhea can be treated with antibiotics such as a single high oral dose of medicines called cephalosporins or fluoroquinolones or a single injection of ceftriaxone. If a young child is infected, she may also be treated with an injection of ceftriaxone. If chlamydial infection cannot be excluded, your child's doctor may recommend treating for both infections.

What Is the Prognosis?

When gonorrhea is treated quickly and properly, the infectious organisms can be eliminated and complications can be avoided.

Prevention

To prevent the transmission of *N gonorrhoeae,* your adolescent should practice safe sex.

Immediately after birth, infants are routinely given either silver nitrate drops or tetracycline or erythromycin ointment in their eyes to protect them from gonorrheal infection.

Human Immunodeficiency Virus

Few infectious diseases have gotten the public attention and caused the public concern that acquired immunodeficiency syndrome (AIDS) has. Human immunodeficiency virus is the organism responsible for AIDS. This infection and disease is a major concern for adults, and it also affects infants, children, and teenagers.

About half of all new HIV infections in the United States occur in teenagers and young adults, most often as an STD spread through body fluids such as semen and vaginal fluids. Acquired immunodeficiency syndrome was once thought of as a disease that primarily affected homosexuals, but it is now increasingly contracted through heterosexual activity. It can also be spread through intravenous drug use and much less commonly, blood, blood products, needles, or other sharp instruments contaminated with infected body fluids or blood.

Children most often get the AIDS virus from a mother with an HIV infection, often during delivery of the newborn or even before birth when HIV can be passed across the placenta to the fetus. It can also be spread through infected breast milk.

The virus *cannot* be spread through hugging or sitting next to a person who is HIV-positive, shaking his hand, playing with his toys, or eating food prepared by a person with the infection. Transmission in schools or child care centers has not occurred.

Signs and Symptoms
Human immunodeficiency virus is an infection that lasts a lifetime. However, symptoms may not appear for many months or years after the virus is acquired. In fact, the average incubation time from getting the virus until developing the signs of AIDS in teenagers and adults is 10 to 11 years. This means that many young adults may not be aware that they are infected and can spread HIV to others.

When children are infected with HIV, the virus attacks their immune system. Signs and symptoms may include

- Swollen lymph nodes
- Recurrent diarrhea
- Minor skin infections
- Persistent fungus infections of the mouth (thrush)
- Failure to gain weight or grow in height at a normal rate
- An enlarged liver and spleen

As the immune system continues to deteriorate, AIDS-related infections and cancers can develop.

How Is the Diagnosis Made?
Blood tests are available to diagnose HIV infections. These tests detect the presence of antibodies to the virus or the virus itself.

If sexually active teenagers test positive for HIV, their sexual partners must be notified and tested immediately.

Treatment
Several anti-HIV medications are approved for use in children. The newest types of these drugs are called highly active antiretroviral therapy. They are designed to lower the levels of the HIV virus in the blood. Acquired immunodeficiency syndrome–related infections, called opportunistic infections, can be treated as well.

Although there are various ways that HIV can be treated, there is no cure.

What Is the Prognosis?

Human immunodeficiency virus is a serious, life-threatening infection. It can leave children vulnerable to serious types of communicable illnesses. For this reason, notify your pediatrician if a child who is infected with HIV has a fever, breathing problems, or swallowing difficulties.

Prevention

A pregnant woman infected with HIV can lower the risk of spreading the virus to her newborn by taking medicine such as zidovudine (AZT), which is commonly prescribed for people who are HIV-positive. The newborn is treated for several weeks until it is clear whether he is infected.

Babies who are born to mothers with HIV are often placed on preventive antibiotics to lower their risk of getting certain AIDS-related infections.

If your teenager is sexually active, he needs to practice safe sex, using a latex condom during every sexual experience. Even when teenagers infected with HIV do not have symptoms, they can still spread the virus to others.

There is currently no vaccine for HIV, although development efforts are underway.

Pelvic Inflammatory Disease

Pelvic inflammatory disease, an infection of the female upper genital tract, is a serious complication of some STDs. It occurs most often in teenaged and young adult females. Pelvic inflammatory disease can affect the uterus, ovaries, and fallopian tubes.

Sexually transmitted organisms, especially those responsible for gonorrhea *(Neisseria gonorrhoeae)* and chlamydial infections *(Chlamydia trachomatis)*, are thought to be the cause of most cases of PID, although other organisms are associated with some cases. The germs from these infections travel from the vagina and cervix into the upper genital tract.

Signs and Symptoms

In some cases, no signs or symptoms are present, but the infection can still harm the reproductive system. In most cases, however, PID causes persistent lower abdominal or pelvic pain and tenderness, with an intensity that can range from mild to severe. These symptoms often begin about a week after the onset of a period. Additional symptoms may include

- Fever
- Vomiting

- An abnormal vaginal discharge
- Irregular menstrual bleeding
- Right upper abdomen pain (uncommon)

When to Call Your Pediatrician
If your daughter complains of symptoms associated with PID, she should be seen by her pediatrician immediately, even if she denies sexual activity.

How Is the Diagnosis Made?
Pelvic inflammatory disease is not easy to diagnose. There is no single sign, symptom, or laboratory test that provides a definitive diagnosis of PID. Your doctor will make the diagnosis based on a physical examination and laboratory evaluations of cervical secretions. Sometimes the pediatrician may use an ultrasound, an endometrial biopsy, or an examination of the abdominal and pelvic organs using a tiny flexible tube called a laparoscope. These methods can help distinguish PID from conditions with similar symptoms, such as appendicitis, a ruptured ovarian cyst, or ectopic (tubal) pregnancies.

Teenaged girls with PID should be tested for syphilis and gonorrhea as well as chlamydial, hepatitis B, and HIV infections.

Treatment
Oral antibiotic treatment, typically with more than one medicine, is prescribed for most cases of PID. Patients should be rechecked within a few days to make sure the treatment is working.

On occasion, especially when symptoms are severe or antibiotics need to be given intravenously rather than as pills, the patient must be hospitalized. Sexual partners within the previous 60 days of any girl with PID should be tested for chlamydial infection and gonorrhea, even if they have no symptoms.

What Is the Prognosis?
Antibiotic treatment successfully resolves most PID infections. As part of this treatment, the patient with PID should refrain from having sex until she and her sexual partner(s) have completed the course of the prescribed medications.

Complications may develop even if PID is treated. Some teenaged girls and adult women experience recurrent infections and chronic pelvic pain. Females with PID have an increased risk (6 times more likely) of an ectopic or tubal pregnancy, as well as a higher risk of infertility because of scarring of the fallopian tubes.

Prevention

Teenagers should be instructed on how to practice safe sex to avoid STDs. Teenaged girls and young women can also lower their chances of developing PID by not using douches. Some research suggests that douching spreads bacteria into the upper genital tract.

Syphilis

Syphilis is an STD caused by *Treponema pallidum* bacteria. It is spread through direct contact with the sores or lesions that are part of the infection. When present between early infancy and puberty, syphilis may be a sign of sexual abuse.

A pregnant woman with syphilis can spread the disease to her fetus through the placenta or during birth. It can result in stillbirth, a premature birth, and various birth defects.

After infection, it takes about 3 weeks for the first signs of syphilis to appear.

Signs and Symptoms

The first signs of infection, primary syphilis, begin with painless sores (chancres) on the skin or the lining of the genitals. The sores will be visible when they're present on the penis or a woman's outer genitals, but they can also be hidden from view in a woman's vagina or cervix or under a male's foreskin.

After a month or two without treatment, other signs and symptoms (secondary syphilis) will develop, including

- A skin rash that can occur anywhere on the body, but is usually present on the palms of the hands and soles of the feet
- Sores in the mouth and on the genitals or anus
- Swollen lymph glands
- Mild fever
- Sore throat
- Headache
- Fatigue
- Joint aches

These symptoms may come and go over a period of 1 to 2 years. If the infection is still untreated, the organisms may spread throughout the body over time, damaging many organs and causing chronic conditions ranging from heart disorders to neurologic problems and even death in some cases (late syphilis).

A newborn who acquires a syphilis infection from his mother often appears completely well. About half the time, however, he may have signs and symptoms such as a yellow-mucous nasal discharge (snuffles), rashes, skin ulcers, fluid retention, bone infection, fever, swollen spleen and liver, low red blood cell count (anemia), and jaundice (yellowing of the skin). These findings may be present at birth or develop within the initial months of life.

When to Call Your Pediatrician
If your teenager complains of having a sore in the genital area or other symptoms associated with syphilis, he should see his pediatrician.

How Is the Diagnosis Made?
The pediatrician will evaluate your child's signs and symptoms and conduct blood tests that can identify the presence of syphilis. Secretions from sores can be examined under the microscope for the syphilis bacteria to provide further evidence of the infection.

Your child and his sexual partner(s) should be tested for syphilis as well as other STDs such as gonorrhea and chlamydial, hepatitis B, and HIV infections. If necessary, his partner(s) should be treated.

All pregnant women should receive a blood test for syphilis early in their pregnancies. Treatment of an infected pregnant woman will also treat the developing baby.

Treatment
Most often, syphilis is treated with penicillin given by a shot. This treatment has been proven effective in teenagers and adults as well as in pregnant women and newborns.

What Is the Prognosis?
The treatment of syphilis with penicillin can resolve the infection. Patients should have blood tests to confirm that the infectious bacteria have been eliminated.

Prevention
Teenagers should be instructed on how to practice safe sex to avoid STDs.

Trichomonas vaginalis Infections

Trichomoniasis is an STD caused by a parasite called *Trichomonas vaginalis*. It can occur in both sexes, but the highest incidence is in teenaged girls and young women. When present between early infancy and puberty, *Trichomonas* infection may be a sign of sexual abuse.

Signs and Symptoms

Many infections with *T vaginalis* have no signs or symptoms. When symptoms do occur, they can include a foul- or strong-smelling vaginal discharge yellow or grayish-green in color, mild vaginal itching, pain during urination, and in rare cases, lower abdominal pain. These symptoms may become more severe just before or after menstruation.

Males can contract the infection from a sexual partner. The symptoms include itching or discharge from the penis, as well as mild burning associated with urination. In most cases, however, boys and men infected with *T vaginalis* have no symptoms.

The incubation period from the time of infection to the beginning of signs and symptoms averages 1 week, although it can range from 4 to 28 days.

When to Call Your Pediatrician

If your daughter notices a vaginal discharge or itching or any of the other symptoms, she should see her pediatrician. Males should be seen as well if they develop symptoms or if their sexual partners have been diagnosed with this infection.

How Is the Diagnosis Made?

The diagnosis of trichomoniasis is usually made through a physical examination and (in females) by examining a smear of vaginal discharge under the microscope. Cultures can be performed but are not usually needed. The diagnosis is more difficult to make in males.

Treatment

Most cases are treated with an antibiotic called metronidazole. The sexual partner(s) of the infected person should be treated at the same time, even if he does not have symptoms.

What is the Prognosis?

Treatment with metronidazole produces a cure in about 95% of patients.

Prevention

Important preventive measures include regular use of latex condoms or
abstaining from sexual activity.

Germs Transmitted by Sexual Activity*

Bacteria: *Treponema pallidum* (syphilis), *Neisseria gonorrhoeae,
Chlamydia trachomatis, Haemophilus ducreyi*
Viruses: Human immunodeficiency virus, herpes simplex type 2,
human papillomaviruses, hepatitis B virus, cytomegalovirus,
hepatitis A virus
Fungi: *Candida albicans*
Parasites: *Trichomonas vaginalis*
Pubic lice and scabies: *Phthirus pubis, Sarcoptes scabiei*

*Many of these germs can be spread in ways other than by sexual activity.

CHAPTER 30

Organisms Associated With International Travel

Chapter at a Glance

There is more to planning an international vacation than reading guidebooks and talking with your travel agent. It's important to know which diseases you and your family may encounter abroad and how to take steps to protect yourselves.

In many cases, simple precautions such as avoiding unsanitized drinking water are necessary for a safe and healthy trip. Wearing protective clothing to lower the risk of mosquito bites is another good idea.

In this chapter, you'll find information about some infections that may be encountered when traveling abroad and how to keep your family disease free. Keep in mind that in other chapters of this book, you'll find descriptions of other illnesses that can be contracted in foreign countries, from cholera to leptospirosis to hepatitis.

Keeping Safe While Traveling
Wash your hands.
Wash foods.
Peel, if possible.
Avoid street vendors.
Use bottled, boiled, or treated water.
Avoid ice, unless made with bottled, boiled, or treated water.
Get immunized before traveling (see www.cdc.gov/travel).
Take prophylactic medicines, if needed (see www.cdc.gov/travel).

Amebiasis

Amebiasis may not be a familiar name, but the microscopic parasite that causes it is found worldwide. This organism, called *Entamoeba histolytica*, is most common in developing nations, often in areas where there are crowded and unclean living conditions. If you and your family travel to foreign countries, you could be at risk for contracting amebiasis, either through person-to-person contact or, less often, through contaminated food and water. The infection can also be spread when your child touches a surface contaminated with the parasite and then brings his fingers to his mouth or nose.

Signs and Symptoms

Children and adults with intestinal amebiasis often have no symptoms. For other people, the illness can be serious, occasionally involving major inflammation of the colon (colitis). Diarrhea is the most common symptom, and it can become increasingly severe over a 1- to 3-week period. Someone with intestinal amebiasis may have many bowel movements a day that contain blood and are accompanied by abdominal cramps. In some cases, a fever may develop. Other symptoms include weight loss and pain during defecation.

Symptoms are more severe in the very young, as well as the elderly and pregnant women.

In a small number of cases, the infection may spread outside the intestines to other organs, most often the liver, but also the lungs, skin, heart, and brain, among others. A liver abscess could develop, accompanied by a fever, abdominal pain, and irritability.

The incubation period for amebiasis is usually 1 to 4 weeks but can extend for months or even years.

When to Call Your Pediatrician

Contact your pediatrician if your child has symptoms such as bloody diarrhea that may indicate amebiasis or another potentially serious infection or illness. Many of the other symptoms, such as abdominal pain, also need a doctor's attention. When discussing your child's illness with your doctor, don't forget to tell the pediatrician about your foreign travel.

How Is the Diagnosis Made?

Stool specimens will be tested in the laboratory for signs of an amebiasis infection. A blood test can also be given and is most often recommended when your doctor suspects that the infection has spread to the intestinal wall or liver.

Treatment

Treatment is aimed at eliminating the invading organisms. One or more antibiotics such as metronidazole are given, as well as oral antiparasitic medicines (eg, iodoquinol, paromomycin).

Antidiarrheal drugs are usually not prescribed or helpful—they can actually make the symptoms worse. In any case of diarrhea, especially bloody diarrhea, do not give your child antidiarrheal or anti-motility drugs before speaking with your pediatrician.

What Is the Prognosis?

With proper treatment, most children fully recover from this infection.

Prevention

To prevent the spread of amebiasis, you should take precautions when traveling to underdeveloped countries. For example, children should

- Wash their hands thoroughly after using the bathroom and before eating.
- Avoid eating and drinking water in unsanitary areas, only drinking water that has been boiled or purified. Raw vegetables and fruits should be washed with boiled or purified water or peeled before eating.
- *Not* consume unpasteurized milk, cheese, or dairy products.
- *Not* eat food or drink bought from street vendors.

    Latex condoms can reduce the risk of sexual transmission of amebiasis. There is no vaccine against amebiasis.

Malaria

Malaria is a serious and potentially fatal disease caused by 1 of 4 species of the *Plasmodium* parasite *(P falciparum, P vivax, P malariae,* and *P ovale)*. Your child can get malaria from the bite of an infected female mosquito from the *Anopheles* species.

Malaria is widespread in the tropical areas of the world, and there are a startling 300 to 500 million cases worldwide each year. According to the World Health Organization, the annual death rate from malaria is greater than 1 million men, women, and children.

Although there are about 1,200 cases of malaria reported in the United States each year, nearly all of these infections are contracted while traveling abroad. Occasionally, a person may get the infection from mosquitoes that have arrived in the United States on airplanes arriving from tropical regions. On rare occasions, malaria is spread through blood transfusions.

Most deaths related to malaria occur in infants and children. The disease can also cause serious complications in pregnant women and their fetuses, including spontaneous abortions and stillbirths.

Signs and Symptoms

In the majority of cases of malaria, symptoms begin from 10 days to 4 weeks after a child becomes infected. Many of the most common symptoms of malaria are flu like. They include

- High fever
- Shaking chills
- Sweats
- Headaches

The fever may come in cycles, appearing every other day or every third day, only to go away and then come back. In between episodes of fever, the child can appear relatively healthy.

In some children, symptoms such as nausea, vomiting, diarrhea, cough, muscle aches, and pain in the abdomen or back may develop. Malaria can also cause declines in the number of red blood cells (anemia) and blood platelets (thrombocytopenia), as well as paleness and jaundice (yellow coloring of the skin and eyes).

When to Call Your Pediatrician

If your child has traveled to a part of the world where malaria infections are common and shows flu-like symptoms, contact your pediatrician.

How Is the Diagnosis Made?

Your pediatrician will evaluate your child's symptoms and ask about recent travel abroad, particularly to tropical regions. Blood tests, usually using smears from a finger prick that are placed on a microscope slide, can identify the parasite responsible for malaria.

Treatment

A prescription medicine called chloroquine is commonly used for treating malaria. However, the particular choice of drugs will depend on the type of malaria infection involved and drug-resistance patterns known to be present in the areas where you traveled.

Treatment sometimes requires hospitalization. Children with serious cases of malaria may need blood transfusions.

What Is the Prognosis?

When malaria is treated promptly, the therapy is usually successful, although recuperation time can last for several weeks. Relapses can occur in some people, sometimes months or even years after the first infected mosquito bite.

When a person is infected with certain species of the *Plasmodium* parasite, the disease is potentially deadly. In its most severe forms, malaria can cause conditions such as cerebral malaria, which can lead to seizures, mental confusion, and a coma. Some types of malaria are associated with kidney failure, respiratory failure, or other life-threatening conditions.

Prevention

Before your child travels to an area with an increased risk of malaria, ask your pediatrician whether your youngster should take preventive medicines such as chloroquine or other antimalarial drugs before you leave on your trip and while you're traveling. Your pediatrician may advise you to continue taking the medicine for a few weeks after your return. Check the Centers for Disease Control and Prevention Web site, www.cdc.gov, for the current guidelines on the use of these preventive treatments.

Other precautions should be taken to reduce your child's chances of getting mosquito bites.

- Your child should wear protective clothing (ie, pants and long-sleeved shirts) that covers her arms and legs.
- She should sleep under insecticide-impregnated mosquito netting.
- She should have mosquito repellents containing a chemical called DEET applied to exposed skin and then reapplied according to instructions on the product label.
- She should remain in well-screened areas whenever possible, especially at dusk and continuing through the night (mosquitos tend to feed during these hours).

Currently, there is no licensed vaccine available to protect against malaria, but several possible vaccines are being studied.

See Also

CHAPTER 31

Agents Potentially Used for Bioterrorism

Chapter at a Glance

The threat of bioterrorism has been on the minds of many parents, particularly since September 2001. Several infectious organisms have the potential to be used in acts of terrorism, and children are considered to be particularly vulnerable to these germs. Children tend to be more sensitive to many infectious diseases and toxins because of their more rapid breathing rate and, depending on their age, inability to describe symptoms to their parents, which might delay appropriate treatment. This chapter discusses some of the most common germs, from anthrax to smallpox, that could be used in a terrorist attack.

Germs That Could Be Used for Bioterrorism

Disease	Germs
Anthrax	*Bacillus anthracis*
Botulism	*Clostridium botulinum*
Hemorrhagic fever	Ebola virus, Marburg virus, Lassa virus
Plague	*Yersinia pestis*
Smallpox	Smallpox virus
Tularemia	*Francisella tularensis*

Anthrax

Anthrax is a serious infection caused by a bacterium called *Bacillus anthracis*. Since 2001, when 22 cases of the disease were reported in the United States after anthrax spores were sent through the mail, most Americans have been aware of this infection and its possible use as a biological weapon.

At the same time, naturally occurring anthrax infections in humans or animals remain very rare in the United States. Both 2000 and 2001 had one such case of this form of anthrax. These natural infections in humans can be spread through contact with infected animals or contaminated animal products such as hides, wool, hair, and undercooked meat.

Signs and Symptoms

Anthrax bacteria can be contracted in 3 ways—through breaks in the skin (cutaneous anthrax), by being breathed in (inhalational anthrax), or by swallowing (gastrointestinal anthrax). Each type of infection has its own set of signs and symptoms.

- In cutaneous anthrax, anthrax spores (dry resting forms of the bacteria) enter the skin through a cut or abrasion, causing swollen, itchy sores or bumps on the skin. Within a day or two, the center becomes black. In most cases, the sore is not painful.
- Inhalational anthrax develops when a child breathes anthrax spores into his lungs. Early symptoms are similar to those of the flu, including fever, chills, cough, chest pain, headaches, muscle pain, and weakness. Two to 5 days later, the symptoms get worse and may include excessive sweating, a bluish tint to the skin from not receiving enough oxygen, serious breathing difficulties, mental disorder, and shock.
- Gastrointestinal anthrax can be caused when your child eats undercooked meat from an infected animal. Its symptoms include nausea, loss of appetite, vomiting, and fever. As the child's condition gets worse, he may have severe stomach pain, bloody diarrhea, and vomiting of blood. Some youngsters have sores in their mouths and throats and swelling of their necks.

Although the skin sores are infectious, person-to-person transmission of any type of anthrax is rare. The incubation period for all forms of anthrax is usually less than 2 weeks, although it can be as long as months for the inhalation variety.

How Is the Diagnosis Made?
If your pediatrician believes an anthrax infection may be present, perhaps because your child has been exposed to anthrax or has developed the symptoms described here, your pediatrician may order special diagnostic laboratory tests of your youngster's blood, respiratory fluids (sputum), or skin lesions. If inhalational anthrax is suspected, your doctor will recommend a chest x-ray film or a computed tomography scan to look more closely at the lungs and other areas inside the chest.

Your pediatrician will report any suspected cases of anthrax to public health officials.

Treatment
When an anthrax infection occurs, your child needs to be treated right away.

- Naturally occurring cutaneous anthrax is typically treated with a variety of antibiotics such as penicillin, erythromycin, or tetracycline for 7 to 10 days. In the cases of anthrax associated with bioterrorism in 2001, doctors often prescribed oral ciprofloxacin or doxycycline medicine instead.

Although drugs such as ciprofloxacin and tetracycline are generally not recommended for use in children, they may be appropriate choices in serious infections in which the benefits of these antibiotics outweigh any real or possible side effects. However, the drugs such as ciprofloxacin or tetracycline that are usually given to adults for these anthrax infections are prescribed more cautiously in children and pregnant women because of safety concerns.

■ For inhalational and gastrointestinal infections, your pediatrician may first recommend that antibiotics be given intravenously in the hospital. Treatment for these more serious infections usually lasts 2 months or longer.

What Is the Prognosis?

When treatment for anthrax is provided early, it is usually effective. However, if the infection is untreated, it is very serious and can cause death. Of the 3 types of anthrax infections, inhalational anthrax is the most dangerous. This type of anthrax can prove to be deadly within days after symptoms appear in as many as half of those with the infection.

By contrast, cutaneous anthrax poses a very small risk of death. In fact, deaths are rare when cutaneous and gastrointestinal anthrax infections are treated right away.

Prevention

An anthrax vaccine is available in the United States, but it is not approved for use in children or pregnant women because it has not been tested enough in these groups. Newer, more efficient anthrax vaccines are currently being studied.

Do not give your child antibiotics as a preventive measure because you are afraid that he might be exposed to anthrax at some time in the future. Antibiotics can lead to resistance, which makes them less effective. They can also sometimes cause serious side effects. Your doctor should prescribe these medicines only if your child has actually come in contact with anthrax bacteria. If your pediatrician thinks your child has been exposed to anthrax spores, the doctor may consider prescribing preventive antibiotics against inhalation anthrax, even though this approach has not been approved for use in children. If a terrorist attack should occur, pediatricians will decide whether antibiotics should be used as a preventive measure.

For additional information about anthrax, especially if a bioterrorist attack should occur, contact

- Centers for Disease Control and Prevention
  800/CDC-INFO (800/232-4636)
  www.bt.cdc.gov
- US Department of Health and Human Services
  877/696-6775
  www.hhs.gov

Hemorrhagic Fevers Caused by Arenaviruses

A number of viruses can cause infections called hemorrhagic (bleeding) fevers. A family of viruses called arenaviruses is responsible for causing lymphocytic choriomeningitis and 5 hemorrhagic fevers—Bolivian, Argentine, Sabia-virus associated, Venezuelan, and Lassa. In some parts of the world, especially South America and the African continent, these infections are much more common, but they can be seen in the United States. Lassa fever, for example, occurs primarily in West Africa, but has been diagnosed in the United States among people who have traveled to Africa.

Arenaviruses are carried by rodents and can be spread to humans who breathe in tiny particles of the virus or have skin contact with the urine or saliva of the rodents. The virus then enters the body through a cut or scratch.

Signs and Symptoms

Some hemorrhagic fever infections cause only mild illness, but in other cases, they can be much more serious. At times, they can be fatal. An infection with an arenavirus often begins with symptoms such as

- Fever
- Headache
- Muscle aches
- Eye inflammation
- Abdominal pain

Respiratory tract symptoms, including a sore throat and pus, can occur in people with Lassa fever. Arenavirus infections can also cause bleeding from the mucous membranes (the nose and mouth) and red spots called petechiae and purpura that indicate bleeding under the skin.

In the most severe infections, patients can develop shock about 7 to 9 days after the illness begins. Other serious findings may include seizures, tremors, and changes in consciousness.

Person-to-person transmission through body fluids or respiratory secretions is uncommon, but can occur. The incubation periods for the arenavirus diseases are about 1 to 2 weeks.

How Is the Diagnosis Made?
Children and adults suspected of having hemorrhagic fever can be tested for antibodies to the virus.

Treatment
Sometimes an antiviral medication called ribavirin, given intravenously, is used to lower the death rate among people with severe Lassa fever, especially if the medicine is given during the first week of the illness. Ribavirin also may be helpful in treating other types of arenaviruses. Transfusions of plasma from patients who have recovered from arenavirus infection are sometimes given as part of the treatment.

Prevention
The best way to avoid arenaviruses is to keep away from rodents that may carry the disease. Make efforts to prevent rodents from entering homes and nesting in areas near people.

Argentine and possibly Bolivian hemorrhagic fever can be prevented with a vaccine that is still being studied. No vaccines are available for other hemorrhagic fevers associated with arenaviruses.

Do not allow your child to be in close contact with people already infected with a hemorrhagic fever virus.

In case of a bioterrorist attack involving arenaviruses, follow the instructions from public health officials to reduce your family's risk of exposure.

Plague
Once called "Black Death," plague killed millions of people in earlier times. In the 1300s, for example, it was responsible for the deaths of 20 to 30 million people in Europe. Although improvements in living conditions and rodent control have dramatically reduced the number of cases today, there are still 1,000 or more new cases worldwide each year, including some in the United States. The bacteria responsible for plague are called *Yersinia pestis*.

Cases of plague have been reported in several western states in the United States, primarily New Mexico, Arizona, California, and Colorado. The disease occurs in rural areas and the incidence tends to be higher in the summers, especially those that follow mild winters and wet springs.

Bubonic plague is the most common form of plague, and it infects the lymph nodes. It is usually spread when humans are bitten by fleas that have fed on infected rodents (most often, rats) or animals such as pet cats and dogs that have been in close contact with rodents. Less frequently, it is spread when humans come in contact with the tissues and body fluids of infected rodents and other animals, including pets. The germs typically enter the human body through a cut or abrasion in the skin. Some cases of plague are transmitted when people are bitten by an infected animal such as a ground squirrel or prairie dog. Person-to-person transmission can occur from contact with drainage from infected lymph nodes or droplets coughed up by patients with lung infection.

Other forms of the disease can be spread to humans in the following ways:

- Although septicemic plague, which affects the bloodstream, occurs most often as a complication of bubonic plague, it can occur from direct contact. Once bacteria invade the bloodstream, the disease can cause serious illness.
- Primary pneumonic plague infecting the lungs is spread when an individual breathes in airborne droplets from a person or animal with the plague. As its name suggests, it can lead to pneumonia.

In recent years, concerns have been raised about the possible use of *Y pestis* in bioterrorism because it can be spread through the air.

Signs and Symptoms
Bubonic plague begins with symptoms such as

- Fever
- Painful, swollen lymph nodes called buboes

Buboes tend to develop in the groin area or regions of the armpit or neck. Other common symptoms associated with bubonic plague, as well as other forms of plague, include

- Chills
- Headache
- Extreme weakness or exhaustion

When a person has plague that infects the bloodstream (septicemic) and spreads through the body, it can cause serious problems such as low blood pressure and breathing difficulties. Pneumonic plague can have serious complications as well, such as a cough, breathing difficulties, and bloody sputum.

The incubation period for bubonic plague is always less than a week and possibly as little as 2 days.

When to Call Your Pediatrician
Contact your pediatrician if a rodent bites your child or if she develops symptoms like those described in this section.

How Is the Diagnosis Made?
Plague is usually diagnosed with laboratory tests that can detect *Y pestis*, including evaluations of samples from sputum and the lymph nodes, as well as blood specimens.

Treatment
Children with plague are most often treated with antibiotics such as streptomycin or gentamicin given as a shot. In some cases, other drugs may be chosen instead. This treatment usually continues for 7 to 10 days or until several days after the fever breaks.

Your doctor also may recommend draining the pus from lymph nodes in children with bubonic plague.

What Is the Prognosis?
If treatment is given promptly, it can keep plague from getting worse. If not properly treated, however, the disease can result in death related to infections in the lungs and bloodstream.

Prevention
If you live in parts of the United States where plague has been reported, such as the southwest, take steps to lower your risks for the disease. Do not leave out pet food that can attract rodents. Remove brush and rock piles that can serve as rodent nesting sites. Use insecticides to destroy fleas. Regularly treat the family pets to remove fleas. Children should be told to avoid any contact with sick and dead animals.

If your child has had close contact with a person with plague, call your pediatrician if she develops a fever or other symptoms that may indicate that she has become infected. Antibiotics may be prescribed as a preventive (prophylactic) measure in these cases.

Although plague has not been used as a bioterrorist weapon, government officials have noted its possible use in this way. If the threat ever turns into reality, guidelines may be issued on steps to take to protect your child. There is no vaccine presently available to protect against plague.

Smallpox

Many Americans grew up in an era when there was no apparent danger of contracting smallpox. In fact, in 1980, the World Health Organization declared that smallpox had been eradicated worldwide. In the United States, doctors stopped giving routine smallpox vaccines to children in 1971.

After the terrorist attacks of September 2001, however, concern about smallpox reemerged because the disease is considered a possible weapon for use in a bioterrorist attack. As a result, even though the smallpox vaccine is not recommended for universal use, public health officials are developing recommendations for when such a vaccine should be given.

The variola virus, part of a family of viruses called *Poxviridae,* causes smallpox. It is highly contagious and is spread by airborne saliva droplets from an infected person. In a small number of cases, it can be spread by direct contact with a smallpox lesion, clothing, or bed linens. Only humans can get smallpox.

Signs and Symptoms

A child with smallpox will develop the illness after a 7- to 17-day incubation period. He will become so severely ill that he'll be left bedridden with symptoms such as

- A high fever (102°F–104°F or 38.9°C–40.0°C)
- Severe headaches
- Backache
- Abdominal pain
- Physical exhaustion
- Vomiting
- Seizures

After about 2 to 5 days, the child will develop blisters or ulcers in the mouth or throat. At this point, he will become contagious and able to spread the infection. In the next 24 hours, a rash will develop, usually beginning on the face and spreading rapidly to the forearms, torso, and legs. This rash will progress to raised bumps and then pus-filled blisters that soon become crusty. Rarely, the blisters will be filled with blood. Scabs will form, which will fall off approximately 3 to 4 weeks later, sometimes leaving behind pitted scars.

About 3 to 4 weeks after the rash first appears, the scabs will separate. At this point, the child will no longer be contagious.

When to Call Your Pediatrician
If your child develops this illness, especially a rash with a fever, contact your pediatrician.

Early chickenpox can be confused with smallpox, but the rashes look very different. The blisters of chickenpox are more concentrated on the face and torso than the arms and legs. The rashes appear in waves rather than all at once and are in different stages of development at the same time (eg, bumps, blisters, scabs). Chickenpox is more delicate, and appears to be on the skin more than in the skin.

How Is the Diagnosis Made?
A doctor will suspect smallpox if the symptoms described previously are present, particularly the characteristic rash associated with the infection. Diagnostic tests for smallpox, which include analyzing fluid from the rash and blisters, can only be conducted at the Centers for Disease Control and Prevention.

If a child or adult is suspected of having smallpox, health departments should be contacted immediately.

Treatment
Currently, no effective treatment is available for smallpox. An antiviral medicine called cidofovir may be useful but has not been tested in actual cases. Children and adults with the infection will be given supportive treatment such as intravenous fluids in the hospital, as well as medication to manage the fever and other symptoms. Patients and their close contacts will immediately be placed in isolation so they will not spread the infection to others.

What Is the Prognosis?
A death rate as high as 30% has been reported with smallpox, especially in infants before their first birthdays and adults older than 30 years. Nevertheless, the majority of children and adults with this disease recover, although they may be left with scars associated with the rash.

Prevention
Immunizations against smallpox are not presently recommended for the general public, and the vaccine is not available from your pediatrician.

Military personnel and first responders such as ambulance drivers, emergency medical technicians, some nurses, and doctors have received the vaccine. In the United States, the government has stockpiled large supplies of smallpox vaccine to be used in an emergency, including a smallpox-related terrorist attack, if it should ever occur. The vaccine can reduce the seriousness of a smallpox infection or even prevent it if it is administered within 4 days after a person has been exposed to the variola virus. However, the vaccine itself has potentially serious side effects.

See Also

CHAPTER 32

Bacterial Infections

Chapter at a Glance

Bacteria are single-celled organisms that are present everywhere, including in and on the human body. These bacteria, called normal flora, are beneficial to the body and usually do not cause health problems. Normal bacteria in the bowels help us by breaking down foods to produce vitamin K. The normal flora also helps protect the body from attack by other bacteria that cause infection and illness. These illness-causing bacteria are referred to as pathogens. Normal flora bacteria can cause problems when they grow in large numbers. Pathogens cause illness when they enter the body through a cut or wound on the skin or by eating contaminated food. Although antibiotics can cure many bacterial illnesses, these infections remain a major concern, in part because of the increasing problem of antibiotic resistance (see Chapter 21).

This chapter describes some of the more common (and a few unusual) bacterial infections that your youngster may encounter during childhood.

Arcanobacterium haemolyticum Infections

Arcanobacterium (formerly classified as *Corynebacterium*) *haemolyticum* is an organism that most often causes infections and illnesses in teenagers and young adults. The infection is spread from person to person, apparently through respiratory tract droplets that carry the bacteria directly to the next person's eyes or nose. The droplets can fall onto hands and then get into eyes and noses.

The most common symptom associated with *A haemolyticum* is a sore throat, although other symptoms such as a fever, swollen lymph glands, and an itchy skin rash occur frequently as well. The rash begins on the extremities and spreads to the chest and back. It will not be seen on the face, palms, or soles. It looks very similar to the rash of scarlet fever.

Strep throat is much more common than an *A haemolyticum* infection. If necessary, your pediatrician can do a test to distinguish between a sore throat caused by *A haemolyticum* and one associated with a streptococcal organism.

Antibacterials, typically erythromycin, can be used to treat this infection. The symptoms quickly clear up when taking these medicines, although the disease is likely to get better on its own without treatment.

Burkholderia Infections

If your child is healthy and has a normal immune system, you usually do not have to worry much about infections caused by *Burkholderia cepacia* bacteria. In the United States, these germs most often cause problems in circumstances such as the following:

- *B cepacia* can produce severe lung infections in young people with cystic fibrosis, often late in the course of the disease.
- It is associated with blood infections (bacteremia) in premature babies who are hospitalized for long periods of time.
- It can cause infections in children with cancer and blood disorders such as chronic granulomatous disease.

Burkholderia organisms are found in soil and water. The germs can be spread through person-to-person contact. The initial symptoms may be a low-grade fever, progressing to much more serious conditions, including pneumonia and other lung disorders that can sometimes be deadly.

Other types of *Burkholderia* infections, such as *B pseudomallei,* are most common in rural parts of southeast Asia. These germs can cause pneumonia as well as skin and skeletal infections.

Depending on the specific type of the infection, cultures of sputum or blood samples may be collected and tested to identify the organism. A medicine called meropenem is the most active drug used to treat *B cepacia.* This antibacterial is typically given intravenously in the hospital and often prescribed in combination with other drugs.

Some strains of *Burkholderia* bacteria are spread from person to person or by contamination of disinfectants, including in hospital settings. Good personal hygiene, including frequent hand washing, and infection control measures in hospitals can lower the risk of disease transmission. Centers treating children with cystic fibrosis often try to limit contact with other youngsters infected with *B cepacia.*

Botulism and Infant Botulism

Although botulism is a rare illness, most parents have heard of it and know that it is often related to eating contaminated food. Botulism can be a very serious disease that can cause abnormal functioning of the nerves, leading to weakness and paralysis.

Botulism is caused by poisons (toxins) produced by a spore-forming bacteria called *Clostridium botulinum.* Food-borne botulism arises when food becomes contaminated with *C botulinum* spores and then is stored improperly. Improper storage allows the bacteria to grow and make toxins. Outbreaks of this type of botulism have occurred by eating not only home-canned foods, but also potato salad, restaurant-prepared foods such as patty melts, aluminum foil–wrapped baked potatoes, and bottled garlic.

Infant botulism occurs mostly in babies younger than 6 months. It develops when *C botulinum* spores are eaten by a baby and the bacteria grow in his intestines, making toxins within the gut. The source of the spores is usually unclear. They may be present in soil or dust and then become airborne where they are breathed in and swallowed by the child. Honey and light and dark corn syrups are other potential sources of the disease-causing spores.

Another form of botulism, so-called wound botulism, can develop when tissues in a child's wound becomes contaminated with *C botulinum* spores. In certain conditions, the spores can grow within the wound and produce toxins, which then enter the blood stream.

Signs and Symptoms

In patients for whom botulism is a food-borne infection, it may progress rapidly. It often begins with feelings of weakness and loss of muscle tone that spread through the body. Children may have blurred or double vision, a dry mouth, drooping eyelids, and difficulty swallowing and speaking. The toxin can cause paralysis of the trunk, arms, legs, and respiratory system. In these food-borne infections, symptoms start soon after the contaminated food is eaten—typically within 12 to 48 hours.

Infant botulism may range from mild to severe, often beginning with constipation, a weakened cry, loss of facial expression, a reduced gag reflex, slow feeding, and overall weakness or floppiness. The typical incubation period for infant botulism can range from 3 to 30 days after exposure to the spores.

How Is the Diagnosis Made?

A child's symptoms will help your pediatrician diagnose botulism. The diagnosis can be confirmed most often by finding toxin in a youngster's stool, stomach contents, or the foods he has eaten. To diagnose wound botulism, tissue specimens may be examined in the laboratory.

Treatment

Much of the treatment for botulism is supportive. Children should be kept well nourished, their airway should be kept clear, and they need to be watched carefully for breathing problems.

In special circumstances, your pediatrician may be able to give your child an intravenous antitoxin that blocks the activity of the toxin in his bloodstream. This can help ease symptoms when given early in the infectious process. Antibacterials are not helpful in treating most cases of botulism, although they may be used in the management of wound botulism. Antibacterials generally should not be used in cases of infant botulism.

Seriously ill children may need help breathing, using a mechanical ventilator, and eating, using feeding tubes or intravenous feeding.

What Is the Prognosis?
Most children recover fully from botulism, although it can take several weeks to months. In cases in which the condition is untreated, the symptoms of food-borne botulism sometimes progress to a stage in which the breathing muscles become paralyzed, causing death from respiratory failure.

Prevention
The American Academy of Pediatrics (AAP) recommends that you do not give honey to a baby younger than 12 months. (Honey is safe for children 1 year and older.)

Food preparation and home canning can be made safer from botulism by following guidelines such as

- Boil foods for 10 minutes, which can destroy toxins.
- Do not feed your child any foods that appear to be spoiled.
- Discard any food containers that are bulging. They may contain gas produced by *C botulinum*.

There is no vaccine available to prevent botulism.

Making Good Use of a Powerful Toxin
The toxin that causes the paralysis of botulism has some medical uses! It is used in eye surgery to correct crossed eyes (strabismus). It can also help decrease muscle spasms in some patients with neurologic problems. This is the agent used in some cosmetic surgery—*Botox* injections.

Escherichia coli and Other Gram-negative Bacilli

In Chapter 25, "Organisms Associated With Infections of the Gastrointestinal Tract," we described *Escherichia coli* (or *E coli*) as a large group of bacterial strains, some of which are identified with food-borne diseases that cause diarrhea. *E coli* and other gram-negative bacilli, such as strains of *Klebsiella, Enterobacter, Proteus,* and *Pseudomonas,* can also cause non–food-related illnesses, including blood infections (septicemia), inflammation of the covering of the brain and spinal cord (meningitis) in newborn children, and urinary tract infections in children and adults of all ages.

In most newborn infections, *E coli* or other gram-negative bacteria have usually been passed from the mother's genital tract to the newborn during childbirth. They can also sometimes be spread through person-to-person contact with caregivers or other children.

Signs and Symptoms

A baby who develops septicemia often demonstrates signs and symptoms such as

- Fever, including a temperature that goes up and down
- Breathing characterized by grunting
- Listlessness
- Irritability
- Lack of appetite
- Vomiting
- Jaundice (yellowing of the skin and eyes)
- A swelled abdomen
- Diarrhea

Meningitis in newborns with an *E coli* or other gram-negative infection may not cause all of the signs usually associated with an infection of the central nervous system. Signs of meningitis can include fever or an abnormally low temperature, listlessness or coma, vomiting, a bulging soft spot (the technical term for the soft spot on the head is the fontanelle), and seizures.

Signs of urinary tract infection (UTI) include pain when urinating, increased frequency of urinating, and wetting bed or clothes in a previously dry child.

When to Call Your Pediatrician

Contact your pediatrician promptly if your baby develops symptoms such as those described here.

How Is the Diagnosis Made?

To diagnose these infections, your pediatrician will order tests of your baby's blood, cerebrospinal fluid, and urine.

Treatment

If your newborn has septicemia or meningitis, your doctor will first prescribe ampicillin and aminoglycosides. (Sometimes, cephalosporin drugs will be used instead of aminoglycosides.) Laboratory tests can identify the exact organism causing the infection. Treatment lasts 10 to 14 days for most cases of septicemia and at least 21 days for meningitis.

Urinary tract infections usually can be treated with oral antibiotics. If your child has a UTI, your pediatrician will order some tests to evaluate your child's bladder and kidneys. Some tests are performed at the time of the infection, but others are done after your child recovers.

Listeriosis (*Listeria monocytogenes* Infections)

Listeriosis is a potentially serious disease caused by *Listeria monocytogenes* bacteria. This infection is uncommon, but certain children and adults have an increased chance of getting this illness, including pregnant women and their fetuses, as well as newborns and children with weakened immune systems. Pregnant women can spread the organism across the placenta and infect their unborn babies.

If a woman becomes infected with *L monocytogenes* early in her pregnancy, perhaps by eating contaminated food, she may have a high risk of a miscarriage. Late in pregnancy, the infection can cause stillbirth or, at times, serious illness or death in the newborn shortly after delivery. Although healthy children sometimes contract listeriosis, it rarely causes serious illness.

L monocytogenes is found in the environment. A person can get sick from these bacteria by eating contaminated foods such as soft cheeses (eg, feta, Brie, Camembert), unpasteurized milk, prepared meats (eg, hot dogs, deli meat, pâté), undercooked poultry, and unwashed raw vegetables.

Signs and Symptoms

When listeriosis occurs in an infant, the signs and symptoms may include

- Listlessness
- Vomiting
- Loss of appetite
- Jaundice (yellowing of the skin and eyes)
- Skin rash
- Breathing difficulties

Many childhood cases of listeriosis lead to meningitis. In older children and adults, listeriosis sometimes causes diarrhea.

How Is the Diagnosis Made?

Cultures are performed on blood, urine, and cerebrospinal fluid. If your pediatrician suspects that your newborn may have listeriosis, the placenta or amniotic fluid can be tested for the infectious organism.

Treatment

Your pediatrician will prescribe antibacterials to treat *L monocytogenes* infections. For initial therapy, the doctor may recommend treating your baby intravenously with ampicillin plus an additional medication called an aminoglycoside (usually gentamicin). As your baby begins to get better, ampicillin alone can be given.

What Is the Prognosis?

When a fetus becomes infected with *L monocytogenes,* the prognosis is poor. The death rate is as high as 50%. The risk of death is also high when a newborn develops the infection.

Prevention

To protect your child from listeriosis caused by food-borne organisms, you should follow procedures such as

- Thoroughly cook raw food from animal sources.
- Do not give your child unpasteurized dairy products.
- Wash raw vegetables.
- Store ready-to-eat foods at 40°F or lower.
- Keep uncooked meats separate from vegetables.
- Wash your hands, as well as knives and cutting boards, after they've touched uncooked foods.

When listeriosis is diagnosed in a pregnant woman, treatment of her infection can prevent the spread of infection to her newborn. Pregnant women can lower their risk of developing listeriosis by following these steps

- Avoid soft cheeses.
- Thoroughly cook leftover foods and ready-to-eat foods such as hot dogs until they are steaming hot.
- Stay away from foods from delis such as prepared salads, meats, or cheeses, or heat these foods until steaming before eating.
- Avoid unpasteurized or raw milk.

Moraxella catarrhalis Infections

A number of common childhood illnesses, including some middle ear (otitis media) and sinus infections (sinusitis), are caused by *Moraxella catarrhalis* bacteria. On rare occasions, this same organism may cause a blood infection (bacteremia), an eye infection (conjunctivitis), and meningitis in newborns. It is also responsible for some cases of bronchitis and pneumonia in older children and children who have problems with their immune system.

M catarrhalis ear infections and other respiratory tract illnesses are often treated with amoxicillin clavulanate. Alternative drugs include cefuroxime, cefprozil, erythromycin, azithromycin, and trimethoprim sulfamethoxazole, among others.

Non-tuberculosis Mycobacteria

A germ from the mycobacterium family, *Mycobacterium tuberculosis,* causes tuberculosis (TB). A related species of *M tuberculosis,* which doctors call non-TB mycobacteria (NTM), can cause other illnesses in children and adults.

Although there are many species of NTM (more than 80, according to the Centers for Disease Control and Prevention), the most common in childhood are *M avium, M intracellulare,* and *M fortuitum.* Many of these species are found in soil, food, and water. They enter the body through cuts in the skin, via the gums during teething, or through the respiratory tract during normal breathing. Even though many children are exposed to these germs, only a few ever develop a chronic infection or disease.

In youngsters, the most common NTM infection is called cervical lymphadenitis, an inflammation of the lymph nodes in the neck. Other infections occur much less commonly, including bone inflammation (osteomyelitis), ear infections, lung disease, and skin infections.

These NTM illnesses sometimes occur in children with human immunodeficiency virus (HIV) infections. In fact, children and adults with weakened immune systems may be at a higher risk for NTM diseases.

Signs and Symptoms
The signs and symptoms of NTM infections depend on factors such as the specific site involved and species of the bacteria. They may include

- Swollen lymph nodes
- Fever
- Weight loss

How Is the Diagnosis Made?
Your pediatrician will take cultures from the lymph nodes, blood, or lungs to test for NTM.

Treatment
If your child has lymphadenitis, your pediatrician may recommend surgically removing the lymph nodes that have become infected. Antibacterials such as clarithromycin, azithromycin, and ciprofloxacin are often prescribed for other forms of NTM.

Choosing the best medicines for NTM infections depend on factors such as the specific species of germ causing a child's illness and part of the body that has become infected. Some strains of NTM are resistant to most medicines. Your doctor will choose medicines carefully to make sure that they'll be effective.

Prevention
For children 6 years or older with an HIV infection, pediatricians may prescribe preventive use of certain medicines such as azithromycin or clarithromycin to prevent *M avium* illnesses from developing.

Salmonella Infections

Salmonella bacteria are best known for the gastrointestinal problems they can cause. This type of illness, called gastroenteritis, usually affects the small intestine and is a common reason for diarrhea in children.

However, *Salmonella* (specifically, so-called non-typhoidal *Salmonella* organisms) can cause a variety of other disorders as well, including bacteria in the blood (bacteremia), inflammation of the membranes of the brain or spinal cord (meningitis), and inflammation of the bone (osteomyelitis). Other types of *Salmonella* can cause other illnesses, such as an especially long-lasting bacterial illness known as typhoid (or enteric) fever. Typhoid fever is rare in the United States, but is a problem for travelers to areas of the world where typhoid fever is common (eg, India, Latin American, Africa, parts of the Far East).

Salmonella infections occur most often in children younger than 4 years. They are usually spread to humans by animal products such as poultry, beef, fish, eggs, and dairy products. At times, however, other foods such as fruits, vegetables, and bakery products have caused outbreaks, most often when contaminated by contact with an animal product. The bacteria can also be spread by drinking contaminated water, as well as through contact with infected pets such as chicks, snakes, turtles, lizards, and other reptiles. Typhoid fever is only spread through contact with an infected person or an item contaminated by an infected person.

Signs and Symptoms

When your child has a *Salmonella* infection that causes gastroenteritis, she may have symptoms such as

- Diarrhea
- Abdominal cramps and tenderness
- Fever

Typhoid fever develops gradually, with signs and symptoms that may include fever, headache, loss of appetite, lethargy, abdominal pain, changes in mental status, an enlarged spleen, and constipation or diarrhea.

The incubation period for gastroenteritis ranges from 6 to 48 hours, while typhoid fever has a longer incubation period of 3 to 60 days.

When to Call Your Pediatrician

Contact your pediatrician if your child shows no improvement within 2 to 3 days of symptoms appearing or if she has blood in her stools or shows signs of dehydration (eg, the absence of tears when crying, a decline in urination).

How Is the Diagnosis Made?

Your pediatrician can test for *Salmonella* organisms from cultures of stool, blood, or urine that are examined in the laboratory.

Treatment

Antibacterials do not help treat *Salmonella*-caused gastroenteritis because they will not shorten how long the disease lasts. However, antibacterials are needed when the infection is found in the blood, brain, bone, or other organs. Antibiotics may be given to infants younger than 3 months because of the risk of the infection spreading into the blood and other organs in the body.

A child with severe diarrhea may get very dehydrated and need intravenous fluids or extra fluids given by mouth.

What Is the Prognosis?

Most *Salmonella* gastrointestinal infections last for 4 to 7 days and clear up on their own without treatment.

Prevention

Salmonella infections can often be prevented by practicing good hygiene techniques during food preparation, as well as regular hand washing. Be sure to thoroughly cook eggs, poultry, and ground beef. Hands should always be washed after playing with pets, especially lizards and pet turtles. If your child has a problem with her immune system, you should avoid reptiles used as pets, such as lizards and snakes. Children with sickle cell anemia are at risk for *Salmonella* infection of the bones. Parents of these children should avoid having reptiles and amphibians as pets.

Two typhoid vaccines are approved for use in the United States, although they may provide only limited protection and are only recommended before traveling to areas where the risk of typhoid fever is high. Talk with your pediatrician before traveling to other countries.

Staphylococcal Infections

Infections caused by staphylococcal organisms can lead to a variety of diseases, including pneumonia, abscesses, bone infection (osteomyelitis), joint infection (arthritis), and a number of skin infections (eg, impetigo, pimples, boils). *Staphylococcus aureus* also causes toxin-related illnesses, including toxic shock syndrome (see page 328), scalded skin syndrome, and staphylococcal-related food poisoning (see page 91). In fact, staphylococcal bacteria are the leading cause of food poisoning. Many of these staphylococcal infections, including their treatment and prevention, are described elsewhere in this book.

Some of the childhood infections associated with *Staphylococcus* that you should be familiar with include the following:

- Cellulitis is a bacterial skin infection that first affects the outer layers of the skin and then may spread more deeply into body tissues under the skin. Although other types of bacteria can cause cellulitis, *S aureus* is responsible for many childhood cases. Symptoms include redness, swelling, warmth, and tenderness of the skin. Your pediatrician may diagnose the infection by examining the area. The doctor may take a culture of the skin or wound, and blood tests may be ordered to identify the organism involved. Antibiotics taken by mouth are usually prescribed for mild cellulitis. Some severe cases require hospitalization with intravenous antibiotics. With proper treatment, most cases clear up in 7 to 10 days.
- Impetigo is a common and contagious skin infection in young children, developing most often during hot, humid summers and usually appearing on the face around the nose, mouth, and ears. It can be caused by staphylococcal or streptococcal bacteria. (More often, it is caused by a staphylococcal infection.) Staphylococcal organisms sometimes can cause blisters. Your pediatrician may diagnose the infection by taking a sample of the material from within the blister and having it tested in the laboratory. Antibiotics should be prescribed for this condition and are usually taken by mouth. In mild cases, an antibiotic cream or ointment can be applied to the skin. Until the rash heals or for at least the first 2 days of antibiotic treatment, your child should avoid close contact with other children.
- Staphylococcal scalded skin syndrome is a disease that affects infants and young children. It tends to begin with a single staphylococcal skin

infection, often in a baby's diaper area, in which bacteria produce a toxin that reddens and damages the skin. Large sections of the top layer of skin (epidermis) can be peeled or slipped away just by pressing down lightly or rubbing the affected area, exposing a raw and red layer that is vulnerable to other infectious organisms. These children can also run a fever. Your pediatrician may put your child on intravenous antibiotics. Warm compresses can be placed on the skin to ease any discomfort. Staphylococcal scalded skin syndrome usually heals without scarring.

Group A Streptococcal Infections

The most common infection caused by group A streptococci is a sore throat known as strep throat. Streptococcal sore throats (pharyngitis) are especially common among school-aged children and teenagers.

Group A streptococcal (GAS) organisms are also responsible for skin infections, including some cases of impetigo and cellulitis. Many GAS infections are spread when a child comes in direct contact with the skin lesions or secretions from the throat or nose of an infected person.

Other GAS infections include blood infections (septicemia), pneumonia, arthritis, and scarlet fever (strep throat with a rash caused by a toxin the germ releases into the body). Some children get sick because of their bodies' reaction to the streptococcal infection. These illnesses affect the kidney (glomerulonephritis) and heart (rheumatic fever). Treatment of the streptococcal infection can prevent rheumatic fever, but not glomerulonephritis.

While some GAS illnesses tend to be mild, others are much more serious. For example

- Necrotizing fasciitis is a severe streptococcal infection that kills tissue very quickly. It is sometimes called flesh-eating disease. Infants and the elderly are most at risk.
- Streptococcal toxic shock syndrome is a serious illness, caused when a toxin made by bacteria gets into the body and causes a dangerous decline in blood pressure and other symptoms.

Signs and Symptoms

When group A streptococcus infects a child younger than 3 years, the symptoms tend to be milder than in older children. Infants with a streptococcal infection may have a low fever and thickened nasal discharge. Toddlers may have a fever, irritability, a decreased appetite, and in some cases, swollen glands in the neck.

When a child is older than 3 years, he may have more serious streptococcal-related symptoms such as a red and very painful sore throat, a high fever (greater than 102°F or 38.9°C), white patches of pus on the tonsils (but not always), and swollen glands in the neck.

An infected child will become ill 2 to 5 days after being exposed to streptococcal bacteria.

What You Can Do
Home remedies such as gargling with warm salt water may relieve some of your child's throat pain. Acetaminophen can lower his temperature and lessen the pain.

When to Call Your Pediatrician
If your child has a sore throat, especially with pus on the tonsils or swollen glands, contact your pediatrician.

How Is the Diagnosis Made?
Your doctor will swab your child's throat and tonsils to test whether he has a GAS infection. Some pediatricians' offices have quick-result streptococcal tests that can help diagnose streptococcal infection in several minutes.

Treatment
The primary treatment for GAS sore throats is penicillin taken orally or by a shot. Ampicillin, amoxicillin, or oral cephalosporins are sometimes used as alternatives. If your child is allergic to penicillin, oral erythromycin is usually chosen.

What Is the Prognosis?
When antibiotics are given to treat a GAS infection, your child should recover fully. However, if his throat infection goes untreated, the infection may spread to other parts of the body. He can develop an ear or sinus infection. Group A streptococcus can also lead to rheumatic fever, a rare disease affecting the heart and joints, or glomerulonephritis, a kidney problem in which urine turns a brownish color and blood pressure increases.

Prevention
Group A streptococcal infections are very contagious. Throat infections, for example, are passed through the air by sneezing, coughing, or touching an infected child.

Children with GAS pharyngitis or skin infections should not return to school or child care until they've been taking antibiotic treatment for at least 24 hours.

Group B Streptococcal Infections

Group B streptococcus (GBS) is bacteria that can cause serious illness, particularly in newborns. It is responsible for many cases of meningitis, an inflammation of the membranes surrounding the brain and spinal cord, in infants, as well as some cases of blood infections (sepsis) and pneumonia. These infections often occur very soon after birth. Infections that take place in the first week of life are called early onset disease. These babies typically contract GBS from their mothers before or during birth. Premature newborns are more likely to develop GBS infections than full-term infants. Infections that occur a bit later, after a week of age and through the first 3 months of life, are called late onset disease. In late onset disease, bacteria can be contracted from the mother, other children, family members, and other caregivers.

Signs and Symptoms
A baby infected with GBS may have symptoms such as

- Fever
- Feeding difficulties
- Irritability
- Lethargy

Most pregnant women who are carriers of GBS will not have symptoms. Sometimes, however, these women may have urinary tract or blood infections while pregnant.

When to Call Your Pediatrician
If your newborn has any of these symptoms, contact your pediatrician at once.

How Is the Diagnosis Made?
If your doctor thinks that your baby could have a GBS infection, the pediatrician will take a culture from the infant's blood or spinal fluid and send it to the laboratory for testing and diagnosis.

Treatment
Newborns with GBS infections should be treated with intravenous antibacterials such as ampicillin, gentamicin, penicillin, or another antibiotic such as a cephalosporin.

Prevention

Early onset GBS infections in newborns can often be prevented if infected pregnant women take intravenous (never by mouth) antibacterials when they are giving birth, typically when labor begins. For this reason, the Centers for Disease Control and Prevention recommends that pregnant women be tested for GBS organisms in the vagina and rectum late in their pregnancy (during the 35th to 37th week). Unfortunately, treating the mother does not prevent late onset infections.

There are currently no vaccines against GBS infections, although several are being studied.

Non–group A or B Streptococcal and Enterococcal Infections

While many streptococcal infections can be categorized as Group A or B, other streptococcal infections do not fall into either category. In infants and children, these non-GAS and non-GBS infections can cause urinary tract infections, inflammation of the heart's lining (endocarditis), respiratory tract infections, and meningitis.

Enterococcus, a bacterium that was once categorized as a streptococcal organism, can cause blood infections in newborns, as well as other infections such as urinary tract infections in older children. The most prevalent enterococci species are *Enterococcus faecalis* and *Enterococcus faecium.*

If your child is sick and your pediatrician suspects a streptococcal or enterococci infection, the doctor will take samples of body fluids to test and identify any organisms that may be present. For most streptococcal infections, your child will be treated with penicillin. Because enterococcal infections are often resistant to penicillin, other drugs may be chosen. For example, when endocarditis and pneumonia are caused by enterococcal organisms, combinations of medications may be used. One combination that is used frequently is ampicillin or vancomycin with gentamicin.

Toxic Shock Syndrome

Toxic shock syndrome (TSS) is a potentially deadly illness that is caused by toxins (poisons) made by 2 types of bacteria, *Staphylococcus aureus* and *Streptococcus pyogenes* (GAS). It was first recognized in 1978 in children and adults. The vast majority of early cases were associated with *S aureus* in menstruating teenaged girls and young women who used highly absorbent vaginal tampons.

Although the use of tampons (particularly extended use) can still increase the chance of getting TSS, there are now fewer cases associated with tampons. Other risk factors have been identified, including recent use of barrier birth control methods (eg, diaphragm, vaginal sponge), surgical procedures, recently giving birth to a baby, and a current infection with bacteria such as *S aureus*. When TSS occurs in young children, it is sometimes present at the same time as a varicella infection (the virus that causes chickenpox).

Signs and Symptoms

The signs and symptoms of TSS develop rapidly, often beginning with a high fever (at least 102°F or 38.9°C) that sometimes includes chills.

Other signs and symptoms can vary, depending on the type of bacteria involved. They may include

- Red skin rash that looks like sunburn
- Red eyes (conjunctivitis)
- Watery diarrhea
- Vomiting
- Severe muscle aches
- Confusion
- Low blood pressure

A week or more after the beginning of the skin rash, the skin around the nails may begin to peel. Then, as the infection progresses, the skin around the soles of the feet and palms of the hands also begins to peel.

Toxic shock syndrome can affect many organs in the body, including the lungs, bowel, brain, and kidneys. Complications are caused by a decline in blood pressure (hypotension) as well as the direct action of the toxin, which makes organs of the body more likely to fail, leading to the need for respirators and dialysis. Some people die from TSS, but the overall mortality rate is less than 5%. The risk of death is higher in adults than children and depends on which organs in the body are involved.

When to Call Your Pediatrician

Toxic shock syndrome is a serious condition that requires a doctor's prompt attention. If your child has these symptoms, contact your pediatrician immediately.

How Is the Diagnosis Made?

Your doctor will evaluate your child's signs and symptoms. The pediatrician will order blood tests and cultures to look for the effects of the toxin and presence of the bacteria *(S aureus* and *S pyogenes)* responsible for TSS.

Treatment

If your child develops TSS, she will need to be hospitalized. She will be treated with antibacterials such as nafcillin, penicillin, or clindamycin for at least 10 to 14 days.

Supportive treatment, such as giving intravenous fluids and stabilizing blood pressure with medicines, will be necessary. Kidney dialysis may be required in cases of kidney failure and ventilators (respirators) are used for failure of the lungs.

Intravenous immune globulin treatment may be given to get rid of bacterial toxins in the bloodstream and help speed up recovery.

Prevention

If your teenaged daughter uses tampons, she should choose them with care. Tampon manufacturers have changed the way they make their products to decrease their absorbency, and this has significantly lowered the number of TSS cases associated with tampon use. Make sure your daughter uses tampons with low absorbency and changes them often.

Bacterial Infections

Bacteria	Infections	Usual Antibiotic	Comments
Actinomyces israelii	Actinomycosis, lumpy jaw disease, abscesses	Penicillin	An anaerobic infection
Arcanobacterium haemolyticum	Pharyngitis	Erythromycin	Rash similar to scarlet fever
Bacillus anthracis	Anthrax	Penicillin, ciprofloxacin, doxycycline	Rare in nature; was used as a bioterrorism weapon
Bacillus cereus	Diarrhea	Supportive care	Food borne
Bacteroides species	Abscesses	Metronidazole	Anaerobes; part of normal flora of the bowel
Bartonella henselae	Cat-scratch disease	None or azithromycin	Kittens are the usual transmitters.

Bacterial Infections, *continued*

Bacteria	Infections	Usual Antibiotic	Comments
Bordetella pertussis	Whooping cough	Erythromycin, azithromycin	Infection can be prevented by immunization.
Borrelia burgdorferi	Lyme disease	Doxycycline, amoxicillin, ceftriaxone	Transmitted by ticks
Borrelia recurrentis	Relapsing fever	Penicillin	Transmitted by body lice and ticks
Brucella species: *abortus, melitensis, suis, canis*	Brucellosis: flu-like symptoms	Doxycycline	Rare in the United States; acquired by animal contact or drinking unpasteurized milk
Burkholderia cepacia	Pneumonia	Meropenem	Causes illness in people with cystic fibrosis or chronic granulomatous disease
Campylobacter species: *fetus, jejuni, coli*	Diarrhea	Azithromycin	Transmitted by food and animals
Chlamydia psittaci	Psittacosis (pneumonia)	Doxycycline	Acquired from birds
Chlamydia trachomatis	Genital tract infection, newborn conjunctivitis, infant pneumonia, trachoma	Erythromycin, doxycycline	Sexually transmitted infection; newborns are infected during birth; trachoma rare in the United States.
Clostridium botulinum	Botulism	Supportive care; antitoxin or antibody	Food-borne and infant botulism
Clostridium difficile	Diarrhea	Stop antibiotics, metronidazole	Occurs in children who have been on antibiotics
Clostridium perfringens	Food poisoning, diarrhea	Supportive care	Food-borne infection
Clostridium species: *perfringens, sordellii, septicum, novyi*	Gas gangrene	Surgery, penicillin	Anaerobic bacteria; uncommon infection of muscles
Clostridium tetanus	Lockjaw	Antitoxin, metronidazole	Rare in United States because of immunization

Bacterial Infections, *continued*

Bacteria	Infections	Usual Antibiotic	Comments
Corynebacterium diphtheriae	Diphtheria	Antitoxin, erythromycin	Rare in United States because of immunization
Escherichia coli	Sepsis, meningitis, urinary tract infection, diarrhea, others	Depends on site of infection	Can be part of normal flora of the bowel
Francisella tularensis	Tularemia	Streptomycin	Transmitted by fleas or ticks or contact with infected wild animals
Haemophilus ducreyi	Chancroid	Azithromycin	Sexually transmitted ulcer disease; unusual in the United States
Haemophilus influenzae nontypeable	Otitis media (ear infection)	Amoxicillin clavulanate	Not all ear infections require antibacterial therapy.
Haemophilus influenzae type b	Meningitis, epiglottitis, arthritis, pneumonia	Ceftriaxone	Now rare because of immunization
Helicobacter pylori	Ulcers	Combinations: amoxicillin, tetracycline, metronidazole, clarithromycin	Persistent infection increases the risk for cancer.
Kingella kingae	Joint and bone infections	Penicillin	Not very common
Legionella pneumophila	Legionnaires disease (pneumonia)	Erythromycin	Rare in children
Leptospira species	Leptospirosis: fever, rash, flu-like illness, organs	Penicillin, doxycycline	Acquired through contact with dog or wild animal urine
Listeria monocytogenes	Sepsis, meningitis	Ampicillin	Occurs in pregnant women, newborns, and children with immune problems
Moraxella catarrhalis	Otitis media, sinusitis	Ampicillin clavulanate	Not all infections require antibacterial therapy.

Bacterial Infections, *continued*

Bacteria	Infections	Usual Antibiotic	Comments
Mycobacterium leprae	Leprosy	Dapsone	Rare in the United States
Mycobacterium tuberculosis	Tuberculosis	Combinations: isoniazid, pyrazinamide, rifampin, ethambutol	Most infected people have no symptoms; one third of the world's population is infected.
Mycoplasma pneumoniae	Bronchitis, walking pneumonia	Doxycycline, erythromycin	Common cause of pneumonia in school-aged children
Neisseria gonorrhoeae	Gonorrhea, newborn eye infection, joint infection	Ceftriaxone, cefixime	Sexually transmitted infection; newborns can acquire it during birth.
Neisseria meningitidis	Sepsis, meningitis, other	Penicillin or a cephalosporin	Vaccination can prevent many cases.
Nocardia species	Pneumonia, skin	Trimethoprim sulfamethoxazole	Serious infection; usually in children with weakened immunity
Nontuberculous mycobacteria: *Mycobacterium fortuitum, kansasii, marinum, avium-intracellulare*	Lymph glands in the neck, pneumonia, blood	Surgery; antibiotic depends on the organism and infection	Lymph node infections in toddlers; invasive infections in children with weakened immunity
Pasteurella multocida	Bite wound infection	Penicillin	Common in cats and dogs
Prevotella species	Abscesses (dental and lung)	Clindamycin	Anaerobic; part of normal flora of the mouth
Salmonella species	Diarrhea, bone, joint, kidney, meningitis	None for diarrhea; depends on site for other infections	Acquired by contact with animals or contaminated foods
Shigella species: *sonnei, flexneri, boydii, dysenteriae*	Diarrhea	None, trimethoprim sulfamethoxazole, others	Food borne or contact with infected person

Bacterial Infections, *continued*

Bacteria	Infections	Usual Antibiotic	Comments
Staphylococcus aureus	Diarrhea, skin, pneumonia, joint, bone, heart	Nafcillin, vancomycin; depends on susceptibilities	Becoming more and more resistant to usual antibiotics
Streptobacillus moniliformis and *Spirillum minus*	Rat-bite fever	Penicillin	*S moniliformis* in United States; *S minus* in Asia
Streptococcus agalactiae (group B streptococcus)	Meningitis, sepsis, pneumonia, skin, urinary tract infection	Penicillin	Serious in babies and pregnant women
Streptococcus pneumoniae	Pneumonia, otitis media (ear infection), joint infection, meningitis	Penicillin, ceftriaxone, cefotaxime	Most serious infections (85%) prevented by immunization
Streptococcus pyogenes (group A streptococcus)	Pharyngitis, skin, pneumonia, joint	Penicillin	Rheumatic fever and glomerulo-nephritis can follow an infection.
Treponema pallidum	Syphilis	Penicillin	Sexually transmitted disease; can affect the fetus
Ureaplasma urealyticum	Urethritis	Doxycycline	Sexually transmitted disease
Vibrio cholerae	Diarrhea	Fluids, doxycycline	A risk for travelers
Vibrio parahaemolyticus	Diarrhea, skin	Doxycycline	Acquired from seawater or seafood
Yersinia enterocolitica	Diarrhea	Trimethoprim sulfamethoxazole	Food borne from pork, especially chitterlings
Yersinia pestis	Plague	Streptomycin	Rare in the United States; transmitted by rodent fleas

See Also

CHAPTER 33

Viruses

Chapter at a Glance

There are thousands of viruses that live among us. Viruses are the tiniest of life-forms, about 10 to 100 times smaller than bacteria. Despite their microscopic size, they are responsible for many childhood illnesses.

Viruses cannot reproduce on their own. They need the help of other cells to multiply. When viruses invade human cells, they take over the cell's machinery to reproduce. As they grow in number, they can cause illnesses, some of them serious.

This chapter describes a number of common viral illnesses that your child may get.

Adenovirus Infections

Adenoviruses are a family of viruses that can infect people of all ages. These infections most often affect the upper respiratory tract. They are slightly more common in the late winter, spring, and early summer months, but can develop at other times of the year as well. Different adenoviruses cause illness at different areas in the body. Some strains cause infection of the eyelids, breathing passages, and lungs, while others affect the bowel or bladder.

The adenoviruses are spread by person-to-person contact, including through secretions that are sneezed or coughed into the air or onto hands and faces. Some adenoviruses are present in the bowels and stools. A person who gets the virus on his hands while bathing or using the bathroom can spread these viruses. The virus can go from one set of hands to the next and then into the mouth or nose or onto the eyes. Children who are in child care, especially those from 6 months to 2 years of age, have a greater chance of getting these viruses. The viruses also are spread in schools or summer camps. On occasion, children may get the infection through contaminated swimming pool water or by sharing towels.

Signs and Symptoms

The signs and symptoms of adenovirus infections are similar to those of the common cold. Sick children may develop a stuffy or runny nose as well as a sore throat (pharyngitis), eyelid inflammation (conjunctivitis), infection of the small breathing tubes in the lungs (bronchiolitis), pneumonia, a middle ear infection, or a fever. Some youngsters may have a harsh cough similar to that of whooping cough. Sometimes there is bleeding into the covering of the swollen eyes. This virus may cause eyes to look very sick, but vision is not affected. Children infected with some strains of adenovirus develop inflammation of the stomach and intestinal tract, which can cause diarrhea and abdominal cramps (gastroenteritis). This virus can also infect the bladder and cause blood in the urine and pain while urinating. Occasionally, the virus causes infection in or around the brain (meningitis or encephalitis). In children with an organ transplant or other conditions in which the immune system is weakened, adenovirus infection can be quite severe and result in an overwhelming infection and death.

Once a child is exposed to the virus, there is an incubation period of 2 to 14 days before he has symptoms. The incubation period for gastroenteritis can range from 3 to 10 days.

What You Can Do

Make sure your child gets extra rest and drinks plenty of fluids. If he is uncomfortable, you can consider giving him acetaminophen to reduce his fever or ease the pain of a sore throat.

When to Call Your Pediatrician

If your school-aged child has a sore throat and fever, contact your pediatrician to be sure the illness is not caused by group A streptococcus bacteria (strep throat). Call if your child has symptoms that last more than a few days, he has difficulty breathing, or he appears to be getting worse. Also, let your pediatrician know if your youngster shows signs of dehydration, such as a decreased output of urine or crying without tears.

How Is the Diagnosis Made?

Most times your pediatrician will examine your child and make the diagnosis based on the signs and symptoms. If your child's throat is inflamed, the pediatrician may check for strep. There are special tests for virus detection, but because there is no specific medicine to fight these viruses, it is usually not worth the pain of getting the specimen or the cost of the tests. If your child is very ill or has an underlying problem, your pediatrician can take a sample of secretions from the throat, eyes, and other body regions for laboratory testing to identify the presence of adenoviruses. Tests can also be conducted on stool, blood, or urine samples.

Treatment

As of 2005, there is no specific treatment for adenoviruses. Your pediatrician will suggest supportive care that helps ease your child's symptoms and makes him more comfortable.

What Is the Prognosis?

Most children with adenovirus infections tend to get better in a few days, although coughs and eye infections often last longer. Complications occasionally develop, particularly in young infants and children with weakened immune systems. These may include severe pneumonia leading to respiratory failure or an overwhelming infection leading to failure of multiple organs and subsequent death.

Prevention

Frequent hand washing can help reduce the chances of spreading adenovirus infections. Toys and other objects handled by children should be kept clean and disinfected. Your child should swim only in swimming pools that have been adequately chlorinated.

Coxsackieviruses and Other Enterovirus Infections

Enteroviruses are a group of organisms that include

- Polioviruses
- Coxsackieviruses
- Echoviruses
- Enteroviruses

This section describes the many non-polio enteroviruses. There are more than 60 distinct enteroviruses responsible for a wide variety of illnesses.

Enterovirus infections are common, especially in young children. They can be spread through saliva that becomes airborne by sneezing and coughing or is present on surfaces or objects that children may touch. These viruses can also be transmitted through contact with the stool of a person with the infection or from mother to infant at the time of birth. Infections are most common during summer and early fall.

One of the most common coxsackie infections is hand-foot-and-mouth disease, most often caused by coxsackievirus A16. It is most often seen in infants and children younger than 10 years. Despite the similarity in names, hand-foot-and-mouth disease is a completely different infection than foot-and-mouth disease, which occurs only in animals and is caused by another type of virus.

The usual incubation period of enteroviral infections is 3 to 6 days from exposure to the initial symptoms.

Signs and Symptoms

Although some children with enteroviral infections may have no signs and symptoms, other youngsters can develop a high fever as well as a wide range of other symptoms, including a sore throat, vomiting, diarrhea, abdominal pain, skin eruptions, eye inflammation (conjunctivitis), and sharp pains in the muscles between the ribs. Eye inflammation is sometimes accompanied by bleeding into the outside lining of the eye. Although the eye may look very sick, it does not interfere with vision. These viruses can also produce serious infections such as myocarditis (infection of the heart muscle) or meningitis (infection of the lining of the brain). Signs of myocarditis include chest pain and an irregular heart rate. Stiff neck, headache, and pain related to bright lights (photophobia) are signs of meningitis. Newborns who get the virus from their mothers at birth may have an overwhelming infection with fever that leads to liver failure, bleeding, and sometimes death.

The signs and symptoms of hand-foot-and-mouth disease include a fever and small but painful sores on the throat, gums, and tongue and inside the cheeks. It also may cause a rash, often with blisters, on the hands, soles of the feet, and diaper area, as well as headaches and a poor appetite.

When to Call Your Pediatrician

Call your pediatrician if your child complains of neck pain, chest pain, difficulty breathing, listlessness, or lethargy. Also consult your pediatrician if your child's mouth sores are causing difficulty swallowing, which may lead to dehydration.

How Is the Diagnosis Made?

Your pediatrician will conduct a physical examination that evaluates signs and symptoms which may indicate an enteroviral infection. If the doctor suspects that your child has hand-foot-and-mouth disease, your pediatrician will look for the rash associated with this infection as well as sores in the mouth and throat.

To confirm the diagnosis, your doctor can test specimens from the throat or stools, as well as other areas of the body. Also, tests of the blood and urine may indicate the presence of enteroviruses. If meningitis is suspected, the pediatrician will perform a lumbar puncture (spinal tap) so that the spinal fluid can be examined in the laboratory. If myocarditis is suspected, a chest x-ray film will be taken and an electrocardiogram (EKG) will be performed.

Treatment

There is no licensed specific treatment available for infections caused by enteroviruses. An antiviral drug, pleconaril, has been tested, but is not yet licensed for general use. Your pediatrician may recommend the use of acetaminophen to reduce your child's fever and ease the discomfort of the mouth sores.

What Is the Prognosis?

In most cases, children recover from these infections within 7 to 10 days without problems. Complications do occur on occasion, including heart failure related to myocarditis and even sudden death related to abnormal heart rhythms. Newborns with enteroviruses can get severe infections leading to liver failure and massive bleeding, which may be fatal.

Prevention

Children and adults should adopt good hand-washing habits to reduce the chances of spreading these viruses. In particular, parents and other caregivers who change baby diapers should wash their hands frequently. When a child becomes ill with an enteroviral infection, she should be kept out of school, swimming pools, and child care settings for the first few days of her illness.

Cytomegalovirus Infections

Cytomegalovirus (CMV) is a common virus that is part of the family of herpesviruses. It infects most people at some point in their lives. It can be spread to children through body fluids like saliva, tears, urine, blood, and even breast milk. It is often transmitted during diaper changes, while bathing, and during other close contact. Teenagers and adults transmit the virus during close contact such as kissing and sexual intercourse.

Cytomegalovirus is responsible for the most common congenital (present at birth) infection in the United States. Infants can contract CMV infections from their infected mothers, sometimes before birth when the virus is passed to the fetus through the placenta, or during delivery if the mother's genital tract is infected. It can also be transmitted through CMV-infected breast milk.

Children who have a human immunodeficiency virus (HIV) infection or whose immune system is weakened for another reason (eg, because of cancer treatment) are also particularly susceptible to CMV infections and their complications.

Once a person is infected, CMV stays within the person, usually in a resting or inactive (latent) state, and can intermittently become active and appear in that person's secretions. The virus can reactivate and cause illness if a person's immune system becomes weakened by a disease or medicine.

Signs and Symptoms

When a child contracts a CMV infection, he usually has mild symptoms or even no symptoms at all. However, some infections do cause symptoms. For example, when teenagers develop a CMV infection, it can look like infectious mononucleosis because of the prolonged fever, sore throat, body aches, and fatigue.

Most babies born with a CMV infection have no apparent symptoms at birth and remain well. However, a few are found to have hearing loss or a learning disability. In a smaller number of cases, these babies have symptoms at birth such as low birth weight, jaundice (yellowing of the skin and eyes), swollen lymph nodes, and a skin rash. These babies are likely to have problems throughout life such as deafness and mental retardation.

In children with weakened immune systems, CMV infection can affect many organs of the body including the lungs, liver, kidneys, bone marrow, and bowels. In children with organ transplants, CMV infections are linked with rejection or malfunction of the transplant.

The incubation period for most CMV infections is between 4 and 16 weeks.

How Is the Diagnosis Made?

Evidence of a CMV infection can be found through special viral cultures of urine, saliva, or other body fluids. Blood tests will show whether a person has made antibody to the virus. There are a variety of special tests that measure parts of the virus and allow doctors to predict whether CMV is the cause of a particular illness.

Treatment

In most children, there is no need for specific treatment for CMV infections. However, serious infections in children with weakened immune systems, such as those with HIV infection or an organ transplant, can be treated with a medicine called ganciclovir. Studies are being done to see if treatment of newborns with serious CMV infection may be helpful.

What Is the Prognosis?

Most children with CMV infections remain symptom free and lead completely normal lives, even though the virus remains inactive in the body. However, youngsters who contract a CMV infection at birth may develop a hearing impairment or mental retardation.

Prevention

Good personal hygiene habits, particularly regular hand washing, can lower the risk of spreading CMV. When you're caring for a child with a CMV infection, be sure to wash your hands frequently, particularly after changing diapers. Most children with CMV have no symptoms but do pass the virus in their urine, so it is important to remember to wash your hands every time you change a child's diaper. Children should be told not to share their cups and utensils because they are contaminated with saliva and can spread viruses from person to person.

Fifth Disease (Parvovirus B19)

Fifth disease, also called *erythema infectiosum,* is usually not a serious infection. Its most notable symptom is a bright red patch or rash on your child's cheeks. It is caused by a virus called parvovirus B19 and can be spread from one person to another through droplets or secretions (eg, saliva, sputum). It can also be passed from a pregnant woman to her fetus. The virus can cause serious illness in a fetus or any child who has a certain type of anemia (low red blood cell count).

Outbreaks of parvovirus B19 infections occur from time to time in elementary and middle schools during the late winter and early spring months.

Signs and Symptoms

In the initial stages of fifth disease, your child may develop mild cold-like symptoms including a stuffy or runny nose, sore throat, mild fever, muscle soreness, itching, fatigue, and headaches. Less commonly, your child may experience aches in the knees or wrists.

After 7 to 10 days of these first symptoms, the distinctive rash of fifth disease may appear. It typically starts on the face, giving the child a "slapped cheek" appearance. A slightly raised rash in a lacelike pattern may develop on the torso and then spread to the arms, buttocks, and thighs. Five to 10 days later, the rash will tend to fade. It may reappear briefly weeks or months later, especially when your youngster becomes hot while exercising, bathing, or sunbathing.

Parvovirus infections can make certain types of anemia, such as sickle cell anemia or hemolytic anemia, much worse. This complication may lead to an aplastic crisis in which blood counts drop to dangerously low levels. This can happen to the fetus when a pregnant woman has a parvovirus infection. The fetus can develop heart failure related to the low blood counts. This condition is called hydrops fetalis and can cause fetal death. Transfusions are often needed in the fetus or child with aplastic crisis.

The incubation period from exposure to the virus to the beginning of symptoms usually ranges from 4 to 14 days. The rash appears 2 to 3 weeks after your child becomes infected. Once the rash is present, your youngster will no longer be contagious.

When to Call Your Pediatrician
If your child's symptoms seem to get worse with time or if she develops joint swelling, contact your pediatrician. If your child has sickle cell disease, contact your doctor whenever your child gets a fever or seems especially pale.

How Is the Diagnosis Made?
Your pediatrician will diagnose fifth disease by examining the rash, which has a distinctive look. In some cases, your doctor will conduct a blood test that can detect antibodies to parvovirus B19.

Let your pediatrician know about any medications your child may be taking because the rash associated with fifth disease can look like rashes that are side effects of certain drugs.

Treatment
Most children with fifth disease are treated only with symptomatic care to make them feel more comfortable. If a fever is present, your pediatrician may recommend acetaminophen to lower the temperature as well as to reduce the intensity of any aches and pains that are part of the illness. Your pediatrician also may advise using antihistamines to relieve any itching associated with the rash. In children with serious anemias, hospitalization and blood transfusions are often needed.

What Is the Prognosis?
Most children infected with parvovirus B19 have only a mild illness that goes away on its own. However, children with blood disorders such as sickle

cell anemia or a weakened immune system can become seriously ill if they develop fifth disease and should be seen by a doctor immediately. The infection can also be serious if it is contracted by pregnant women. Fifth disease can result in serious complications such as damage to the fetus, miscarriages, or stillbirths.

Prevention
To reduce the risk of spreading fifth disease, good hygiene is important, including frequent hand washing.

Children who have fifth disease rash are no longer contagious and may attend child care or school. However, during the early stages of the virus when she may have a fever, keep her away from other children until her temperature is normal or she feels well enough to go back to school.

Herpes Simplex Viruses (Cold Sores)

Herpes simplex viruses (HSVs) cause raised and oozing sores or blisters. When these sores erupt on or close to the lips or inside the mouth, they are commonly called cold sores or fever blisters. In most cases, these facial sores are caused by the HSV type 1 (HSV-1) strain. Herpes infections can also affect the genitals. These sores are usually caused by another herpes strain, HSV type 2 (HSV-2). However, both strains of the virus can cause sores in any part of the body. Herpes simplex viruses can involve the brain and its lining to cause encephalitis and meningitis. In the newborn, herpes viruses cause severe infections along with brain, lung, and liver disease as well as skin and eye sores.

The herpes virus is very contagious. It can be spread from one child to another or from parent to child through direct contact with a herpes sore or by contact with the saliva of someone with the infection (eg, through kissing). In athletes, especially wrestlers and rugby players, the virus can be transmitted during the physical contact of competitive events. The genital form of the infection is a sexually transmitted disease (STD). Babies can be infected during the birth process. The incubation period of these infections averages 6 to 8 days.

Signs and Symptoms
When your child develops a herpes infection for the first time (primary HSV infection), mouth sores, fever, and swollen, tender lymph glands are the most common symptoms, usually seen after swelling and reddening

of the gums. These sores slowly heal over 7 to 14 days. During a herpes flare-up, children develop 1 or 2 sores around the mouth. In some young-sters, however, the symptoms are so mild that no one is even aware that an infection is present.

After your child's initial herpes infection occurs and has run its course, the virus itself will remain in the nerve cells of his body in an inactive or dormant (latent) form. He will be a carrier of the herpes virus for life. From time to time, the virus may become active again (sometimes in response to cold, heat, fever, fatigue, stress, or exposure to sunlight), causing a return of a cold sore (secondary HSV infection). These outbreaks often begin with a tingling or itching sensation in the area where the sores are about to break out. The sores and blisters often become crusty before healing.

When the genitals are affected, the herpes lesions are found on the penis, vagina, cervix, vulva, buttocks, or other nearby parts of the body. As with the oral sores, someone with genital herpes may have repeated outbreaks over a lifetime.

When an HSV infection occurs in newborns, it tends to develop in the first few weeks of life. The baby becomes infected while passing through the birth canal. The virus attacks the liver, lungs, and central nervous system as well as the skin, eyes, and mouth. This is a life-threatening infection that can lead to permanent brain damage or even death.

Herpes simplex viruses also cause encephalitis, an infection of the brain. Children with encephalitis have fever, headache, irritability, and confusion. Seizures are common. Herpes simplex type 2 often causes a mild form of meningitis that does not cause long-term problems or brain damage.

What You Can Do

Serious herpes infections, such as those affecting newborns or the brain, will require hospitalization and intensive care. Superficial infections of the mouth can usually be treated at home. After a few days, most cold sores will go away on their own. During the outbreak, prevent your child from scratching or picking at the sores.

When your child has a cold sore, make him as comfortable as possible. Avoid foods and drinks that irritate the sores. Help prevent dehydration by giving him extra fluids. Apple juice will cause less irritation than drinks such as orange juice or lemonade that are more acidic.

When to Call Your Pediatrician

If your child develops signs and symptoms of a first herpes infection, contact your pediatrician. If your youngster has fever, swollen glands, or trouble eating because of mouth sores, your pediatrician may suggest an office visit. Watch your child for dehydration and call your pediatrician if you are concerned about this. Keep in mind that most cases of herpes do not cause serious illness. If your teenager develops genital herpes, contact your pediatrician to arrange for a visit. An antiviral medicine can speed healing.

If your newborn develops a rash, fever, or irritation of the eyelids or eyes in the first month of life, contact your pediatrician immediately. The doctor will probably want to examine the baby in the office or emergency department. If your infant, child, or teenager has a seizure or fever, headache, and confusion, contact your pediatrician without delay.

How Is the Diagnosis Made?

Your doctor will usually diagnose a herpes infection through visual examination of the sores. Laboratory tests are available and can be used to confirm the diagnosis, although they are not always necessary. In these tests, a tissue scraping of the sores may be examined under the microscope, or a blood test is given. In the case of brain infection, an electroencephalogram (EEG) and imaging studies may be done to help with the diagnosis. In addition, a lumbar puncture (spinal tap) will be done to examine the spinal fluid for signs of infection. Newborns will have a variety of tests performed to look for evidence of viral infection of the brain, lungs, and other organs.

Treatment

If your child complains of pain and discomfort related to the sores during a herpes outbreak, talk to your pediatrician about giving him acetaminophen. Your pediatrician can also prescribe a number of antiviral medicines, such as acyclovir, for HSV infections. These prescription drugs keep the virus from multiplying and, if given early, reduce symptoms and heal the sores more rapidly. Sometimes special numbing liquid, prescribed by your pediatrician, can be applied to the mouth sores to relieve pain. However, most children with oral herpes outbreaks are not given these medicines because they recover quickly on their own.

Antiviral drugs can be lifesaving for newborns with the infection, as well as for older children with more severe infections such as in and around the brain and children whose immune systems are weakened because of an HIV infection or cancer treatments.

Antiviral drugs are used more frequently for genital herpes and may be prescribed for the first genital outbreak. Antiviral drugs can be given continuously to prevent outbreaks from returning. However, there is limited information about the success of long-term therapy in children. In adults with frequent genital herpes outbreaks, an antiviral is given continuously for a year to decrease the outbreaks.

What Is the Prognosis?

While most cold sores are uncomfortable and may be cosmetically unattractive, they are usually not a serious problem. Most outbreaks run their course in several days and have no lasting effects.

When herpes infections affect newborns, they can be more dangerous. They can cause serious illness and sometimes death, even when appropriate medicines are given. In older children, a form of encephalitis can develop and must be treated effectively to avoid long-term neurologic problems such as seizures and weakness. The mild form of meningitis caused by HSV-2 infections usually goes away in a few days to a week.

Prevention

To prevent the spread of HSV, your child should avoid contact with the sores of someone with an outbreak. Remember that many people will have the virus in their saliva even when sores are not present. Do not allow your child to share eating utensils or drinking glasses with others. In most cases, your youngster can attend school with an active infection, but your pediatrician may suggest keeping him home if he has a primary outbreak.

Sexually active teenagers should use a latex condom during every sexual experience.

Infectious Mononucleosis (Epstein-Barr Virus Infections)

Infectious mononucleosis is sometimes called mono or the kissing disease. It is caused most often by the Epstein-Barr virus (EBV), which is in the herpesvirus family of organisms. Most people become infected with EBV at some point in their lives. Like all herpesviruses, EBV stays within the body once a person is infected. Most of the time, the virus is in an inactive (latent) state, but occasionally the virus multiplies and is shed in saliva and other body fluids.

Epstein-Barr virus is spread from one person to another in saliva, blood, and other body fluids. Close contact is usually required, such as kissing or sexual contact.

Although the infection can occur at any age, mononucleosis is most common in people between 15 and 30 years of age.

Signs and Symptoms

Many infants and young children infected with EBV have no symptoms or only very mild ones. When there are signs and symptoms of mononucleosis, they usually include the following:

- Fever
- Sore throat, including white patches in the back of the throat
- Swollen lymph glands in the back of the neck, groin, and armpit
- Fatigue

In addition to these classic symptoms, some children may also have one or more of the following signs and symptoms:

- Chills
- Headache
- Decreased appetite
- Puffy eyelids
- Enlargement of the liver and spleen
- Oversensitivity to light
- Anemia

Some children with EBV infection develop meningitis, brain inflammation (encephalitis), and a paralyzing disorder called Guillain-Barré syndrome. Occasionally, EBV can cause myocarditis (inflammation of the heart muscle), an abnormal decline in the number of blood platelets (thrombocytopenia), and inflammation of the testes (orchitis).

This virus can cause several types of cancer. In Africa, EBV causes Burkitt lymphoma; in Asia, nasopharyngeal cancer; and in the United States, a type of lymphoma. However, cancer caused by EBV is rare. It is not clear why some people infected with the virus get cancer while the vast majority does not. In patients with organ transplants, EBV can cause a malignant disorder called lymphoproliferative disease.

There is a rare genetic disease, seen mostly in boys, in which the body cannot control the EBV infection. This serious infection may lead to liver failure, decreases in the blood cells, or cancer and is often fatal.

The incubation period of infectious mononucleosis ranges from 30 to 50 days.

When to Call Your Pediatrician

Contact your pediatrician if your child has the major symptoms described here, especially a fever, sore throat, fatigue, and enlarged glands.

How Is the Diagnosis Made?

The diagnosis of infectious mononucleosis is usually made through a medical history, physical examination, and blood tests. These tests may include a complete blood count to check for unusual looking white blood cells (atypical lymphocytes). Blood tests can also detect increases in antibodies against EBV.

Treatment

Much of the treatment for mononucleosis is aimed at making your child more comfortable until the infection goes away on its own. For example

- Some pediatricians may recommend giving your youngster acetaminophen to reduce the fever and ease pain.
- Sore throats can be treated by gargling with warm water and salt.
- Bed rest can be important for a child feeling fatigued.

Because a virus causes mononucleosis, infected children should not be treated with antibacterials. In a small percentage of EBV-infected children, corticosteroids such as prednisone are given, but only if certain complications are present, such as inflamed tonsils that may block the breathing passages.

Children with infectious mononucleosis should not participate in contact sports until the swelling of their spleens subsides. If the body is hit in the area of an enlarged spleen, the spleen can rupture or tear open, causing internal bleeding that can lead to death. Keep in mind that this is uncommon and that mononucleosis rarely results in death.

What Is the Prognosis?

Most cases of infectious mononucleosis clear up in 1 to 3 weeks (although symptoms, particularly fatigue, can last for several additional weeks in some children). Patients with abnormal immune systems can have a more severe infection that further weakens the immune system, resulting in cancers or death caused by liver failure and bacterial infections.

Prevention

It is difficult to prevent the spread of this virus because people who have been infected can spread the virus for the rest of their lives. Your youngster should avoid infected saliva by not sharing drinking glasses, water bottles, or eating utensils.

No vaccine is available to protect against infectious mononucleosis.

Prevention Tip
When to share and when not to share? Your child should *not* share drinking glasses, water bottles, or eating utensils, which can carry infected saliva.

Rhinovirus Infections

More than any other illness, rhinoviruses *(rhin* means "nose") are associated with the common cold. Rhinoviruses may also cause some sore throats, ear infections, sinus infections, and to a lesser degree, pneumonia and bronchiolitis (infection of the small breathing passages of the lungs).

The average child has 8 to 10 colds during the first 2 years of her life. If she spends time in child care settings where she'll be exposed to other children with colds, she may catch even more colds.

Rhinoviruses are spread easily through person-to-person contact. When a child with a rhinovirus infection has a runny nose, nasal secretions get onto her hands and from there onto tables, toys, and other surfaces. Your child might touch the hands or skin of another youngster or toys that have been contaminated by the virus and then touch her own eyes or nose, infecting herself. She might breathe in airborne viruses spread by a sneeze or cough.

Although your child can develop a cold at any time of the year, these infections are most common during autumn and spring.

Signs and Symptoms

The signs and symptoms of the common cold are familiar to everyone. Your child's cold may start with a watery, runny nose that has a clear discharge. Later, the discharge becomes thicker and is often colored brownish, gray, or greenish. This colored nasal discharge is normal as the child begins to get over the cold.

Children may also develop symptoms such as

- Sneezing
- A mild fever (101°F–102°F or 38.3°C–38.9°C)
- Headaches
- Sore throat
- Cough
- Muscle aches
- A decrease in appetite

In some children, pus will appear on the tonsils, which could be a sign of a streptococcal infection (strep throat; see page 325).

The incubation period for a rhinovirus infection is usually 2 to 3 days. Symptoms generally persist for 10 to 14 days, sometimes less.

What You Can Do
When your child has a cold, make sure she gets enough rest. She should drink extra fluid if she has fever. If she is uncomfortable, talk to your pediatrician about giving her acetaminophen to reduce her fever. Don't give her over-the-counter cold remedies or cough medicines without first checking with your doctor. These over-the-counter medicines do not kill the virus and, in most circumstances, do not help with the symptoms.

When to Call Your Pediatrician
If your infant is 3 months or younger and develops cold symptoms, contact your pediatrician. Complications ranging from pneumonia to bronchiolitis are much more likely to develop in very young children.

Older youngsters generally don't need to be seen by a pediatrician when they have a cold. Nevertheless, contact your doctor if your older youngster has symptoms such as

- Lips or nails that turn blue
- Noisy or difficult breathing
- A persistent cough
- Excessive tiredness
- Ear pain, which may indicate an ear infection

How Is the Diagnosis Made?
Colds are typically diagnosed by observing your child's symptoms. In general, it is impractical to conduct laboratory tests to identify the organism that may be infecting a child with cold symptoms.

Treatment

Most rhinovirus infections are mild and do not require any specific treatment. Antibacterials are not effective against the common cold and other viral infections.

What Is the Prognosis?

Most colds go away on their own without complications.

Prevention

Keep an infant younger than 3 months from having close contact with children or adults who have colds.

Make sure your child washes her hands frequently, which will reduce the chances of getting the virus.

Roseola (Human Herpesvirus 6)

Roseola, also called exanthem subitum and sixth disease, is a common, contagious viral infection caused by the human herpesvirus (HHV) 6. This strain of the herpesvirus is different than the one that causes cold sores or genital herpes infections.

Roseola occurs most often in children aged 6 to 24 months. Youngsters typically have a high fever (greater than 103°F or 39.5°C) for 3 to 7 days. After the fever disappears, a rash will develop on the torso and spread to the arms, legs, back, and face. This rash usually only lasts for hours, but in some cases persists for several days. Some children have seizures associated with the high fever, but more often the fever is accompanied by a decrease in appetite, a mild cough, and a runny nose. This pattern of a high fever followed by a rash will help your pediatrician make the diagnosis of this infection. However, HHV-6 can also cause fever without rash or rash without fever.

Human herpesvirus 6 is spread from person to person via secretions from the respiratory tract. You can reduce the chances of your child becoming infected by making sure that he washes his hands thoroughly and frequently. There is no specific treatment for roseola, and it usually goes away without causing any complications. If your child's fever makes him uncomfortable, ask your pediatrician about lowering his temperature with acetaminophen.

Similar symptoms are associated with another herpesvirus infection caused by HHV-7. Many children infected with HHV-7 have only a mild illness. Human herpesvirus 7 may be responsible for second or recurrent cases of roseola that were originally caused by HHV-6. Like all of the viruses in the herpes family, these viruses will stay within the body for life. If a person's immune system becomes weakened by disease or medicines, the virus can reappear to cause fever and infection in the lungs or brain.

West Nile Virus

You might not be familiar with the term *arbovirus,* but thanks to widespread media coverage in recent years, most people now know about the arbovirus called West Nile virus.

Arboviruses are spread to humans by mosquitoes, ticks, and sandflies and can cause infections of the central nervous system, inflammation of joints, or fever with bleeding and liver infection. West Nile virus is now the most common arbovirus in the United States. Although other arboviruses occur in isolated parts of the United States, including the St Louis encephalitis virus, California encephalitis virus, and eastern equine encephalitis virus, West Nile virus has received the most attention. The first outbreak was in 1999 on the East Coast. Every year since then, the virus has moved across the United States and the number of people who become infected has increased.

Mosquitoes contract the virus by feeding on infected birds, or occasionally on other infected animals like horses, bats, and squirrels, and pass it along to humans. If an infected mosquito bites your child, the virus will multiply in her bloodstream, which could eventually cause her to become ill.

Signs and Symptoms

Most children who get West Nile virus have only mild symptoms or no symptoms at all. Symptoms may include

- Fever
- Headaches
- Body aches
- Nausea
- Vomiting
- Skin rash

In a very small number of infected children (fewer than 1% of cases), the illness can become severe and involve the brain (West Nile Virus encephalitis or meningitis). Symptoms involving the brain include high fever, stiff neck, severe headaches, muscle weakness, mental confusion, tremors, vision problems, convulsions, paralysis, and loss of consciousness.

When to Call Your Pediatrician
If your child experiences any of the symptoms that are associated with a severe West Nile virus infection, such as high fever, severe headaches, and a stiff neck, contact your pediatrician.

How Is the Diagnosis Made?
Your doctor will perform a lumbar puncture (spinal tap) to see if meningitis is present. The pediatrician may also order blood tests to help diagnose a West Nile virus infection. An EEG and imaging studies (computer tomography [CT] scan or magnetic resonance imaging [MRI]) are often done to help identify the type of brain infection.

Treatment
No specific medicine is available to treat West Nile virus infections. Fortunately, mild cases of West Nile virus infection do not require treatment. However, children who become severely ill will require hospitalization and supportive care.

What Is the Prognosis?
In most children with West Nile virus infections, the symptoms disappear in a few days.

Prevention
To protect your child from a West Nile virus infection, keep her away from places where mosquitoes gather or lay their eggs, such as standing water in bird baths and flower pots. Be sure to remove standing water in your yard and house.

Particularly if you live in a region where West Nile virus has been reported, apply insect repellent to your child's exposed skin when she's outdoors. Choose a repellent that contains the chemical DEET. However, products containing DEET should not be applied to infants younger than 2 months and be used only lightly around the eyes and mouth in all children. Because mosquitoes are most likely to bite at dawn and in the early evening, consider keeping your child indoors during these times of day.

West Nile virus can't be spread from person to person, so there's no need to keep your child away from someone who has the infection.

No vaccine has been developed to protect your child from West Nile virus.

Viral Infections

Virus	Infections	Usual Treatment	Comments
Adenovirus	Pneumonia, conjunctivitis, bladder infection, diarrhea	Supportive care	Common viral infection
Arboviruses: California encephalitis, eastern equine encephalitis, western equine encephalitis, Powassan encephalitis, St Louis encephalitis, Venezuelan equine encephalitis, West Nile encephalitis, Colorado tick fever, dengue, Japanese encephalitis, yellow fever	Encephalitis, meningitis, fever, fever and rash, hemorrhagic fever, joint infection	Supportive care	All these viruses are spread by mosquitoes; different viruses are present in different locations.
Arenaviruses: Junin, Machupo, Guanarito, Lassa, lymphocytic choriomeningitis	Meningitis, hemorrhagic fever	Supportive care	Lymphocytic choriomeningitis virus is the only one common in the United States; rodents are the usual host.
Astrovirus	Diarrhea	Supportive care	Not usually diagnosed because there is no simple laboratory test
Caliciviruses	Diarrhea	Supportive care	Not usually diagnosed because there is no simple laboratory test
Coronaviruses	Common cold, severe acute respiratory syndrome (SARS); may be a cause of Kawasaki disease	Supportive care	Not usually diagnosed because there is no simple laboratory test

Viral Infections, *continued*

Virus	Infections	Usual Treatment	Comments
Cytomegalovirus	None, mononucleosis-like illness, fetal infection, pneumonia	None, ganciclovir	Very common infection; can cause severe illness in fetuses and children with weakened immunity; causes latent infection
Enteroviruses: coxsackieviruses, echoviruses, enteroviruses, polio	Fever, meningitis, heart infection	None	Polio now eliminated from the Western hemisphere because of immunization
Epstein-Barr virus	Infectious mononucleosis	Supportive care	Causes latent infection; linked to some cancers
Hantaviruses: Sin Nombre, Bayou, Black Creek Canal, New York	Pneumonia, hemorrhagic fever	Supportive care	Outbreak in southwest related to mice
Hepatitis A virus	Hepatitis	Supportive care	Can be prevented with immunization
Hepatitis B virus	Hepatitis	Supportive care; some antiviral drugs are beginning to be used in children.	Infections decreasing because of immunization
Hepatitis C virus	Hepatitis	Supportive care; some antiviral drugs are beginning to be used in children.	Often causes chronic infection
Hepatitis D virus	More severe hepatitis in people with hepatitis B virus	Usually supportive care	Needs hepatitis B virus to infect, so this is prevented by the hepatitis B vaccine.
Hepatitis E virus	Hepatitis	Supportive care	Travelers are at risk.
Herpes simplex type 1 virus	Cold sores, mouth infection	None or acyclovir	Once you are infected, the virus stays with you and can reactivate.

Viral Infections, *continued*

Virus	Infections	Usual Treatment	Comments
Herpes simplex type 2 virus	Genital ulcers	None or acyclovir	Once you are infected, the virus stays with you and can reactivate.
Human herpesviruses 6 and 7	Fever with rash	Supportive care	Once you are infected, the virus stays with you and can reactivate.
Human herpesvirus 8	Kaposi sarcoma (a type of cancer)	None known	Rare in children; occurs in people with acquired immunodeficiency syndrome (AIDS)
Human immunodeficiency virus	AIDS	Many antivirals, combinations used	Infection rate decreasing in children because pregnant women are screened and treated; sexually transmitted disease
Influenza virus	Flu	Supportive care; antivirals: amantadine, rimantadine, oseltamivir, zanamivir	Can prevent or decrease illness by immunization
Measles virus	Measles	Supportive care, vitamin A	Almost gone in the United States because of immunization
Molluscum contagiosum	Skin infection	None, curette	This pox virus causes minimal illness but long-lasting small skin lesions (raised bumps with a center core where the virus lives).
Mumps	Mumps	Supportive care	Almost gone in United States because of immunization

Viral Infections, *continued*

Virus	Infections	Usual Treatment	Comments
Papillomavirus	Warts	Topical agents	Common; some types are sexually transmitted and associated with cancer of the cervix.
Parainfluenza virus	Croup, colds	Supportive care	Autumn and spring
Parvovirus B19	Fifth disease	Supportive care, transfusion	Serious illness in the fetus and children with hemolytic anemias such as sickle cell disease
Rabies virus	Rabies	None known to be effective	Preventable with immunizations
Respiratory syncytial virus	Cold, bronchiolitis, pneumonia	Supportive care	Passive immunization decreases severe illness.
Rhinoviruses	Colds	Supportive care	More than 100 types
Rotavirus	Diarrhea and vomiting	Supportive care	A vaccine was available, but was withdrawn; another vaccine is being tested.
Rubella virus	German measles	Supportive care	Serious infection in the fetus; can be prevented by immunization
Varicella-zoster virus	Chickenpox, shingles	None, acyclovir	Incidence of infection is decreasing because of immunization; the virus stays in the body once a child is infected and can reactivate as shingles.
Variola virus	Smallpox	Unclear; cidofovir may be useful.	Eliminated by immunization, but feared as a weapon of bioterrorism

See Also

CHAPTER 34

Fungi

Chapter at a Glance

There are thousands of types of fungi, and you're probably familiar with many of them—from mushrooms to mold to mildew. Some antibiotics, including penicillin, are actually produced by fungi.

Many fungi normally live on or in the human body, on the skin or in the intestinal tract, without causing any illnesses. If they overgrow, infections can occur. In other parts of this book, you'll find descriptions of fungal infections like ringworm of the scalp (tinea capitis), athlete's foot, and jock itch. Here are some others that may cause illness.

Aspergillosis

Aspergillosis is an infection that frequently affects the lungs. It is caused by the fungus *Aspergillus*. Species of *Aspergillus* are found on decaying vegetation and in soil. When the mold becomes airborne in dust, it can make its way into homes through open windows or air vents. In certain children, it can lead to allergic reactions and infections.

When aspergillosis causes an allergic reaction, it affects the lungs, triggering symptoms such as wheezing, coughing up of brown mucus, and a low-grade fever. This form of aspergillosis is called allergic aspergillosis and occurs most often in children with chronic asthma or cystic fibrosis.

Aspergillus species can form fungus balls called aspergillomas. These form within preexisting holes in the lungs. Such holes are found in children who have lung cysts or cystic fibrosis. Aspergillomas can also be found in the lungs of adults with cavities formed during tuberculosis or other types of pneumonia.

Aspergillus species can cause severe disease in children whose immune systems are weakened. The lungs are often involved, as are the sinuses and ear canals. This is a serious infection (*invasive* aspergillosis) that often destroys the lungs and can result in death.

To diagnose aspergillosis, your pediatrician will evaluate your child's symptoms. If he has the allergic type of aspergillosis, your pediatrician will order blood tests to measure immunoglobulin E levels and antibodies to the fungus. If your child has an impaired immune system and aspergillosis is suspected, the doctor will order an x-ray film or computed tomography (CT) scan of the infected area. Cultures of sputum or lung tissue are needed to identify the fungus. Treatment for invasive infection involves the use of antifungal medications such as amphotericin B. Treatment of allergic aspergillosis involves steroids as well as antifungal agents.

Thrush and Other *Candida* Infections

The fungus *Candida* is normally found on and in the body in small amounts. It is present on the skin and in the mouth, as well as in the intestinal tract and genital area. Most of the time, *Candida* does not cause any symptoms. When these organisms overgrow, they can cause infections (candidiasis), which sometimes can become chronic. If the fungus enters the bloodstream, the infection can spread to other parts of the body. Bloodstream infections are most common in newborns, children with long-term intravenous catheters, and children with weakened immune systems caused by illnesses or medicines.

Candidiasis can affect the skin, mucous membranes (eg, mouth, throat), fingernails, eyes, and skin folds of the neck and armpits, as well as the diaper region (eg, vagina, folds of the groin). The oral infection, called *thrush,* frequently occurs in infants and toddlers.

If *Candida* infections become chronic or occur in the mouth of older children, they may be a sign of an immune deficiency, such as human immunodeficiency virus (HIV) infection. Very low birth weight babies are susceptible to candidiasis as well. Newborns can acquire the infection from their mothers, not only while they're still in the uterus, but also during passage through the vagina during birth.

Most of these infections are caused by *Candida albicans,* a yeast-like fungus, although other species of *Candida* are sometimes responsible. In some cases, children can develop candidiasis after being treated with antibacterials.

Signs and Symptoms

When an infant develops a *Candida* infection, symptoms can include painful white or yellow patches on the tongue, lips, gums, palate (roof of mouth), and inner cheeks. It can also spread into the esophagus, causing pain when swallowing. Candidiasis can make a diaper rash worse, producing a reddening and sensitivity of the affected area and a raised red border in some cases. Teenaged girls who develop a yeast infection of the vagina and the surrounding area may have symptoms such as itching; pain and redness; a thick, "cheesy" vaginal discharge; and pain when urinating.

Infection of the bloodstream occurs in children who are hospitalized or at home with intravenous catheters. A yeast infection often follows antibiotic therapy. Infections occur in children with cancer who are receiving chemotherapy. In these cases, the fungus in the gut gets into the blood system. Once in the blood, the yeast can travel throughout the body, causing infection of the heart, lungs, liver, kidneys, brain, and skin. The early signs of infection are fever and blockage of the intravenous catheter.

How Is the Diagnosis Made?

Your pediatrician will often make the diagnosis by examining your child and her symptoms. Scrapings of *Candida* lesions inside the mouth or elsewhere can be examined under the microscope for signs of the infection. An ultrasound or CT scan can detect candidal lesions that have developed in the brain, kidney, liver, or spleen. Cultures of the blood or mouth lesions are taken to grow the fungus in the laboratory and identify the type and sensitivity of the yeast.

Treatment

Antifungal drugs are used to treat candidiasis. The antibiotic nystatin is often prescribed for children with superficial infections such as oral thrush or a *Candida*-related diaper rash.

The specific medicines given for candidiasis vary, depending on the part of the body where the infection is concentrated. For example

- *Mouth and airway* (associated with a weakened immune system): nystatin, clotrimazole, fluconazole, itraconazole
- *Esophagus:* nystatin, fluconazole, itraconazole
- *Skin:* topical medicines such as nystatin, miconazole, clotrimazole, naftifine, and ketoconazole, among others
- *Vagina:* topical clotrimazole, miconazole, butoconazole, terconazole, tioconazole

If candidiasis has spread through the bloodstream to various parts of the body, your pediatrician will usually recommend treatment with an intravenous medicine such as amphotericin B. This medicine causes many side effects, but it is still a reliable medicine for serious, invasive fungal infections.

What Is the Prognosis?

Once treatment starts, most candidiasis infections get better within about 2 weeks. Recurrences are fairly common. Long-lasting thrush is sometimes related to pacifiers. The infection is much more difficult to treat in children with catheters or weakened immune systems. The catheter usually must be removed or replaced and tests are done to determine whether infection has spread to other parts of the body. Antifungal therapy may need to be given for weeks to months.

Prevention

To reduce the risk of candidiasis in your baby's diaper area, keep the skin as clean and dry as possible, changing diapers frequently. Fungal infections (thrush or vaginitis) often follow courses of antibacterials. To avoid this, it is important to use antibiotics only when necessary.

Oral nystatin and fluconazole are often used to prevent candidiasis in children with weakened immune systems.

Other Fungal Diseases

At times, children may become infected with fungi that only rarely infect people. In many instances, the children most susceptible to these infections have weakened immune systems because of cancer, chemotherapy, corticosteroids, organ transplantation, or an HIV infection. However, even children with normal disease-fighting systems can get these infections by breathing in the fungi. Certain organisms can enter the body through cuts or abrasions in the skin.

Here are some brief descriptions of some of the fungal diseases that your child could develop. In some cases, they occur so uncommonly that treatment recommendations are not clear, especially for children. Ask your pediatrician for a referral to a pediatric infectious disease specialist if your youngster is diagnosed with one of the following fungal infections:

Hyalohyphomycosis

Fungi from the *Fusarium* species may cause this infection. These fungi can enter the body through the respiratory tract, sinuses, or skin. It may cause signs and symptoms associated with a sinus infection (sinusitis), a urinary tract infection, a blood infection, or meningitis. These infections may occur in children with weakened immune systems. Your pediatrician will diagnose hyalohyphomycosis by taking a blood culture or tissue specimen and having it tested in the laboratory. High-dose amphotericin B or fluconazole have been used in treating hyalohyphomycosis.

Malassezia species cause a common, superficial skin infection known as tinea versicolor or pityriasis versicolor. The skin of the face, torso, arms, and neck is covered with many round and scaly red areas. These areas fail to tan during the summer, but are relatively darker in the winter. The infection is most common in teenagers and young adults. Your pediatrician will make the diagnosis based on the appearance of the rash. A culture can be taken, if needed. Selenium sulfide lotion or shampoo is used for treatment. Ketoconazole shampoo is also effective, as are several other antifungals that are applied directed onto the affected area. Oral antifungals such as ketoconazole, fluconazole, and itraconazole have been shown to be effective in adults. These drugs are used less commonly in children.

Penicilliosis

Children infected with HIV may be susceptible to a fungal disease called penicilliosis caused by *Penicillium marneffei*. This fungus is found in soil and decaying vegetation as well as in the air. It can cause signs and symptoms such as lung inflammation (pneumonitis) and acne-like skin lesions on the face, torso, arms, and legs. Your pediatrician may have a blood culture or tissue sample tested in the laboratory as part of the diagnostic process. Amphotericin B or itraconazole are commonly prescribed treatments for penicilliosis.

Phaeohyphomycosis

Phaeohyphomycosis is a large category of fungal infections that are caused by organisms from the *Bipolaris, Curvularia, Exserohilum, Pseudallescheria,* and *Scedosporium* species. These infections often involve the skin and, in some cases, the nasal passages and sinuses. They also can infect the brain, bones, and heart (endocarditis). Superficial infections can occur in children with healthy immune defenses, while more serious infections occur in children with weakened immune systems. To make the diagnosis, your doctor will order tests that examine affected tissues under the microscope. The pediatrician may also take cultures of the tissue to try to grow the fungi in the laboratory. Your child's doctor will recommend treatment with medicines such as itraconazole or amphotericin B or the surgical removal of infected tissue.

Trichosporonosis

Children with weakened immune systems are susceptible to trichosporonosis, which can infect the lung, heart, or bloodstream. The fungus *Trichosporon beigelii*, which can produce skin lesions on the torso, face, and arms, causes trichosporonosis. Other symptoms include a cough, fever, and bloody sputum. This organism is found in soil and can enter the body through the respiratory tract, gastrointestinal system, or skin wounds. When it infects humans, it is potentially life threatening. Treatment typically involves the use of amphotericin B or fluconazole.

Zygomycosis

As with many other fungal infections, zygomycosis is most likely to occur in children with weakened immune systems. It may develop in children with leukemia, lymphoma, or diabetes and those who have used nonsterile bandages on wounds or cuts. Zygomycosis is caused by fungi from the *Rhizopus, Mucor, Absidia,* and *Rhizomucor* species and can cause nose and sinus infections. Affected children may have a fever, nasal congestion, and sinus discomfort. If the infection spreads, it can affect the lungs and brain and, in the worst cases, cause pneumonia, infection of the brain, seizures, paralysis, and death. This infection is diagnosed with laboratory tests examining nasal discharges and phlegm, as well as by conducting biopsies of, for example, lung lesions. Treatment includes surgical removal of the infected tissue, if possible, and use of medicines such as high-dose amphotericin B.

Fungal Infections

Fungus	Infections	Usual Treatment	Comments
Aspergillus species: *fumigatus, flavus, teres, niger*	Aspergillosis: allergic, fungus ball, invasive	Amphotericin B, itraconazole	Allergic type occurs in children with cystic fibrosis and some children with asthma; invasive disease occurs in children with weakened immunity.
Blastomyces dermatitidis	Blastomycosis	Amphotericin B	Found only in certain geographic areas—southeast United States, Great Lakes, central United States
Candida albicans	Thrush, diaper rash, blood and organs	Nystatin, amphotericin B, fluconazole	Minor infections in children; serious infections in premature babies and children with weakened immunity or intravenous catheters

Fungal Infections, *continued*

Fungus	Infections	Usual Treatment	Comments
Candida species other than *albicans: tropicalis, parapsilosis, glabrata, krusei, guilliermondii, lusitaniae, dubliniensis*	Blood and organ infections	Amphotericin B, fluconazole or other azoles	Infections occur in premature newborns and children with weakened immunity.
Coccidioides immitis	Coccidioidomycosis	None, amphotericin B	Found only in certain geographic areas—California, Arizona, New Mexico, Texas, Mexico, and Central and South America
Cryptococcus neoformans	Cryptococcosis: meningitis, bone, joint, skin infections	Amphotericin B	Uncommon in children; occurs in people with weakened immunity
Fusarium species	Pneumonia, skin, sinusitis	Amphotericin B	Occurs in children with weakened immunity
Histoplasma capsulatum	Pneumonia	None, amphotericin B	Found only in certain geographic areas—Ohio, Mississippi, Missouri river valleys
Malassezia species	Blood infection, skin (tinea versicolor)	Remove catheter, fluconazole	Blood infection in children who are receiving feedings by vein
Paracoccidioides brasiliensis	Pneumonia	Amphotericin B	Found in Mexico and Central and South America
Penicillium marneffei	Pneumonia	Itraconazole	Occurs in children with AIDS
Phaeohyphomycosis: *Bipolaris, Curvularia, Exserohilum, Pseudallescheria boydii, Scedosporium*	Sinusitis	Itraconazole	Occurs mostly in children with weakened immunity

Fungal Infections, *continued*

Fungus	Infections	Usual Treatment	Comments
Pneumocystis jiroveci	Pneumonia	Trimethoprim sulfamethoxazole	Has properties of a parasite; occurs in children with weakened immunity
Rhizopus, Mucor, Absidia, Rhizomucor	Pneumonia, skin	Amphotericin B	Occurs in children with weakened immunity
Ringworm fungi: *Trichophyton tonsurans, Microsporum canis, Microsporum audouinii, Trichophyton mentagrophytes, Trichophyton rubrum, Epidermophyton floccosum*	Ringworm: head, body, groin, feet; jock itch, athlete's feet	A variety of anti-fungal creams or oral antifungals (eg, griseofulvin, fluconazole)	Spread by direct skin contact or contact with contaminated towels
Sporothrix schenckii	Skin	Itraconazole	Present in soil and on thorny plants (roses)
Trichosporon beigelii	Blood, lungs, heart	Amphotericin B	Occurs in children with weakened immunity

See Also

CHAPTER 35

Parasites

Chapter at a Glance

Infections caused by parasites are common in many parts of the world. These types of infections are less common in the United States and other developed countries, however, largely as a result of improved sanitation methods. The eggs of these parasites are usually found in feces. The parasites can enter the human body through the mouth (the fecal-oral route), or sometimes the larva of the parasites enters the body directly through the skin.

Some parasites are single-celled protozoa that can only be seen under the microscope. Others, such as tapeworms, can reach several feet in length. Parasites cannot live on their own and must live in and off another animal, often called the host animal. Furthermore, the parasite causes harm to its host. The amount of harm varies dramatically depending on the parasite and, of course, the host animal. Parasites that use humans as their host are discussed in this chapter. Many of these parasites use more than one type of animal as a host at different stages of life. Sometimes humans are accidental hosts rather than the preferred host.

Parasites go through a life cycle that is sometimes complex. There may be eggs (ova), which hatch to form larvae, which, in turn, can form cysts or develop into the adult organism.

In this chapter, you'll read about several diseases caused by parasites that can make your child sick. Descriptions of other parasitic infections, including malaria, giardiasis, amebiasis, and trichomoniasis, appear in other chapters of the book.

Ascariasis (*Ascaris lumbricoides* Infections)

A large roundworm, *Ascaris lumbricoides* is the cause of a parasitic infection of the small intestines called ascariasis. Humans are the preferred hosts for this parasite. Children become infected with this disease more often than adults. The illness often develops after a child puts his hands in his mouth after playing in soil contaminated by feces containing the roundworm eggs. Eating unwashed fruit or vegetables that were grown in contaminated soil can also cause ascariasis. Although the infection can occur in any part of the world, it is more common in developing countries with poor sanitation and areas where human feces are used as fertilizer.

The entire life cycle for this parasite occurs within humans. The adult worm in the bowels of a child lays thousands of eggs a day, which then pass into the stools. In areas with poor sanitation or where human feces are used as fertilizer, the eggs will mature for 2 to 3 weeks in the soil and become infectious on the surface of unwashed fruits or vegetables. If a child plays in the contaminated soil, he can get the eggs directly onto his fingers and put his fingers into his mouth, or a person could eat the parasite's eggs that may end up on the surface of unwashed vegetables. After the eggs hatch in the bowel, the larvae burrow through the bowel wall and into the bloodstream. The blood carries the larvae to the lung, where the parasites can enter the breathing sacs. The larvae then crawl up the breathing tubes and into the throat, where they are swallowed. Once they are back in the gut, the larvae mature to adult worms.

Signs and Symptoms
Most children with *A lumbricoides* infections do not have any signs and symptoms. Sometimes youngsters have stomach cramps and, in the more serious cases, even intestinal obstruction that could lead to vomiting. Worms that travel into the bile ducts can cause blockage and infection of the liver, pancreas, or both. When the roundworm's larvae migrate through the lungs, they can cause an allergic lung inflammation (pneumonitis) along with fever, cough, and wheezing. Sometimes, the worms are seen coming out of the anus, mouth, or nose.

When to Call Your Pediatrician
Contact your pediatrician if your child has any of the symptoms or signs described here, especially if they continue to get worse. Let your doctor know if your child has traveled to parts of the world where parasitic infections are common (ie, areas of poor sanitation, the tropics).

How Is the Diagnosis Made?
Most often, this infection is diagnosed by seeing a worm or worms in the diaper or toilet bowl or detecting eggs in a sample of your child's stool. The eggs are microscopic in size, while the worms are several inches in length and have an appearance similar to an earthworm.

Treatment
To treat *A lumbricoides* infections, your pediatrician may prescribe a single dose of medicine called albendazole or 3 days of pyrantel or mebendazole. These treatments should be given whether the infection causes symptoms.

Surgery is occasionally needed to relieve an intestinal or bile duct blockage.

What Is the Prognosis?
With proper treatment, children fully recover from ascariasis.

Prevention
Reinfection is common. Keep your child away from soil that could be contaminated with human feces. Make sure you wash vegetables and fruits prior to eating.

Hookworm Infections

Hookworms are small (less than 0.5 inches long) parasitic worms that can cause infections in the small intestines. The major species of hookworms associated with infections in humans are *Ancylostoma duodenale* and *Necator americanus*. They get their name from the teeth ("hooks") or cutting plates in their mouths by which they attach themselves to the intestinal wall.

Hookworm diseases are most common in tropical and subtropical climates. These infections develop after a person has contact with soil contaminated with human feces. Children are at high risk because they often play barefoot in areas with contaminated soil. In soil, hookworm eggs hatch and form larvae, which then burrow through the skin of a person's foot and crawl into the blood. The blood carries the larvae to the lungs, where they enter into the air sacs. The hookworms then crawl up the breathing tubes to the throat, where they are swallowed. The larvae pass through the stomach and mature into adult worms in the bowel. The worm holds onto the bowel wall with hooks, which cause minor bleeding. Adult hookworms live in the bowel and lay eggs that pass out of the child with the stool.

Signs and Symptoms
Most children with hookworm infections have no signs or symptoms. However, especially when the infection is long term, it can cause iron deficiency and anemia (low red blood cells) because of bleeding from the bowel wall where the worm is attached. Other symptoms include mild diarrhea and stomach cramps. An itchy, red skin rash (ground itch) can appear on the feet where the larvae entered the body. Lung inflammation with cough, wheezing, and fever rarely occur while the larvae migrate through the lungs. Some infections can produce a hoarse voice, nausea, and vomiting after directly eating and swallowing larvae. Several weeks after exposure to this hookworm, a loss of appetite and weight loss may occur. Chronic infections can lead to poor nutrition and growth.

How Is the Diagnosis Made?

A stool sample from your child will be tested in the laboratory to look for evidence of hookworm eggs.

Treatment

Antiparasitic drugs are used to treat hookworm infections. The oral medicines commonly prescribed include a single dose of albendazole or 3 days of mebendazole or pyrantel. One to 2 weeks following treatment, your pediatrician may test another stool sample from your child. The drug therapy should be repeated if the infection persists.

Iron supplements are recommended if your child develops anemia.

What Is the Prognosis?

Proper treatment of hookworm infections results in a high recovery rate.

Prevention

Reinfection is common. Wearing shoes prevents the larvae from entering the body through the feet. If your child goes barefoot, make sure she avoids contact with soil that may be contaminated with human feces.

Tapeworm Diseases

Tapeworms can cause intestinal infections. When they do, any of a number of tapeworm species may be involved. These may include *Taenia saginata* (beef tapeworms), *Taenia solium* (from pork), or *Diphyllobothrium latum* (from fish). Tapeworms require human hosts to live out their life cycles. They affect people through contact with contaminated human feces found in soil, fresh water, or food. Children can develop these diseases by eating raw or undercooked meat from animals or fish that are infected with tapeworms. Contaminated food contains cysts of the parasite. Your child may have a tapeworm infection and have no symptoms.

When a child eats tapeworm cysts in undercooked beef, pork, or fish, the cyst survives the stomach acids and releases the larvae. The parasite grows within the child's bowel to become an adult tapeworm. The adult tapeworm has up to 1,000 segments called *proglottids,* each of which contain 30,000 to 100,000 eggs. A proglottid separates from the adult and travels out of the intestines with the stool. The segment is about 0.5 to 1 inch in length and can sometimes be seen moving in the stool or on the anus. If a child or adult has an adult tapeworm, they will pass segments filled with eggs in their stools. These eggs are then released onto soil and eaten by cattle or pigs, in which they hatch, enter the bloodstream, and form cysts in the meat, completing the parasitic life cycle.

These eggs can also get onto the hands of humans and then into foods that they are preparing. The eggs of the fish tapeworm do not affect humans. These eggs need a different host called a copepod, which is a small fresh-water shrimplike animal. The copepod is eaten by a fish, which then becomes contaminated with the tapeworm, thus completing the life cycle. The eggs of the beef tapeworm also do not affect people. However, when a person eats an egg from pork tapeworms, the egg hatches in the bowel and the larva emerges. The larva then burrows through the wall of the bowel to enter the bloodstream. Because the larva is not in a pig (the preferred host of a pork tapeworm), it cannot go through its normal life cycle. Thus, in its human host, the larva gets stuck in tissues such as the muscles, liver, and brain. Within the tissue, the larva forms a cyst. Cysts within the brain can cause seizures.

When adult tapeworms cause human illness, doctors use the name taeniasis to describe the infection. In contrast, when pork tapeworm larvae lead to illness, it is called cysticercosis.

Tapeworm infections tend to be more common in parts of the world with poor sanitation systems or where beef, pork, and fish are eaten raw or poorly cooked. Some tapeworms can grow up to 30 feet and live as long as 25 years!

Signs and Symptoms

Many tapeworm infections are symptom free. When symptoms are present, they often include

- Nausea
- Diarrhea
- Stomach pain

Fish tapeworm competes with its human host for vitamin B12 in the intestine and, in prolonged cases, can cause pernicious anemia.

Children who ingest pork tapeworm eggs can develop tapeworm cysts (cysticercosis) within their internal organs. If these cysts occur in the brain, they can cause serious symptoms such as seizures, behavioral disturbances, and even death.

When to Call Your Pediatrician

Contact your pediatrician if you notice something moving in your child's stool that could be a worm segment, your youngster has prolonged stomach pain, or any of the other symptoms appear without another, more obvious cause. If you think your child might have been exposed to tapeworms within the past 2 to 3 months, let your pediatrician know. Make sure your doctor is aware if your child has traveled recently to a developing country.

How Is the Diagnosis Made?

To diagnose a tapeworm infection, your pediatrician will send your child's stool sample for tests to detect eggs or worm segments of the suspected tapeworm. Children with cysticercosis usually do not have adult tapeworms. Therefore, eggs are not usually found in the stool. Blood tests can be done to look for antibodies to the tapeworm. In patients with seizures, imaging of the brain with computed tomography (CT) or magnetic resonance imaging (MRI) is performed to look for cysts or other abnormalities.

Treatment

Your pediatrician may prescribe oral drugs such as praziquantel or, as an alternative, niclosamide to treat a tapeworm infestation. These medicines are typically given in a single dose.

Other antiparasitic drugs, including albendazole and praziquantel, are available specifically for treating cysticercosis. Anticonvulsant medications should be used to control seizures if they occur.

What Is the Prognosis?

Drug treatment for tapeworms is very effective and can completely kill the parasite. Treatment for the cysts will get rid of them, but the area of the brain may remain abnormal and seizures may continue.

Prevention

To reduce your child's risk of developing tapeworm infections, do not allow him to eat raw or undercooked fish, beef, or pork. Be sure he always practices good hygiene, including regular hand washing, especially after using the bathroom. To avoid cysticercosis, be sure that all food handlers wash their hands. Proper sanitation is the key to the elimination of tapeworm infestation worldwide.

Toxoplasmosis (*Toxoplasma gondii* Infections)

The infection toxoplasmosis is caused by the *Toxoplasma gondii* parasite. Cats are the usual host for these parasites, but children, adults, and other animals can also be infected. Humans and animals can become infected if they swallow the microscopic eggs of the parasite or eat cysts in under-cooked meats from cattle, sheep, pigs, or wild animals such as deer.

The *T gondii* parasite can only mature to an adult in the body of a cat. The adult parasite lives in the gut of cats, and the eggs enter the environment through the cat feces. The eggs must mature in the soil for 1 to 5 days before they become contagious for people or other animals. When a person or an animal other than a cat eats the mature egg, it hatches within the bowel and burrows through the bowel wall. When the parasite is in a human (the non-preferred host), it cannot mature to an adult, but instead becomes a cyst in a muscle or organ. These cysts can become reactivated later in life, especially if a person's immune system is weakened by illness or medicines.

Humans can get the parasite by

- Eating raw or undercooked meat that contains cysts
- Drinking untreated water contaminated with mature eggs
- Eating unwashed fruits and vegetables grown in contaminated soil
- Touching your mouth with your hand after handling soil or sand that contains mature eggs

If a pregnant woman becomes infected with *T gondii,* she can pass the infection to her unborn fetus.

Signs and Symptoms

When the parasite is passed from the pregnant mother to the unborn fetus, the infections are less frequent but more severe early in pregnancy, and more frequent but less severe in the later months. Most infants born with toxoplasmosis have no signs or symptoms at birth. Some babies will have signs and symptoms that include

- Rash
- Swollen lymph glands
- Jaundice
- Low number of blood platelets
- Enlargement of the liver and spleen
- Tiredness

Although 70% to 90% of the infants born with toxoplasmosis do not have any signs or symptoms of infection, serious complications caused by inflammation of the eye and brain often appear in the ensuing months and years. These can include vision problems, varying levels of developmental delay, seizures, deafness, and extra cerebrospinal fluid in the brain (hydrocephalus). Some infected fetuses may die in the uterus or within the first few days after birth.

When children or adults develop toxoplasmosis, illness is uncommon. When it does occur, it may look similar to infectious mononucleosis and include

- Fever
- Swollen lymph glands, particularly in the region of the neck
- Headache
- Muscle aches and pains
- Sore throat
- Enlargement of the liver and spleen
- General feelings of being ill

A pregnant woman with toxoplasmosis may be symptom free, but she can still pass the infection to her unborn baby. This is most common when the infection occurs near the end of the pregnancy.

People with weakened immune systems can develop blindness because of cysts within the retina (the part of the eye involved in vision). Meningitis or encephalitis may be caused by cysts within the brain. Other complications include pneumonia or, less often, widespread infection involving many organs in the body.

How Is the Diagnosis Made?

The diagnosis of toxoplasmosis is made by blood tests that can detect antibodies to the parasite. These tests can be difficult to perform and interpret and should be done with the guidance of specialists in this field.

If you are pregnant and believe you may have become infected with *T gondii,* ask your doctor to test you for the presence of this parasite.

Treatment

Older children and teenagers with a normal immune system do not require specific medical treatment for toxoplasmosis unless they are pregnant. All infected newborns should be treated to avoid eye problems and inflammation of the brain. Patients with a weakened immune system usually require treatment. Your pediatrician will often call in a specialist in infectious diseases to help decide on management.

The most common medicines used are a combination of pyrimethamine and sulfadiazine or clindamycin. Treatment continues for several months. Newborns may require treatment for a year. Pyrimethamine is always given with folinic acid (leucovorin) to prevent damage to the liver and bone marrow. In certain patients, corticosteroids may be prescribed for eye problems caused by the infection.

What Is the Prognosis?
Early treatment can be very successful for babies who are infected before birth, although many will develop eye or brain problems despite treatment.

Toxoplasmosis acquired after birth generally goes away on its own without any lasting complications. However, if your child has a weakened immune system because of, for example, a human immunodeficiency virus (HIV) infection or cancer chemotherapy, she is more likely to develop a severe form of the disease that can damage the brain, eyes, or other organs.

Prevention
Pregnant women should not change cat litter boxes or do any gardening and landscaping to avoid being exposed to cat feces, which may contain these parasites. If these activities are unavoidable, wear gloves and wash your hands thoroughly afterward. If you do catch toxoplasmosis, early treatment can prevent many of the complications to the fetus.

Prevention Tip: Women during pregnancy should not change cat litter boxes or engage in any gardening and landscaping to avoid contracting toxoplasmosis from cat feces. A pregnant woman with toxoplasmosis may be symptom free, but she can still pass the infection to her unborn baby.

To reduce the chances of ingesting foods with *T gondii*, cook all meat—beef, pork, lamb, and wild game—to an internal temperature of 150°F to 170°F until the meat is no longer pink. Also, follow these recommendations

- Wash or peel all fruits and vegetables.
- Take steps to prevent contaminating other foods with raw or undercooked meat.
- Wash your hands, cutting boards, other kitchen surfaces, and kitchen cutlery and utensils after handling and preparing raw meat, fruits, and vegetables.

- Wash your hands after gardening or having other contact with soil or sand in sandboxes.

To reduce the chances that your pet cats will become infected, feed them only commercially made cat food. Keep them from eating undercooked kitchen meat scraps or hunting wild rodents. Cats who go outdoors may be exposed to soil contaminated by eggs from infected cats' feces.

Parasitic Infections

Parasite	Infection	Usual Treatment	Comments
Ancylostoma duodenale	Hookworm	Albendazole	Can cause anemia
Ascaris lumbricoides	Ascariasis	Pyrantel pamoate	Uncommon in the United States
Babesia microti	Babesiosis	None	Transmitted by ticks
Balantidium coli	Balantidiasis (diarrhea)	Tetracycline	Uncommon infection
Blastocystis hominis	Diarrhea	Unclear	Role as a pathogen not clear; may be an innocent bystander
Cryptosporidium parvum	Cryptosporidiosis (diarrhea)	Nitazoxanide	Outbreaks caused by contamination of water; chronic diarrhea in children with weakened immunity
Cyclospora cayetanensis	Cyclosporiasis (diarrhea)	Trimethoprim sulfamethoxazole	A cause of traveler's diarrhea
Diphyllobothrium latum	Tapeworm	Praziquantel	Fish tapeworm; acquired by eating raw or undercooked fish
Dipylidium caninum	Tapeworm	Praziquantel	Dog tapeworm; child is infected by eating a flea.
Echinococcus granulosus and *Echinococcus multilocularis*	Hydatid disease; cysts in the lung or liver	Surgery, albendazole	Southwest United States; dogs and sheep are the usual hosts.
Entamoeba histolytica	Amebiasis, diarrhea, abscesses	Metronidazole plus iodoquinol	Rare in the United States; travelers are at risk.

Parasitic Infections, *continued*

Parasite	Infection	Usual Treatment	Comments
Enterobius vermicularis	Pinworm	Mebendazole	Infection very common; usually there are minimal or no symptoms.
Filariasis: *Wuchereria bancrofti, Brugia malayi, Brugia timori*	Lymphatic infection, elephantiasis	Diethylcarbamazine	Risk for travelers; transmitted by mosquitoes
Giardia lamblia	Giardiasis (diarrhea)	Metronidazole	Common in child care, campers, travelers
Hymenolepis nana	Tapeworm	Praziquantel	Smallest of the tapeworms
Isospora belli	Diarrhea	Trimethoprim sulfamethoxazole	Occurs mostly in children with weakened immunity
Leishmania species	Leishmaniasis: skin, mouth, organs	None, special drugs from the Centers for Disease Control and Prevention	Not found in the United States; found in the Middle East, India, and some parts of Africa
Microsporidia: *Encephalitozoon, Enterocytozoon, Nosema, Pleistophora, Trachipleistophora, Brachiola, Vittaforma*	Diarrhea	None known	Occurs most often in children with weakened immunity
Naegleria fowleri, Acanthamoeba species, *Balamuthia mandrillaris*	Meningitis, eye infection	Difficult to treat meningitis; topical medicines used for the eye infection	Rare; swimmers in warm lakes at risk; contact lens users at risk for the eye infection
Necator americanus	Hookworm	Albendazole	Can cause anemia
Onchocerca volvulus	River blindness	Ivermectin	Transmitted by a type of black fly; found in Central and South America and Africa

Parasitic Infections, *continued*

Parasite	Infection	Usual Treatment	Comments
Paragonimus westermani	Pneumonia	Praziquantel	Found in Asia
Plasmodium species: *falciparum, vivax, ovale, malariae*	Malaria	Depends on the type	Risk to travelers; transmitted by mosquitoes
Schistosoma species: *mansoni, japonicum, haematobium, mekongi, intercalatum*	Fever, diarrhea, blood in the urine	Praziquantel	Found in Africa, South America, and Asia; acquired while swimming
Strongyloides stercoralis	Strongyloidiasis	Ivermectin	Can cause severe infection in people with weakened immunity; found in the tropics
Toxocara species: *cati, canis*	None, flu-like symptoms	None, albendazole	Roundworms of dogs and cats; children inadvertently eat the eggs present in the soil.
Toxoplasma gondii	Mononucleosis-like syndrome; eye and brain infection	Pyrimethamine, sulfadiazine, clindamycin, spiramycin	Causes serious infection in the fetus and children with weakened immunity
Trichinella spiralis	Diarrhea, rash, muscle aches	Mebendazole	Acquired by eating undercooked wild game
Trichomonas vaginalis	Vaginitis	Metronidazole	Sexually transmitted disease
Trichuris trichiura	Whipworm, diarrhea	Mebendazole	Most common in the tropics
Trypanosoma brucei gambiense and *Trypanosoma brucei rhodesiense*	African sleeping sickness	Pentamidine	Found in Africa
Trypanosoma cruzi	Chagas disease	Benznidazole	Transmitted by the kissing bug; found in Mexico and Central and South America

See Also

CHAPTER 36

Rickettsia

Chapter at a Glance

Although you may not have heard the term *rickettsia,* you're probably familiar with some of the diseases that fall into this category of infections. Rickettsia is a group of very tiny organisms that are spread through the bites of ticks, lice, and fleas. These organisms can infect human cells, including those that line the blood vessels. All rickettsial diseases can be treated with antibacterial medicines.

Human Ehrlichioses (*Ehrlichia* Infections)
Human ehrlichioses are rickettsial infections caused by at least 3 different species of bacteria called *Ehrlichia* that are spread to humans through the bites of infected ticks. Most cases occur in the spring and summer months. Infected ticks usually are found in specific areas of the country. The lone star tick is most common in southeastern and south central United States, while deer ticks are common in the northeast and north central United States.

Signs and Symptoms
Although the 3 types of human ehrlichioses are caused by different organisms *(Ehrlichia chaffeensis, Ehrlichia ewingii,* and *Anaplasma),* the infections they cause have similar signs and symptoms. These symptoms are similar to those of influenza.

- Fever
- Headache
- Chills
- Muscle and joint aches and pains
- A general feeling of sickness (malaise)
- Loss of appetite

    Laboratory abnormalities include

- Low red blood cell count (anemia)
- Low white blood cell count (leukopenia)
- Inflammation of the liver (hepatitis)

In some cases there may be a rash. Nausea and vomiting are common, as well as sudden weight loss because of lack of appetite. On rare occasions, these infections may cause stomach pain, cough, or confusion (a change in mental status).

These symptoms typically begin 5 to 10 days after the tick bite. It is important to remember that tick bites often go unnoticed. Many people with tick-borne infections do not realize that a tick has bitten them.

How Is the Diagnosis Made?
It can be difficult to make a diagnosis of ehrlichioses. There are blood tests that measure antibodies, but these are not generally available. Other blood tests do not give clear results.

Treatment
Most often, human ehrlichioses is treated with an antibacterial called doxy-cycline. It should be started immediately after the disease is diagnosed and given orally or intravenously for 5 to 10 days. Although doxycycline and other tetracycline antibacterials are not normally used in children younger than 8 years, in this case, the need for treatment of the bacteria outweighs the small risk of staining the teeth. Currently, there is no effective alternate antibiotic.

What Is the Prognosis?
Most children infected with human ehrlichioses who are treated appropri-ately will recover without any lasting effects within 1 to 2 weeks. In children with severe cases of the disease, there may be damage to the brain. Without treatment, some patients die from ehrlichioses, although this is rare.

Prevention
Limit your child's exposure to ticks as much as possible. In tick-infested areas, he should wear clothing such as long-sleeved shirts and long pants that covers most of his body. Tuck his pants legs into his socks. Apply a repellant containing DEET to the areas of his skin that are exposed, and reapply it every few hours according to the instructions on the product label.

Rocky Mountain Spotted Fever
Rocky mountain spotted fever (RMSF) is a widespread infection that occurs throughout the continental United States. It is caused by *Rickettsia rickettsii* bacteria. Although the name implies that the disease is related to the Rocky Mountains, it is most commonly seen in the southeastern and south central states. The disease is spread to humans through the bite of an infected tick. Most often, the infected tick is a dog tick, but sometimes it can be a wood tick. Cases tend to occur from April through September. The disease most

often affects children and teenagers younger than 15 years, especially those who spend time outdoors or have pets that might carry the ticks.

Signs and Symptoms

Children infected with RMSF first have symptoms common to many other infectious diseases, including flu-like symptoms such as fever, muscle pain, severe headaches, vomiting, nausea, and loss of appetite. A rash develops in most cases of RMSF, typically before the sixth day of the illness. This rash tends to appear first on the wrists and ankles, but within hours it can spread to the torso. It can also spread to the palms of the hands and soles of the feet. The rash is red, spotted, and raised. Other symptoms may include joint pain, stomach pain, and diarrhea. In severe cases, the blood pressure can drop and the patient may become confused. As the infection spreads, many organs, including the brain, can be affected. Laboratory findings include low platelet counts and a low sodium level.

Symptoms usually appear about 1 week after the tick bite occurs. This incubation period, however, can range from 2 to 14 days.

When to Call Your Pediatrician

If your child has been exposed to ticks or you know she has been bitten by a tick, contact your pediatrician if your child develops any of these symptoms.

How Is the Diagnosis Made?

Your pediatrician will evaluate your child's signs and symptoms and also use blood tests to confirm the diagnosis of RMSF. Laboratory findings that could help identify RMSF include decreased blood platelet count (thrombocytopenia), decreased concentration of sodium in the blood (hyponatremia), and increased level of liver enzymes (elevated transaminases).

Treatment

If your pediatrician suspects that your child has RMSF, the doctor will prescribe a course of antibacterials to be started immediately. Most often, doxycycline is the drug chosen to treat RMSF. Treatment with this medication usually continues for 7 to 10 days or until the child's fever has been gone for at least 3 days. Although doxycycline and other tetracycline antibiotics are not normally used in children younger than 8 years, in this case, the need for treatment of the bacteria outweighs the small risk of staining the teeth. The other antibacterial used to treat RMSF is chloramphenicol. This drug is avoided when possible because of possible side effects affecting bone marrow.

What Is the Prognosis?

With early treatment, almost all children will recover completely from RMSF. Even without antibacterial therapy, most children recover. However, the infection can become severe and overwhelming. Although rare, certain patients may have long-term complications that include nerve damage, hearing loss, incontinence, partial paralysis of the lower extremities, and gangrene that can lead to the amputation of toes or fingers. Some children may die from RMSF.

Prevention

The best preventive measure is to keep your child away from areas where ticks are present, such as wooded areas and areas with brush and tall grass. If she spends time in tick-infested regions, apply an insect repellant containing DEET to her exposed skin, following product instructions. Do not use excessive amounts of DEET on children. Regularly inspect your child's clothes and body for ticks, including the scalp and hair. If your child wears light-colored apparel, it will be easier to see ticks that may be crawling on her clothing. Don't forget to check your pets for ticks. Ticks can be brought in to the house on the dog's fur and spread to a child.

Antibiotics should not be taken as a preventive measure after a tick bite because the risk for infection is so low.

Rickettsial Infections

Rickettsia	Infection	Usual Treatment	Comments
Coxiella burnetii	Q fever	None, doxycycline	Acquired by farm animal contact
Ehrlichia species: *chaffeensis, ewingii,* *Anaplasma* *phagocytophila*	Human ehrlichiosis	Doxycycline	Transmitted by ticks
Rickettsia akari	Rickettsialpox (skin rash with flu-like illness)	Doxycycline	Transmitted by mouse mites
Rickettsia *prowazekii*	Typhus	Doxycycline	Transmitted by body lice or contact with flying squirrels
Rickettsia rickettsii	Rocky Mountain spotted fever	Doxycycline	Transmitted by dog ticks
Rickettsia typhi and *Rickettsia felis*	Typhus	Doxycycline	Transmitted by rat fleas

CHAPTER 37

Other Organisms

Chapter at a Glance

A few important disease-causing organisms do not naturally fit into any of the topical groupings discussed in other chapters. In this chapter, you'll read about 2 of these conditions, Kawasaki disease and mad cow disease, both of which have only been identified relatively recently.

Kawasaki Disease

Kawasaki disease is uncommon and presumed to be infectious. The first cases were noted in Japan in the late 1960s. The disease is named after the Japanese doctor who first described the illness. Even though it remains uncommon, doctors are particularly concerned about Kawasaki disease because it has become a leading cause of coronary artery disease in children. In fact, if not recognized and properly treated, it can cause inflammation and abnormalities of the coronary arteries.

Most often, Kawasaki disease affects youngsters between the ages of 1 and 8 years, with the highest number of cases in children between 18 and 24 months of age. About 80% of children who develop Kawasaki disease are younger than 5 years. Most cases occur during the winter and spring months.

The cause of Kawasaki disease is not known, nor is it clear how the illness is spread. Person-to-person transmission has not been found. Its various clinical features suggest it is an infectious disease.

Signs and Symptoms

The first sign of illness with Kawasaki disease is a high, spiking fever, with a temperature usually above 102.2°F (39°C), that lasts at least 5 days. In addition, 4 of the following 5 signs and symptoms must be present for a diagnosis of Kawasaki disease to be made:

- Eye redness and irritation (conjunctival injection) without eye discharge
- Inflammation and redness of the mouth, tongue, lips, and throat
- A rash
- Reddening and swelling of the palms and soles with subsequent peeling of the skin around the nails (peeling occurs in the second week of illness)
- Swollen glands in the neck, with one being more than 0.5 inches in diameter

Other characteristics sometimes associated with Kawasaki disease include irritability, stomach pain, diarrhea, and vomiting.

The signs and symptoms of Kawasaki disease may be less specific in infants younger than 12 months, making an accurate diagnosis more difficult. The diagnosis of Kawasaki disease may be considered in this age group even when all the symptoms are not present.

When to Call Your Pediatrician
Prompt treatment of Kawasaki disease is important. If your child has many of these symptoms, particularly a fever that lasts for longer than 5 days, contact your pediatrician.

How Is the Diagnosis Made?
There is no diagnostic test available for Kawasaki disease. Your pediatrician will make the diagnosis based on your child's signs and symptoms and by excluding illnesses that have some of the same symptoms, such as measles, streptococcal infections, toxic shock syndrome, juvenile rheumatoid arthritis, and certain reactions to medicines. The doctor may order blood tests that can rule out other infectious diseases. Your pediatrician may also perform echocardiography, an ultrasound of the heart, to monitor the coronary arteries.

Treatment
If Kawasaki disease is diagnosed in your child, your doctor may recommend hospitalization to receive medicines to reduce inflammation. In most cases, this treatment will include intravenous immune globulin (purified human antibodies), given along with aspirin. Although parents are usually advised to avoid giving aspirin to children because it may put youngsters at risk for Reye syndrome, doctors agree that the benefits outweigh the risks for Kawasaki disease. Thus, aspirin use is usually recommended for these youngsters. However, you should never give your child aspirin for any condition without first consulting with your pediatrician.

What Is the Prognosis?
With proper treatment, most children recover fully from Kawasaki disease in a few weeks. If untreated, however, about 20% will develop abnormalities of the coronary arteries, including aneurysms (the enlargement or bulging of blood vessels). Even with proper treatment, some children may still develop heart disease. The children at greatest risk are young and male and have signs of heart involvement early in the illness.

Prevention
There are no known preventive measures against Kawasaki disease at this time.

Mad Cow Disease

Occasional news about mad cow disease has caused concern among some parents about buying meat. However, the chance of getting mad cow disease appears to be much smaller than parents may think.

Mad cow disease is the commonly used name for bovine spongiform encephalopathy (BSE). It is one of a number of prion diseases. Prions are a type of infectious particle. Prion diseases are progressive, degenerative infections that affect the central nervous system of cattle. They can be spread to humans who eat the beef of an infected animal or come into contact with tissues of infected animals. The cattle themselves become infected with BSE by eating feed contaminated with the BSE organism. The cattle develop brain disease that results in death. When humans get the disease, it causes a variation of Creutzfeldt-Jakob disease (CJD) called variant CJD (vCJD), which is a fatal brain disorder.

Millions of cattle have been destroyed in Europe since the first cases of mad cow disease appeared in the 1980s. The first BSE case in a dairy cow in the United States was identified by the Department of Agriculture in December 2003. The Food and Drug Administration and other federal agencies have regulations in place to prevent contamination of the US food supply with BSE. At present, the risk of getting BSE from beef available in the United States is considered extremely low.

Worldwide, BSE-related illnesses remain very rare in humans. Through December 2003, there were a total of 143 cases of vCJD reported in the United Kingdom, plus 6 cases in France and 1 each in the United States, Canada, Italy, and Ireland. A person can also become infected if he receives a transplant from someone with the disease or a child receives a growth hormone that was made from the pituitary gland of an infected person. Note that growth hormones are now manufactured rather than taken from human bodies.

Signs and Symptoms
People with mad cow disease can have very serious signs and symptoms, including personality changes, muscle stiffness, involuntary muscle

movements, dementia, and seizures. The disease can affect individuals at a younger age than those with traditional CJD (a median age of 28 years in vCJD, compared with 68 years in classic CJD). Most cases have occurred in adults, but an occasional case has been seen in teenagers. The traditional form of the disease has a hereditary basis. Both diseases involve abnormal proteins that accumulate in the brain.

How Is the Diagnosis Made?
The signs and symptoms of vCJD will help your pediatrician make the diagnosis. However, the only way to definitively diagnose any human prion disease is to examine the brain tissue itself.

Treatment
No treatment is available to slow down or stop the progression of mad cow disease or other prion infections. Studies are currently taking place to investigate a number of experimental treatments.

What Is the Prognosis?
Mad cow disease is fatal. The incubation period for disease related to exposure to infected tissues varies between 1.5 years and more than 30 years.

Prevention
There is no evidence that cooking contaminated meat will destroy the BSE organism. Government regulations of the beef industry make the risk of transmission of BSE to people very unlikely.

Resources for Parents

Organizations

AIDSinfo
PO Box 6303
Rockville, MD 20849-6303
www.aidsinfo.nih.gov

American Academy of Pediatrics
141 Northwest Point Blvd
Elk Grove Village, IL 60007-1098
www.aap.org

- Childhood Immunization Support Program:
  www.cispimmunize.org
- Policies: www.aappolicy.org
- *Red Book®: Report of the Committee on Infectious Diseases:*
  www.aapredbook.org
- Section on Adoption and Foster Care:
  www.aap.org/sections/adoption/default.htm

Canadian Paediatric Society
100-2204 Walkley Rd
Ottawa, Ontario, Canada K1G 4G8
www.cps.ca

Centers for Disease Control and Prevention
1600 Clifton Rd
Atlanta, GA 30333
www.cdc.gov

- National Center for Infectious Diseases Travelers' Health:
  www.cdc.gov/travel
- National Immunization Hotline:
  800/232-4636 (800/CDC-INFO)
- National Immunization Program:
  www.cdc.gov/nip/home-hcp.htm
  — Vaccine Information Statements:
    www.cdc.gov/nip/publications/VIS/default.htm

Food and Drug Administration
5600 Fishers Ln
Rockville, MD 20857-0001
www.fda.gov

- Vaccine Adverse Event Reporting System:
  www.vaers.hhs.gov

Immunization Action Coalition
1573 Selby Ave
Suite 234
St Paul, MN 55104
www.immunize.org

Infectious Diseases Society of America
66 Canal Center Plaza
Suite 600
Alexandria, VA 22314
www.idsociety.org

National Network for Immunization Information
301 University Blvd
CH 2.218
Galveston, TX 77555-0351
www.immunizationinfo.org

National Pediatric & Family HIV Resource Center
University of Medicine & Dentistry of New Jersey
30 Bergen St
ADMC #4
Newark, NJ 07103
www.pedhivaids.org

Other Resources

Immunization Education Program
Pennsylvania Chapter of the American Academy of Pediatrics
www.paaap.org/immunize

Institute for Vaccine Safety
Johns Hopkins University School of Public Health
www.vaccinesafety.edu

National Partnership for Immunization
www.partnersforimmunization.org

Vaccine Education Center
The Children's Hospital of Philadelphia
www.vaccine.chop.edu

Books

American Academy of Pediatrics. *Baby & Child Health: The Essential Guide From Birth to 11 Years.* Shu J, ed. New York, NY: DK Publishing, Inc; 2004

American Academy of Pediatrics. *Caring for Your Baby and Young Child: Birth to Age 5.* Shelov SP, Hannemann RE, eds. 4th ed. New York, NY: Bantam Books; 2004

American Academy of Pediatrics. *El Cuidado De Su Hijo Pequeño: Desde Que Nace Hasta Los Cinco Años.* Shelov SP, Hannemann RE, eds. Elk Grove Village, IL: American Academy of Pediatrics; 2001

American Academy of Pediatrics. *El Primer Año De Su Bebé.* Shelov SP, ed. Elk Grove Village, IL: American Academy of Pediatrics; 2004

American Academy of Pediatrics. *Guide to Your Child's Symptoms.* Schiff D, Shelov SP, eds. New York, NY: Villard Books; 1997

American Academy of Pediatrics. *Immunizations & Infectious Diseases: An Informed Parent's Guide.* Fisher MC, ed. Elk Grove Village, IL: American Academy of Pediatrics; 2006

American Academy of Pediatrics. *Your Baby's First Year.* Shelov SP, ed. 2nd ed. New York, NY: Bantam Books; 2005

Gold R. *Your Child's Best Shot: A Parent's Guide to Vaccination.* 2nd ed. Ottawa, Ontario, Canada: Canadian Paediatric Society; 2002

Humiston SG, Good C. *Vaccinating Your Child: Questions & Answers for the Concerned Parent.* 2nd ed. Atlanta, GA: Peachtree Publishers; 2003

Offit PA, Bell LM. *Vaccines: What You Should Know.* 3rd ed. Hoboken, NJ: John Wiley & Sons, Inc; 2003

Glossary

abdomen. The area of the body between the chest and the pelvis. It holds the stomach and intestines.

abscess. A collection of pus surrounded by inflamed tissue.

active immunization. Use of a vaccine to activate the body's production of antibodies. These antibodies fight off invading bacteria or viruses. Active immunizations produce antibodies that last from months to years to a lifetime, depending on the vaccine and the person being immunized.

Advisory Committee on Immunization Practices (ACIP). Fifteen experts in fields associated with immunization who have been selected by the secretary of the US Department of Health and Human Services to provide advice and guidance to the secretary, assistant secretary for health, and Centers for Disease Control and Prevention on the most effective means of stopping vaccine-preventable diseases.

American Academy of Pediatrics (AAP). An organization of 60,000 primary care pediatricians, pediatric medical subspecialists, and pediatric surgical specialists dedicated to the health, safety, and well-being of infants, children, adolescents, and young adults.

anemia. Low red blood cell count; often called "low blood." Red blood cells carry oxygen from the lungs to the rest of the body.

antibacterials. Medicines that kill or weaken bacteria.

antibiotic resistance. The ability of microorganisms such as bacteria to survive and grow despite the presence of antibiotics.

antibiotics. Medicines that kill pathogens (germs). Types of antibiotics include antibacterials, antivirals, antifungals, and antiparasitic drugs. Most people refer to antibacterials as antibiotics.

antibodies. Proteins that a person makes, also called immunoglobulins, that help immune responses. These immunoglobulins inactivate microbes (germs) and help a person clear the infection. Some antibodies, called autoantibodies, can react to part of a person and cause harm.

antifungals. Medicines that kill or weaken fungi.

antiparasitics. Medicines that kill or weaken parasites.

antivirals. Medicines that kill or weaken viruses.

arthritis. Inflammation of a joint. Manifest by warmth, tenderness, pain, and swelling.

autism. Also called autistic disorder. A developmental disorder that affects language, imagination, and social interactions. Autistic disorder is one of the pervasive developmental disorders of children.

bacteria. Single-celled organisms that are present everywhere, including on and in the human body.

bactericidal. Causing the death of bacteria.

bacteriostatic. Inhibiting or slowing down the multiplication of bacteria.

bladder. The sac that holds and releases urine.

bronchiolitis. Infection or inflammation of the small breathing passages of the lungs.

bronchitis. Infection or inflammation of the tubes leading from the trachea (throat) to the lower breathing passages of the lungs.

bronchodilating medicine. Medicine that increases of size of the bronchi and bronchioles in the lungs. This medicine acts on the muscles surrounding the breathing tubes.

cellulitis. Infection or inflammation of the skin.

Centers for Disease Control and Prevention (CDC). The lead federal agency for protecting the health and safety of people at home and abroad, providing credible information to enhance health decisions, and promoting health through strong partnerships. Serves as the national focus for developing and applying disease prevention and control, environmental health, and health promotion and education activities designed to improve the health of the people of the United States.

central nervous system. The brain and spinal cord.

cervix. The opening of the womb.

cold agglutinins. A special type of antibody usually produced in response to infections. These antibodies cause red blood cells to clump together in the cold.

cold-adapted influenza vaccine. An influenza vaccine in which a live virus has been specially adapted (changed) so that it can't grow at high temperatures (eg, in the body). It is given as a nasal spray. The virus grows in the front of the nose and the person makes antibodies to the virus. These antibodies protect the person against infection from wild influenza viruses.

colitis. Inflammation of the colon. Can be caused by an infection or disease such as ulcerative colitis (inflammatory bowel disease).

complications. Problems that develop as a result of a disease or procedure such as surgery.

congenital. Present at birth.

conjunctivitis. Inflammation of the eyelid, often called pinkeye.

contagious. A condition (in this book, an infection) that can be spread from one person to another.

contaminated. Containing microorganisms. Can refer to food, water, medicine, a surface, or body fluid.

convulsion. Spasm or series of jerking of the face, torso, arms, or legs. Also called a seizure.

corticosteroids. A type of steroid used medically, especially as an anti-inflammatory. Can be produced artificially and given as medicine to stop inflammation (eg, to treat asthma).

croup. Inflammation of the larynx (voice box) and trachea (windpipe). The child will be hoarse, have a barking cough, and may have difficulty breathing.

culture. A laboratory test that involves the growth of microorganisms on or in media of various kinds.

cyst. A sac of fluid.

dehydration. Excessive loss of water.

dementia. Mental deterioration with loss of mental abilities.

donor. An individual who donates blood, tissue, or an organ.

duodenum. The first part of the small intestine (bowel or gut).

ectopic pregnancy. Also called tubal pregnancy. Pregnancy outside the uterus, usually in the tube that extends from an ovary to the uterus or womb.

encephalitis. Brain inflammation.

enteroviruses. A group of viruses that commonly cause infections, especially in young children. These viruses live in the bowel (gut) and cause colds, fevers, rash, pneumonia, heart infection, and meningitis. They are spread from child to child during the spring, summer, and fall.

epidemic. Outbreak of disease.

epiglottitis. Swelling and inflammation of the tissue (epiglottis) over the voice box that can block the breathing passage.

esophagus. The tube connecting the mouth to the stomach.

evidence based. Findings based on scientific research.

extremity. A limb of the body, especially a hand or foot.

fallopian tube. The tube through which the egg travels from the ovary to the uterus (womb).

fatigue. Tiredness.

fever. An increase in body temperature, usually 100.4°F (38°C) or greater. Fever is an indication of the body's response to something, but is not a disease or a serious problem by itself.

fever blisters. Cold sores; herpes simplex of the lips.

flora. In this book, local bacterial life; in nature, local plant life.

fontanelle. "Soft spot" on a baby's or infant's head.

Food and Drug Administration (FDA). Responsible for protecting the public health by ensuring the safety, efficacy, and security of human and veterinary drugs, biological products, medical devices, our nation's food supply, cosmetics, and products that emit radiation. Also responsible for advancing the public health by helping to speed innovations that make medicines and foods more effective, safer, and more affordable and helping the public get the accurate, evidence-based information it needs to use medicines and foods to improve health.

food-borne diseases. Illnesses spread by food.

fungi. Plural of fungus. Plantlike organisms such as yeasts, molds, mildew, and mushrooms that get their nutrition from other living organisms or dead organic matter.

gastroenteritis. Inflammation of the stomach and intestinal tract that can cause vomiting, diarrhea, and abdominal pain and cramps.

gastrointestinal tract. The mouth, esophagus, stomach, small intestine (duodenum, jejunum, ileum), large intestine (colon), and rectum (anus).

genital. Of, relating to, or being a sexual organ.

germ. An organism usually producing disease. Also called a microbe. Bacteria, viruses, fungi, and parasites are examples of germs.

hemorrhage. To bleed, usually a large amount.

host. The organism, usually a person or an animal, in or on which a parasite lives and from whom it gets food and energy.

human T-cell lymphotropic virus (HTLV). A virus in the same family as the human immunodeficiency virus (HIV) that can be transmitted in blood. Sometimes causes a rare type of leukemia or a problem with the nervous system.

hygiene. Protective measures taken by an individual to promote health and limit the spread of diseases.

hypotension. Low blood pressure.

immune globulin. Also called gamma globulin and immunoglobulin. A protein (antibody) made by a person in response to an infection or immunization. Also refers to a preparation of antibodies made from human plasma.

immune system. Part of the body that protects us from foreign substances, cells, and tissues. Includes the thymus, spleen, lymph nodes, lymphocytes (including B cells and T cells), and antibodies.

immunization. A vaccine that is given to children and adults to help them develop protection (antibodies) against specific infections.

immunocompromised. Having a weakened immune system.

immunodeficiency. A condition resulting from a weakened or defective immune system.

impetigo. A common and contagious skin infection that typically appears on the face around the nose, mouth, and ears.

incubation period. The time from exposure to a microbe until the beginning of symptoms.

infection. A condition caused by the growth of an infectious agent in the body.

infectious. Capable of being spread.

infectious diseases. Illnesses caused by organisms.

inflammation. A local response that includes swelling, redness, heat, and pain.

injection. The introduction of a medicine under the skin or into a vein, muscle, or any other body cavity.

inoculation. The introduction of a pathogen or antigen into a living organism to stimulate the production of antibodies.

intramuscular. Within a muscle (as in intramuscular injections).

intravenous. Going into a vein (as in intravenous fluids).

jaundice. Yellowing of the skin and eyes.

larvae. A stage in the life of a parasite, usually after the egg stage.

laryngitis. Inflammation of the larynx (voice box).

larynx. The voice box.

latent. An infection that is in the resting stage.

lesion. A wound, sore, or injury.

lethargy. Extreme tiredness.

leukopenia. Low white blood cell count.

listlessness. Lack of energy.

liver. A large organ on the upper right-hand side of the abdomen that removes toxins from the blood and makes a variety of substances such as proteins and clotting factors.

lungs. The organs in the chest that exchange gases (oxygen and carbon dioxide). What we use to breathe.

lymph nodes. Collections of lymphocytes that are located along the course of the lymphatic vessels. These get bigger during infections.

lymphadenopathy. Enlarged lymph nodes or glands.

lymphocytes. White blood cells that are an important part of the immune system. They make antibodies and kill off viruses, bacteria, and parasites.

meningitis. Inflammation of the covering of the brain.

myocarditis. Inflammation of the heart muscle.

nodules. Small lumps.

nonproductive cough. Dry cough that does not contain mucus.

orchitis. Inflammation of the testis.

organisms. Living things. Often used as a general term for *germs.*

osteomyelitis. Inflammation of the bone.

otitis media. Middle ear infection.

ova. Eggs.

ovaries. The paired female sex organs that produce eggs and female sex hormones.

paralysis. Loss of movement of part of the body.

parasite. Organisms that live in and cause harm to another animal (host).

passive immunization. The process of giving antibodies against a particular infectious agent to a child or adult. This provides short-term protection that lasts just a few weeks.

pathogenic. Causing or capable of causing disease.

pathogens. Microbes (germs) that cause disease.

pharyngitis. Inflammation of the pharynx.

pharynx. The throat.

photophobia. Painful sensitivity to light.

plasma. Liquid part of the blood.

pneumonia. An infection of the lungs.

preterm. Born early (premature birth).

prion disease. A progressive, degenerative disease of the brain caused by infectious particles. Mad cow disease is one example.

prognosis. A description of the likely course and/or outcome of a disease.

prophylactic. Guarding or protecting from disease.

prophylaxis. The use of something to prevent a disease (in this book, antimicrobial drugs to prevent infection).

protozoa. Single-celled microscopic organisms. *Giardia* is one example.

rabid. Acting violently because of an infection with rabies.

reactive airways. Breathing tubes that are extremely sensitive to environmental pollutants and allergy-causing organisms. People with asthma have these.

rheumatic fever. An illness that can affect the heart, joints, skin, and brain following infection with group A streptococcus.

rickettsia. A group of tiny organisms that are spread by the bites of ticks, lice, and fleas.

saliva. Fluid made by salivary glands that goes into the mouth.

scarlet fever. Strep throat with a rash. The rash is caused by a toxin and feels like sandpaper.

secretions. Liquids such as saliva that are produced by cells or glands.

sepsis. A very serious illness with low blood pressure and failure of many organs caused by infection.

sexually transmitted disease (STD). Any of the various diseases transmitted by direct sexual contact.

shingles. An itchy, often painful skin rash caused by reactivation of the chickenpox virus.

sinusitis. Inflammation of the sinuses.

spasticity. Stiffness or rigidity caused by the spasm of a muscle.

species. A type of germ.

specimen. A small part or sample of any substance or material obtained for testing (as in taking a specimen).

sputum. A mixture of saliva and mucus, usually coming from the breathing passages.

stomach. The part of the digestive system between the esophagus and small intestine.

supportive care. Care other than medicines used to make your child comfortable while sick.

suture. To stitch or sew (eg, a wound).

symptom. A complaint that could indicate an illness or a disease.

tapeworm. A type of parasite that lives within the intestines (gut or bowel).

thrombocytopenia. Having a low number of platelets (the cells in the blood that stop bleeding by starting the clot).

ticks. Eight-legged arthropods (often bloodsucking). Some transmit diseases to humans, birds, and other animals.

toxins. Poisons.

trachea. Windpipe. The part of the airway between the voice box and bronchi.

tracheitis. Swelling of the mucous membrane of the trachea.

transmission. The passing of an organism or germ from person to person, person to animal, or animal to person.

ulcer. Sore, crater, or lesion in the skin or mucous membrane that results in tissue damage, usually with inflammation.

urethra. The tube that carries the urine out of the bladder. In males, it carries sperm and other sexual secretions.

urinary tract infection. Infection of the bladder, kidney, or both.

uterus. The womb.

vaccination. Receiving a vaccine that causes the immune system to develop antibodies to specific diseases.

vaccine. A preparation of infectious organisms or parts of organisms that is introduced into the body to produce immunity to a particular disease.

virus. A microscopic organism that may cause disease. It is smaller than bacteria and cannot live on its own.

white blood cell. One of the blood cells that is important for fighting infections.

Index

Page numbers with *f* indicate figures; page numbers with *t* indicate tables.